Our Next Billion Dollar Killing

Leveraging Global Economic System Dynamics
By The Financial Elite

ROBERT LAW

Copyright © 2017 Robert Law

All rights reserved. Printed in the United States of America. Except as permitted under the United States Copyright Act of 1976, no part of this publication may be reproduced or distributed in any form or by any means, or stored in a database or retrieval system, without the prior written permission of the author.

ISBN: 978-1976156984

Contents

INTRODUCTION: FINANCIAL KILLINGS 1
PART 1: SOME EXAMPLES OF FINANCIAL KILLINGS 11
    1A: Risking Our Own Money 14
    1B Risking Other People's Money 34
    1C Having It Both Ways 45
PART 2: KEY COMPONENTS OF KILLINGS 47
    2.1 Business Cycles 47
    2.2 Combinations of Cycles 60
    2.3 Price Spikes, Collapses and Triggers 62
    2.4 Complex Variable Analysis 66
    2.5 Analytical Expertise 73
    2.6 Financial Instruments And Timing 79
PART 3: NEW KILLING OPPORTUNITIES 87
    3.1 Technology 87
    3.2 Geoeconomic Changes 95
    3.3 The Twenty to Fifty Billion Dollar Financial Killing 101
APPENDIX 1: BUSINESS CYCLE GENERATION 109
    Multiplicity of Cycles or Waves 109
    Combinations of Cycles or Waves 111
    Inter-temporal Flows 115
    Generation of Business Cycles 116
    Price Spike Generation 131

APPENDIX 2: LIQUIDITY, SOLVENCY AND CREDIT FAILURE 135
    Impact of Financing on Sales and on Price Collapse 141
    Impact of Financing on Financial Stability................................... 143
    Cash Flow and Price Stability... 168
APPENDIX 3: COMPLEX VARIABLES AND PRICE COLLAPSE 173
    Wave Patterns in Cash Flow and Price... 174
    Risk For Supplier, Buyer and Financing Party............................... 181
    Wave Stability and Business Cycles.. 193
    Complex Numbers - Imaginary Money 198
    Implications of Wave Model 216
    Assumptions of Wave Model 222
APPENDIX 4: MACRO-ECONOMIC STABILITY 237
    Organic Growth Mechanisms.. 237
    Macroeconomic Effects 240
    DSGE Models and Financial Stability... 250
APPENDIX 5: MORE ON SPECIFIC CYCLES... 257
APPENDIX 6: GEOECONOMIC FACTORS –STABILITY OF LINKS.......... 291
    Geoeconomics and Trade 291
    Geopolitical Parallels - Products 304
    Currency Crises.. 305
    Real Estate and Geoeconomics... 307
    General Geoeconomic Comments 318
INDEX.. 323

INTRODUCTION: FINANCIAL KILLINGS

His fund had bought a range of securities, including debt and stock, from various financial firms. His fund was down $600 million soon after they started buying. No one else was buying big and the prices dropped. His fund kept buying. Ordinarily there would be howls from the fund investors and demands to get back in line with the crowd. But they had done that when he had shorted the dot com boom. He had complied with their demands and the investors missed making the fortunes they would have if they had trusted his analysis. This time they did trust it.

Now the payoff was visible to all. The Bank of America shares that the fund had paid an average of $6.73 per share had risen to $15.79 per share. AIG debt that the fund had paid 10 cents on the dollar had risen to 61 cents when he sold them. With all the other financial sector gains, the fund made over seven billion dollars.

If we have the creative, technical and business skills to found a Standard Oil, a General Electric, a Ford Motors, a Microsoft, an Apple Computer, an Amazon, a Google or a Trump Organization we can make billions. It usually takes some years or decades.

But if we belong to the financial elite we can make billions in months or even days. We do it simply by buying and selling financial assets whose real values other parties fail to see. By financial elite we mean elite in skills, access to resources and in understanding of the dynamics of the global financial system.

High Profit, High Risk

One of the more obvious ways to make a fortune is to buy stocks in a new company that is developing some new product that we believe many people will be willing to buy, or that is developing some process that saves someone a lot of money. The problem with both ways is that the success rate is very low. The product or process may ultimately be successful but it is likely to be another company, which had better timing or greater resources, reaping the benefits.

Another way is to buy stocks in a large established company which we believe will gain value based on some scenario described in the financial media. The scenario will involve factors like market growth, cost reduction, economies of scale, improved components and materials, customer capture and regulatory change that will lead to its stock price climbing. It might be GM, IBM, Google, Tesla, Bank of America, Apple, Mobil Oil or some other historically successful large company. And we ignore the alternative scenario described elsewhere in the financial media involving different factors that leads to its stock price falling.

Another way again is to buy gold, oil or some other commodity based on a scenario for increasing value as described in the financial media. And again ignore the alternative scenario described elsewhere in the financial media involving different factors that has its price falling instead of rising.

The problem with these methods is that we can make a fortune but need to risk a fortune to do it. And in each case we depend on the accuracy of a scenario which may be quite invalid.

Note in this book we use the term *company* to mean a non-financial business enterprise and *firm* to mean a financial services business enterprise. This is purely for convenience, as both terms are used for both types of enterprise.

High Profit, Other People's Money

A high degree of risk in such asset purchases is fine if it is other people's money we are risking. We collect a share of the profits when they are made but if things go wrong we do not share any losses. Better still we collect a fee for managing the investment whether there are profits or losses. The key for us to making a lot of money is to have a lot of people risking their money so that we can collect a large quantity of fees. Collecting a large quantity of shares in profits is a bonus.

Many financial sector firms operate on this principle and make a lot of money year after year. Sometimes things go wrong and they go out of business leaving many investors losing money. However, the firm's owners keep the money they made in earlier years.

To attract the customers in the first place we need to appear to know what we are doing. They could invest their money in potentially high profit opportunities if they just wanted to take high risks without needing us (see above). We need to offer them potentially high profits and apparently low risks. That requires that we at least appear to understand risks on a deeper level than the average market participant.

High Profit, Moderate Risk

If we are seeking a multi-billion $US killing with a significant investment of our *own* money, we need to drive the risk right down. We need to align the forces of market competition, business cycles, geo-economics and technology so as to ensure the odds are in our favor. We will not have certainty but high probability is the next best thing.

If the investment is relatively moderate in size and moderate in risk, or low in size and high in risk, and the potential gain is large and/or high in probability, it may be a very attractive investment. What is critical is that our analysis of the downside and upside risks is strong. That requires in depth analysis of factors that are likely to suddenly lead to changes in market demand or supply capacity.

Some financial killings involve making billions in a very short time. Typically a disruptive event occurs, strongly affecting prices of assets of interest and large transfers of wealth occur. If we are suitably prepared for the event, some of those wealth transfers can go to us. By the time people realize what has happened, it is too late to prevent it.

Other financial killings involve making tens and hundreds of millions per year over a longer term. To achieve this we need to minimize the normal competitive forces that would force down profit margins. We use secrecy to exclude as many competitors from the opportunity as possible. And we use political connections and legal maneuvers to obstruct those who do get to know about it.

Key to achieving these is an understanding of the development of price spikes, price collapses, liquidity crises and solvency failures in a cyclical system. Not all killings can be neatly explained in a mathematical model, or set of models, however, but some can and these are the ones we focus on here.

Historical Financial Killings

On one level none of this is new. Killings from price spikes have been made since the Roman Empire and Medieval eras, if not before. Where there was a famine, a war or a plague, there was likely some commodity whose price spiked to great heights. It might be food in a famine, weaponry in a war or a berth on a ship out of a plague city. Whichever it was, people would pay greatly for it. Those who held that commodity could make a fortune.

There were also indirect ways to make killings from price collapses. If a price collapsed and someone lost a lot of money, they might need to raise a lot of cash fast. If another party had the cash they could buy their assets at fire sale prices and resell them at their leisure or keep them for profitable usage. The assets could include forests, mines, landholdings, a county or even a principality.

A relatively recent development allows for killings directly from price collapses, through the evolution of financial securities in the Modern era. These include stocks, bonds, futures, options and swaps. These allow us to buy some commodity at a future price and sell it at the current price. If we expect the price to collapse, this is a way to make a killing. Or we can buy the right to make such a profit if it occurs. If the new price is much lower than the current price we make money. If the price goes up we have the right to opt out. The particular type of security we buy determines whether, if things do not go to plan and the price rises, we lose a lot of money or if our loss is moderate.

Price collapses have a major advantage over price spikes. Spikes generally disappear when the supply constraint causing them is relieved or buyers drop out of the market. Collapses tend to last a lot longer, with large transfers of wealth. They often generate a cascade of continuing collapses. These expand the scale of the opportunity and create new killing opportunities for those who are positioned to profit. The biggest killings usually relate to a collapse event.

Systemic Events

Global trade has been evolving for a long time with connections such as the Silk Road, the Indian Ocean Islamic trading routes, the Venetian and Genoan routes from the Eastern Mediterranean to Western Europe. What has changed since the time that these routes first connected different global regions is the speed that connections now move products and business information. Physical products now move in days or weeks instead of months. Data-carried service products and market information take seconds.

What is also more recent is that the global economic system now generates its own events. We do not need wars, plagues and famines to create a price spike or a price collapse. Combinations of business cycles impacting on demand and capacity can create price spikes in commodities and assets, which can make killings possible. Better still they can create price collapses, which usually create bigger opportunities than spikes. And they can activate cash flow crises to expose valuable assets for plucking.

We refer here to systemic disruptions of a fluid market. These are caused by upper capacity and lower demand limits of the supply system being reached. They usually happen when cyclical peaks and troughs reach unexpected levels or supply lines incur unexpected bottlenecks or incur unexpected expansions of capacity. The effect of these limits being reached is sudden changes in price. Such changes can release billions of $US to those who are prepared.

The global economic system, in conjunction with changing technology, also generates vast amounts of confusing and apparently conflicting information. Will interest rates rise or fall? Will a particular currency value rise or fall? Will more or less businesses fail than usual? Will unemployment increase or decrease? Will a government policy expand the economy or slow it down? All the economic experts have an opinion. This is often expressed with certainty, whether or not the last time that they made such a prediction they were correct.

This confusion is good for those of us seeking to make serious killings because it hides the big opportunities from others in the market. Their participation on our side of the bet would dilute our profits. The less they understand the better.

Seeing The Opportunity

The key factor in making a killing is anticipating the large price movement of some key asset when other parties in the market do not see it.

The asset price can be that of a physical commodity (grain, oil, gas, mineral). It can be that of a security whose value is dependent on that asset price, (credit debt, stock value, bond value, etc). It can be that of a derivative of the security. Once the asset has been identified, we can select a suitable financial instrument whose purchase will allow us to capture the value from the asset price change.

Some people can see hidden patterns behind a price that everyone else misses because it relates to some factor that is inactive until a certain threshold is reached. When the threshold is reached sudden changes in price can occur.

The market players who can see these patterns have an ability to assess capacity available at various costs from diverse sources and to assess demand at various prices from diverse markets. Capacity and demand follow cyclical patterns. Capacity increases in response to higher prices and demand decreases in response to higher prices. However, the speed of these responses varies with the type of supplier and the type of market.

Many people struggle to grasp the significance of business cycles because cycles are not neat and regular in size and timing. They are not regular because they are composites of the activity of many individual businesses. There are many of them and they combine in ways that are hard to predict. But regardless of the irregularity, they have characteristics that can have drastic effect on those unprepared. Simultaneously they offer great opportunities for those who are prepared.

New Opportunities in The Cloud Era

The above types of killing opportunities apply at the local level and at the global level. Spatial economic transport links have their own business cycles overlaying local business cycles. This increases complexity, the potential for unforeseen events, and sometimes the speed and scale of events when they do occur.

The other factor speeding the global economic system and increasing opportunities for financial killings is the Cloud. The founders of companies such as Amazon, Google and Facebook, who have developed Cloud-based technology to develop products, have become billionaires creating great corporations. Even developers of mobile device apps using Cloud data can make millions.

Those of us who may not be such clever technical innovators, but have financial resources and expertise, can still benefit from the Cloud due to its expansion of potential financial killings. The Cloud brings new accelerators to the financial system. These expand the system's throughput, making potential killings larger. More billions move around at high speed in response to more events. The increasing speed and complexity also add destabilizing forces, making those killing opportunities come more frequently.

To exploit these new opportunities, alongside the ones already available before the Cloud arrived, we need to understand the conditions that lead to situations and events that incur large wealth transfers. We can then select the right mechanisms for the applicable market to operate at the right time to capture those billions.

Appendices

This is not a long book as our readers are busy people and may just want to get to the crux, based on which they can make their own decisions. We have included background technical information in appendices, which readers can study at their leisure and according to their level of interest. The appendices often cover the same material but from a different perspective so there is some duplication. Common themes occur in multiple appendices including buyer's risk, the impact of financing on price, economies of scale, instability and price collapse.

Appendix 1 deals with the multiplicity of cycles in business and how they can combine to produce hard-to-predict spikes in the price of products and assets, which can contribute to financial killing opportunities.

Appendix 2 deals with the cyclical relationships between cash flow, liquidity, profits and solvency, which become critical in a financial crisis. It also outlines the role of price collapses which generate many financial killing opportunities.

Appendix 3 deals in detail with the development of investment cycles into price collapse events, which can offer opportunities for great financial killings. While these events can occur for any recurring investment cycles, they are particularly applicable to the working capital cycle. We use complex variable mathematics to indicate how price collapses occur and how they are influenced by varying levels of financing.

Appendix 4 deals with some of the macroeconomic modelling and forecasting by governments and central banks that we can use in predicting situations which lead to financial killing opportunities. It also highlights the limitations of these forecasts in terms of identifying instabilities, which lead to killing opportunities. These limitations create great opportunities for those seeking financial killings. They need to do their own stability analysis, by understanding how particular sectors behave within the wide economy.

Appendix 5 elaborates on some of the more detailed aspects of the various types of business cycles. This helps with recognition of changes in cycles that contribute to killing opportunities.

Appendix 6 deals with geoeconomic factors in terms of how they affect the pricing of products in a global economy, and associated financial stability. This includes consumer products and capital products as well as financial services.

It deals with how geoeconomic factors can affect currency values, which can generate killing opportunities when instability occurs.

Appendix 6 also deals how geoeconomic factors affect real estate prices. Real estate can have a critical role in providing collateral for business and can strongly influence consumer confidence. Changes in real estate values provide financial killing opportunities due to their impact on loan collateral. This is in addition to the killings that can be made from them directly. Understanding how real estate cycles can impact on general business and finance is of great value in identifying certain types of potential killings.

PART 1: SOME EXAMPLES OF FINANCIAL KILLINGS

"We're value-oriented and performance-based like a lot of funds. But I think what differentiates us is that we're not afraid of the downside of different situations when we've done the analysis. Some other people are very afraid of losing money, which keeps them from making money."
David Tepper

The key factor in a financial killing is to ensure that firstly we can profit from an unusual or unexpected price situation and that secondly we can avoid competition which would cut into our profit margin.

We can do this in a quick killing where the vast majority of market participants are not aware of the situation and when it all happens before the victims are aware it is happening.

Or we can do this in a slow killing where we have some kind of monopoly or cartel squeeze on competition over a sustained period. Here the victims do not know it is happening to them before or after because of ignorance or a preconditioned mindset. This mindset can last for months or years and if we do suck our victims dry, new ones come along to replace them as long as the ignorance and mindset prevails.

Financial killings can be made under any business conditions, including rising markets, spiking markets, collapsing markets and long term depressed markets. For example, in the Global Financial Crisis of 2007/08, fortunes were made in the billions from collapsing financial asset prices. It was one of those great transfers of wealth that created opportunities amidst the chaos and collapse, for those suitable prepared to collect huge returns on their investments. But there were also killings in the years that led to the GFC, killings in the months immediately afterward, and killings in the years following it. There were different cyclical forces applying each time.

In the fourteen example types below, all made billions for the leading firms involved and often billions for individual partners in those firms. Cash flow crises, price spikes, price collapses and combinations are all included:

- One type of killing is a bet on the market moving in a certain direction in a particular time frame and in a particular location, but with big downside risks.
- Three types of killings are bets on the market moving in a certain direction where, if we bet correctly, we make a killing but, if we do not bet correctly, our losses are moderate.
- Two more types involve making killings while operating businesses by leveraging off multiple business cycles. These businesses can be in any sector.
- Two types involve making killings by strongly leveraging off political cycles in addition to business cycles. These can occur in a number of sectors.
- Five types are *other people's money* plays where we make various high risk, high reward bets over an extended period and we profit as long as all goes well. But if and when things do not go to plan, some other parties pay. These parties can be customers, stockholders or the government.
- One type where we combine other people's money killings with market movement killings.

With each of these types of killings we look at the key cycles involved leading to the change in price of the targeted asset or product. We see how, as a consequence of this price change, the money flows in a path that can be diverted to those who have purchased the right financial instruments.

Most of these cycles are investment cycles. Investment requires financing, which gives those in the financial sector a big advantage in terms of recognizing opportunities. They are simply exposed to a far wider range of cyclical financial activities than the rest of the business community. And they are familiar with the financial instruments which can be used to capture sudden money flows.

There are some who will criticize the financial firms for taking advantage of this opportunity. But little wealth gets built in the first place without their expertise. The industrial revolutions that brought billions of people out of subsistence living was based on financing. The pharmaceutical revolutions that save hundreds of millions of people from death by disease are based on financing. Earlier technology revolutions could be built on a platform of slave labor under the dictates of some prince or king. But these later technology revolutions needed a more sophisticated approach. Financing borrows from the willing rather than forcing those without choice.

We are not focused here on the particular personalities of the people carrying out killings. We are not concerned about the schools they went to, the firm they first worked for, their starter spouses, their trophy spouses, their eight houses around the power and leisure centers of the world, their 12 Ferraris, their racehorse stable or their superyachts. These things are undoubtedly of interest and entertainment and have an important status-defining function but are only a diversion here. The status defining functions in fact provide camouflage for what is really going on.

What we are focused on is what these rare people understand that the rest of the crowd does not. These are the real financial elite. Somehow along the line they have developed an understanding of a particular type of mathematics that describes the changes in prices that make fortunes.

This mathematics is not taught at business school. The underlying principles might be taught in a math, physics or engineering degree course. However, our practitioners are more likely to have developed an intuitive grasp of the dynamics though experience of many price-changing events.

Central in this is the wave characteristics of business cycles, which can lead to sudden price changes. Different cycles interact with one and other, sometimes combining forces, sometimes one triggering changes in others. If we understand these dynamics we can anticipate the price changes with much lower downside risk than upside risk. We can then capture the price change with a large flow of money into our bank accounts.

1A: Risking Our Own Money

1.   A Currency Value Collapse

"My job for 30 years was to anticipate changes in the economic trends that were not expected by others, and, therefore not yet reflected in security prices."
Stanley Druckmiller

This was a late Twentieth Century financial killing but it highlighted the emerging potential of the big killing, which has since expanded in the early Twenty First Century.

After unification in 1990, Germany had a one-off event, the reconstruction of East Germany, which required large expenditure. To prevent inflation the central bank increased interest rates.

The United Kingdom meanwhile was in a recession. With its currency fixed against the German Mark, it could not stimulate the economy by reducing the currency value. Its interest rates were already high and increasing them to match German increases would deepen the recession.

Currency values go through cycles. The attractiveness of a country's exported products to buyers in other countries rises and falls over time for many reasons. If exports, or sales of assets within the country to foreign buyers, exceed imports, the currency value will tend to rise. This happens in the short term with significant sales of individual items, and over medium and long terms with expanding or contracting foreign markets.

As a currency increases in value, its consumers and businesses find purchase of products from other countries drop in cost. This can help respectively with these parties' sense of well-being and profitability. It tends to improve their satisfaction with the government in power. On the other hand, exporters of products find that they now earn less in their own currency. If their local costs have not reduced, this means their profits are reduced, which may mean layoffs of staff and reduced investment. These results tend to make voters unhappy with the government. The balance of these conflicting forces can affect government popularity.

At certain points in the currency value cycle, governments might want to freeze currency values for reasons that make sense to them. They might want to stop inflation growing, stop unemployment growing or make an industry sector that supports the government party or faction become more profitable. They might want to fix their currency against another currency to enjoy a stable relationship with an important trading partner.

However, what they want for political reasons is not necessarily what is realistic in the prevailing market conditions. If the currency value is moving in a certain direction based on cyclical forces, and the government tries to hold it at a certain level, or reverse its changes, then stresses will build. These create the potential for big shifts in value with associated opportunities for financial killings.

In 1992 managers of the Quantum hedge fund believed that the rate at which the United Kingdom was brought into the European Exchange Rate Mechanism was too high. They borrowed Pounds and converted them to dollars and made a point of telling the media that they expected the UK Government to devalue the Pound. This, as planned, created a run on the Pound.

The UK government bought Pounds to try and hold the value of the Pound but without effect. Traders continued to sell Pounds. Quantum continued to predict a devaluation of the Pound.

The government then raised interest rates. That did not stop the selling of the Pound but it did start taking money out of the accounts of borrowers on floating interest rates, such as businesses and mortgages This reduced company profitability and consumer spending. These are both factors for increasing unemployment. Governments which drive unemployment to high levels need to have someone else to blame or else they risk being voted out of office. The government chose to devalue the Pound rather than taking that risk. Quantum made its billion.

Shorting currency or any other asset is dangerous territory. If we get it wrong, as with any shorting situation, we can lose huge amounts of money. For that reason investors and speculators are cautious about risking a lot of their own money. See Section 2.5, Expertise. But Quantum and the other hedge funds involved could see something that most could not. The government was being squeezed by multiple cycles:

- They needed to reduce the value of the Pound to strengthen their economy with its mix of sectors at the time (see Appendix 5).
- The economy's position in Inventory and Fixed Investment cycles meant that there was already low demand in the economy, reducing employment and business throughput. Increasing interest rates would reduce demand further.
- There are many benefits for certain political factions from a depressed economy (see Example 5 and Appendix 4). But it needs to be periodically eased. Squeezing harder will deepen the collapse to the point where the government gets the blame (see Political Cycle).

So the hedge funds could see that the UK government had no good political options if they defended the currency value. Politicians will almost always choose what is good for their political survival if they are smart enough to work out what that is. They believe that they make a contribution of great value to the country. That value justifies any costs to the economy incurred in protecting their position.

This was a notable event because the hedge funds challenged the government. Usually people do not do this. There are many opportunities for killings due to sudden changes in currency value. Forcing devaluations of currency by government is only one method and one that needs all the factors involved to be understood.

There was a particular set of cyclical circumstances that made in an otherwise risky endeavor a good bet. Some years later, traders trying to short the Hong Kong dollar got burnt (see Short risk in Financial Instruments and Cycles below) when the Hong Kong government responded to different cyclical circumstances in a less cooperative manner. The political situation and the government's resources to undertake a fight were very different.

Even leading liberal economist Paul Krugman, not one to support hedge funds making billions, suggests that it might be argued that Mr Soros and colleagues did the UK a favor by highlighting to them the dangers of a fixed currency rate in Europe. The UK never joined the Euro as the Southern Europe countries Greece, Italy, Portugal and Spain did. When we look at their economic predicaments 20 years later, we see Mediterranean countries trapped in a Euro currency value that damages their economies. Its high value for them is choking their industries and condemning their youth to high levels of unemployment and low level jobs. Simultaneously its low value for Germany supports a huge export economy.

Cycles involved include:
- Currency cycle – the UK Pound was on a natural decline.

- Interest rate cycle – an era of declining interest rates and high sensitivity to rate increases was emerging.
- Inventory cycle and fixed investment cycle – demand for production was low.
- The political cycle - the political forces in this case gave the government little room to fight.

The killing mechanism was the price collapse. Understanding that underlying market forces were too powerful for political wishes was the hedge funds' advantage.

2. Financial Asset Price Collapses (The Big Short)

"When we expressed our concerns about the mortgage markets, many of the most sophisticated investors in the world, who had analyzed the same publicly available data we had, were fully convinced that we were wrong, and more than willing to bet against us."
John Paulson

The currency value example above dealt with shorting a currency where hedge fund managers had strong reasons to think that the currency value would not rise, even for a short period of time. In the following example the hedge fund managers were confident of a collapse at some time. They believed other market participants had an inadequate understanding of what was really going on with the US real estate mortgage market and with the vast amount of securities whose value was linked to those mortgages.

Cyclical Factors included:
- There was a real estate boom/bust cycle due for a bust, but while experts recognized this at a regional level, policy makers denied that it existed on a national scale.
- There was a long term interest rate cycle with a sustained period of low interest rates driven by long term depressed demand. This led to a shortage of quality lending (all the

good lending opportunities had no problem getting low rates) and a demand for poor quality loans. It aggravated the real estate boom bust cycle.
- The leverage cycle for many financial firms had reached very high leverage ratios.
- The financial risk perception cycle had seen a decline in perception of risk over much of two decades. People came to believe that the brilliance of Alan Greenspan as Chairman of the US Federal Reserve could cope with any financial crisis by suitable judicious opening or closing of the money flow.
- The political cycle supported the state of the financial risk perception cycle. Politicians could service their supporters by suppressing mechanisms that highlighted increasing levels of risk.
- There was a commodity price cycle (oil) where the price spiked upwards due to rising Chinese and Indian demand. This led to a big increase in some US commuting costs which was a trigger for the real estate market collapse. The price of oil dropped soon afterwards but by then the real estate security price collapse was under away.
- The working capital cycle was starved of liquidity as the above cycles combined to create a price collapse in collateral values.

The smarter hedge funds could see that this combination of cycles added up to a collapse which created a tremendous opportunity to short related securities.

There were multiple options for securities to short. Collateralized Debt Obligations offered one option. The stock values of financial firms which owned too many of these CDOs offered another. The stock values of financial firms, such as shadow banks which relied on using CDOs as collateral for short term commercial loans, were another. If the CDOs lost value, other firms would be unwilling to continue funding using them as collateral and there would be a liquidity crisis.

However, they knew that simple shorting in these circumstances was extremely risky. Knowing that other market participants did not understand the potential for collapse, they were aware prices could go up before this collapse occurred.

The nature of the expected collapse was such that picking its timing within weeks or months was very difficult. The bubble could continue for an extended period, increasing the reference asset prices as people thought real estate prices could only go up. Logically the financial firms run by brilliant managers could only make money not lose it.

Given that a major price collapse was expected, the Credit Default Swap (CDS) was the optimum instrument (see Section 2.6, Financial Instruments and Cycles below). Shorting would be too risky as the price might go up before it collapsed. A put option would avoid that risk but it would be a lot more costly (see Section 2.6).

The default condition for the CDS on the CDOs was defined by a certain percent of defaults of particular subprime mortgage tranches. The rating agencies had rated these to be low risk based on the input of the investment banks who issued them.

3.   Banking Stock Price Collapse - A Big Long

"When bad becomes good after an inflection, people are still in a bad mood. We are good at the inflection point."
David Tepper

A lot of financial killings by hedge funds are based on shorting some financial asset prior to it undergoing a price collapse. But sometimes hedge funds bet on the opposite, which is a big price surge in financial asset value. This requires betting that the assets price will rise when most market participants think that it will lose value.

Distressed assets are debt, bonds or stocks of companies that have filed for bankruptcy or have a significant chance of filing for bankruptcy in the near future. They all have the potential to become worthless. They also have the potential to increase a lot in price because their price has already collapsed if that collapse can be reversed to some degree, or if it applies to some securities much less than others.

The various values of different securities used to finance a company change in different ways when the company is in distress. They have different positions in the order of repayment. This means some securities may be repaid to varying extents and some may get nothing. Investors who specialize in distressed asset often have the expertise to see these repayment probabilities better than others in the market. This creates opportunities for those with better analytic skills to see a gap in value before the rest of the market does.

A classic financial killing occurred after the Global Financial Crisis when certain large banks had low stock values due to high levels of dubious assets. A big fear held by investors was that the government would nationalize these banks.

The killings due to financial asset price collapse (Example 2) had already occurred. Some hedge fund managers were looking for the next wave of killings.

One hedge fund, a distressed asset specialist, made billions of US$ in the months after the intervention by government agencies in the Global Financial Crisis. It invested in two of the banks that were believed to be likely candidates for nationalization and whose stock prices were plummeting.

It did this because the US Treasury had stated in a Financial Stability Plan Fact Sheet that it would convert convertible preferred securities common equity if needed to preserve lending in a worse-than-expected economic environment. The conversion price would be set at a modest discount from the prevailing level of the institution's stock price as of February 9, 2009. The stock price on March 5 for one of the banks had dropped to approximately a quarter of that price as panic set in. There was a 300% potential upside to buying at the collapsed price.

This reinforced the hedge fund's belief that the government was not going to let the banks fail. Politicians cannot afford to let the banking system collapse. See Political Cycle, Appendix 5.

The hedge fund operator realized a number of things about the cycles affecting their bank's environment:

- The leverage cycle had passed through the point of inflexion from prices plummeting to turning around before the rest of the market. That point was activated by the commitment by US Treasury to support the financial firms. Prices continued to plummet for a period after this point but this made purchases cheaper, leading to an even bigger killing.
- The risk perception cycle had gone from very low to very high. Investors had gone from thinking the banks could never fail to thinking they were much more likely to than the actual numbers suggested.
- The interest rate cycle had gone from low rates to very low rates with continued injection of liquidity by government agencies and deepening loss of demand.
- The political cycle meant that the government remained highly committed to supporting the financial sector.

4. Leveraged Buyouts

"I've lived through periods of illiquidity before. Asset prices come down. The economy slows or even goes into recession. Then the cycle re-starts. We buy at lower prices with less leverage."
Stephen Schwarzman

Leveraged buyouts are company buyouts which are designed to take advantage of multiple business cycles. Financial firms, typically private equity firms, buy companies with low earnings due to outdated and/or badly managed business processes, and due to their sector being in a down phase of its cycle. A firm will buy a company when the business cycle of the company's sector is entering a trough and the market is offering low price: earnings ratios. It borrows most of the money and pays an attractive interest rate on the borrowed money.

The PE firm installs management to modernize the business processes, typically taking advantage of a newer generation of technology to increase output and/or decrease costs. Through direct use of the technology, or through restructuring of the company, this may be advantageous due to effects on the company's environment. These could be cost structures or market demand of suppliers or customers. This increases the earnings as a result. Earnings (improved with modernized business processes) ideally pay the interest on the borrowed money.

The modernization process usually takes two to five years and in that time the business cycle will ideally have come out of its trough and price: earnings ratios will be rising. With the combination of increased earnings and the rise in price: earnings ratio, the market value of the company might have doubled.

For example, imagine the PE firm has bought a five billion market value business putting in $1 billion of its own money and that of its fund contributors. It borrows the rest, and after reorganizing, sells it for $10 billion. It will have increased the fund's stake from $1 billion to $6 billion, a $5 billion profit on the initial $1 billion. This is a fine killing by most standards.

But it can go wrong and many LBOs fail to achieve planned results. Getting the cycles wrong is a big risk when seeking these killings:

- If the sector demand cycle does not return to growth when expected and demand stays depressed, the increase in market value may be significantly deferred. We can hold off the sale but the longer we pay interest on financing, the poorer is the overall result. We may still be profitable but not make the hoped for killing.
- If the enhancement of business processes through updated technology does not work out according to plan, we may have higher costs and/or lower revenues. We might cut costs by removing staff who do not seem necessary for day to day operations. But they may prevent things going wrong in unusual situations, or at times of high demand. This can cause catastrophic failures in product safety, reliability and usability.
- Bringing in new technology to streamline customer engagement is particularly risky, even if the technology is proven elsewhere. A lot of success for new technology being applied to new products and processes depends on where it is in the technology upgrade cycle. New technology platforms may offer big potential gains. However, it may take time to refine the implementation tools to the point they can be used quickly and reliably in diverse applications. It is very easy to underestimate the time it takes to introduce a new technology platform.
- Often introducing new technology reduces flexibility in operation. This is because many of the small enhancements that have evolved over time with the previous platform get left out with the new platform. User interfaces often change with bad results for operational staff and customers.
- If customers have bad experiences dealing with a call center or an on-line transaction process they will hate us and stop buying from us when possible. These are the highly visible

layers of the customer interaction. But the organization may be full of processes that have evolved over time and which can cause problems when we cut them.
- We may have cut out people and processes that were actually necessary to keep our customers happy. Some customers may quickly switch to our competitors. Others who cannot easily do that may reengineer their own products and/or processes to permit substitution of different components to ours. That may take a year or two but will happen if the customers are sufficiently unhappy.

So a lot can go wrong. But if it was easy everyone would do it and compete furiously for the opportunities. Then we would not be able to buy out the company at the collapsed price that makes the killing a big one when we do succeed.

And of course we may have seen the problems coming all along. If we cannot find a better buyout opportunity to make sustained gains from reengineering we may settle for short term gains. Providing initial numbers are good, we can quickly put the business on the market and let the new buyers discover that all is not as it seems.

Refer to Appendix 2 for cash flow, liquidity, profitability and solvency.

Cycles involved include:
- Inventory and/or fixed investment – it is good to buy in when the market is depressed and sell when it is rising.
- Technology platform development - it is good to take advantage of a point in this cycle when the early, difficult and unpredictable developments have been worked through.
- Process development – as for technology development.
- Product development (if applicable) – it is good to have proven market acceptance of a new type of product. A competitor's product is fine if it can be reverse engineered.

- Interest rate cycle – low rates are not essential for buyouts but they help keep the costs down and provide a lot of lenders keen to earn higher than what a bank will offer.

5. **Real Estate Redevelopments**
   "If you want to buy something; it's obviously in your best interest to convince the seller that what he's got isn't worth very much."
   Donald Trump

   A lot of money can be made (and lost) buying up real estate that has decayed in value due to the decline of an industry sector or a commercial area. These redevelopment projects are similar in many ways to leveraged buyouts and some private equity firms have groups which specialize in them.

   In these projects we buy facilities in an area that has lost value and we develop the facilities to raise the market value of the area. This can be a complete repurposing of an area. Abandoned slaughter houses, chemical plants, old wharves or rail depots, slums are the kinds of cheap real estate that can be developed into a new residential, commercial or entertainment area.

   Alternatively we might have an existing commercial area that is simply shabby and out of fashion but we see the potential to breathe life into it due to various changes in its vicinity (see Area Price Relativity Cycle Appendix 6 Geoeconomics). The change in relative values of areas can make a tremendous difference to the profitability of a project.

   Cycles involved include:
   - Real estate cycle – general real estate
   - Sector investment cycle – investment for previous land use sector has moved elsewhere and not reinvested here

- Area price relativity cycle. The belief in the market that a particular area is going to rise in price relative to other areas is central to buying low and maximizing returns.
- Architectural fashion cycle – offices, retail centers, hotels and entertainment centers will attract more customers if their design appears to be new and exciting.
- Interest rate cycle – as for leveraged buyouts, low rates are not essential for buyouts but they help keep the costs down and provide a lot of lenders keen to earn higher than normal rates.

6. **Price Collapse and Asset Fire Sales.**

"We attempt to be fearful when others are greedy and to be greedy only when others are fearful."
Warren Buffet

Warren Buffet is talking here about investing not when the stock market has risen and people are confident but instead investing when the market is down and people have lost confidence in the stock market. But he is talking about securities in firms that own existing production assets, not in building new production assets. Contrary to what politicians like to tell us, smart people do not invest during recessions to increase capacity and create jobs. They invest to take control of existing capacity, reduce capacity to drive up prices and if necessary reduce jobs.

Boom times finishing with crashes are good for financial killings. But sustained recessions are good too. This follows the logic of Warren Buffet's long term investment gains but applies it to hands-on business operations.

When supply capacity exceeds demand with multiple suppliers competing for business, price usually drops, which usually increases demand to some degree. New buyers come into the market attracted by the lower price. If the increase in demand is not enough to meet the available capacity of parties ready and willing to sell, the price will usually drop again. Again there will be new demand but if its volume is still not enough to match supply, supply capacity will be run at lower volume levels. Sooner or later some supply capacity will be shut down. Along the way, if buyers are smart they will anticipate further drops and demand ever lower prices and we will have a price collapse.

A sustained price collapse presents a great opportunity for financial killings by suppliers with lower variable costs than their competition and with the financial resources to operate at low profit margins for periods. If we are in this situation we can reduce the price just to the level that balances supply against demand and no further. This will achieve short term profitability. Or we can reduce price below the variable cost of other suppliers and force them to lose money or shut down. Our short tem profitability is reduced but we ae making some and they are losing money.

We can then selectively swallow up assets of competitors who are struggling after a price collapse, and need to sell it off to survive. Or we can take over the competitors themselves as operating companies. We are selective because we may not want to buy old, inefficient supply facility assets. We may just buy the newer more efficient ones available. Or we may buy the old less efficient assets, take them out of operation and return them to operation when demand builds. The higher costs caused by their inefficiencies may be small compared to the price surge during a shortage of capacity. If we take a sufficient number of competitors out of the market, we can keep supply near or below demand so that prices stay healthy.

Acquisition usually offers a much cheaper way of adding long term capacity than building it. It also offers low cost capacity that we can use in the short and medium term to add and remove from total sector supply capacity. This allows us to damage competitors and produce upward price spikes. If we play the game right, the mix of supply capacity facilities with different operating and maintenance regimes will make it hard to prove any anticompetitive behavior. That assumes anticompetitive behavior is an issue in our environment. If it is not we can be more open about our operations.

We might buy assets worth hundreds of millions, even billions, of US$, for a fraction of that money.

We may buy and keep the new, more efficient facilities. We may buy and mothball old facilities. We may buy and shut down/repurpose old facilities. Which we do depends on our expectations of future demand. When will demand return and how strong will it be?

In a sustained recession, we are squeezing the life out of our weaker competitors and taking their markets and/or their assets. At the same time we are generating enough profit for our own needs. We can have our friendly politicians periodically spend to boost the economy. This provides a burst of money for the members of lower income sector, which they spend immediately and moves money around the economy. It also reassures the middle classes that things are improving after all.

The buyup of assets applies to the development of products, processes and technology as well as to supply capacity. As the recession sets in, expected short/medium term returns on such investment may be much less than they were before the recession set in. Startups are very vulnerable. Should technical problems occur in the development things become difficult. Also should general business conditions decline things could become difficult. Finding money from other investors to fill the revenue gap is no longer easy.

So a lot of new product, process and technology developments will be struggling to survive in a recession, let alone to grow and make billions for their founders. Many will be grateful purely for the chance to continue and bring the development to completion. They will sacrifice most or all ownership rather than let their development fail completely. Even if they walk away without stock or a job they can at least put on their CVs they were involved in something that succeeded. We can buy such companies for much less than the cost of developing new products, processes or technology ourselves.

The great thing about this approach is that we do not need to be a Henry Ford, an Alfred Sloan, a Bill Gates, a Steve Jobs, a Larry Page, a Sergey Brin, or a Mark Zuckerberg developing new products, technologies and industries. We just need to understand the mechanisms of financial killings. We can then buy up the creations of the technically innovative and milk the opportunities.

The key cycles here, in addition to the working capital cycle, which provides price collapse when required, are:
- The inventory cycle, which moves to a recessionary phase when required and helps the price collapse to occur.
- The fixed investment cycle, which provides potential assets for buyup, which have capex burdens for current owners.
- The political cycle, which is key to maintaining an economic environment that keeps the economy in a recessionary state when we need it to be in one.

In the case of the technology buyup, we also use the technology cycle. There are key points in it, particularly relating to missing functionality, which can bring a company to its knees through lost market share. This can often be corrected in the next minor upgrade, provided we have the financial resources to get it to the market.

7. Selectively Awarded Government Supply Contracts
"Never let a good crisis go to waste"
Winston S. Churchill

Government service contracts in most western jurisdictions are supposed to be awarded through scrupulously fair processes. The logic is that this drives down costs and prevents excessive profit levels being attained by private companies at the expense of the taxpayer. Competitive bidding in this environment can mean we often lose money on a particular deal.

However, if we have a supportive government, we can find ways of bypassing this process and making real killings, either in short term or long term contracts:

- Military contracts are excellent for this as they can be applied during some security crisis or other – an act of war, a threat of an act of war, an incursion into some disputed territory, a new defensive deployment.
- Technology development contracts are very good, particularly if associated with military capability during times of security fears. New technology usually involves some kinds of specialist knowledge whose omission removes many competitors.
- Public health emergencies that threaten the voters of our friendly politicians are also good.
- Civil disaster event contracts can be very rewarding – earthquakes, tsunamis, hurricanes, big floods and plagues to name a few. Construction firms can gain huge repair contracts without needing to compete.
- Financial crises can create opportunities where governments reward financial firms for merging with firms that are having difficulties.

The key thing for success in these various sectors is to have a government that will quickly see our company as the solution to the urgent problem and which will award us the contract on a selective basis.

We do not necessarily need to bribe politicians, although in some countries and cultures this is the generally accepted process to win business. When overt bribery is risky, we can be a bit more subtle using a range of methods to achieve desired actions from our politicians (see Political Cycle in Appendix 5).

The key cycles here are:
- The political cycle – we need our faction, or a faction that will share benefits with our faction, in power.
- The working capital/inventory/ fixed investment cycles – to deliver a financial collapse which will give urgency to selected government expenditure.
- The military cycle, if applicable to our opportunity – military spending is usually big and responsive to crisis.

8. Selectively Awarded Privatization Contracts

"Government programs are effectively insulated from the rigors of the marketplace, and therefore are denied the possibility of failure. Sometimes, nothing short of outright privatization can restore the discipline of a bottom line."
Donald Rumsfeld

An extension to the opportunity in Example 6 is to not just supply goods or services to some government agency but to take over the role of the agency itself. The logic here is to get rid of those costly and lazy bureaucrats and replace them with efficient private companies who compete to win contracts from the government. For example, we do not just supply the weapons but supply an operational military unit. We can hire soldiers, already trained by the government's military forces. Perhaps we have already provided that training as another contracted service.

The same can apply to airport security, prisons, schools, highway construction and operation. Military is particularly good though as it offers two opportunities:
- When times are quiet in terms of global strife the military start seeming to spend a lot of money that could be spent elsewhere. So the logic is to cut costs by handing over to the

more efficient private sector. But choose only companies with the right experience, one of which happens to be ours.
- When people feel threatened they want their political leaders to get rid of the threat. They are much less likely than usual to worry about the process. Times of crisis are excellent to avoid the competitive bidding that requires us to cut our profit margins.

Making very good money on these contracts should be the norm. If the service has previously been provided by bureaucrats it should be deliverable at relatively low risk. Bureaucrats are skilled in following rules, not in maximizing revenue and reducing costs. If the service has previously been done by soldiers, a large supervisory overhead can be removed. This is because career soldiers and their civilian masters will not have the same risk of embarrassment if things go wrong as they would if the actual military was involved.

The government's negotiator can be directed to write us a low risk contract with easily achieved performance measures.

If a large financial crisis does occur, which needs expenditure, that expenditure usually creates other effects such as government deficits.

The key cycles here are:
- Political cycle – we want a party or faction in power which will look for privatization opportunities and pick ones which advantage its friends (us). We also need information on what the crises (real or imaginary) are that our politicians can put to good use. This may involve local and/or geopolitical knowledge.
- Working Capital/Inventory/Fixed Investment cycles – a financial collapse which requires government expenditure, as they often do (see Example 14), is excellent. Our political friends can call out for cuts in government costs, replacing lazy, inefficient government servants with private sector efficiency.

- Financial Risk Perception cycle – a sense of panic after a financial crisis can be exploited by our politician friends.

1B Risking Other People's Money

"I made a mistake in presuming that the self-interests of organizations, specifically banks and others, were such that they were best capable of protecting their own shareholders and their equity in the firms."

Alan Greenspan

All of the examples so far involve risking our own money to make killings. This is fine if we really know what we are doing, which means we can:

- Identify stability conditions combined with an impending event that will create a killing opportunity.
- Understand the factors that affect the timing of an event.
- Know what financial instruments we need to use to catch the money flow.

A lot of financial people do not have this complete skillset but do have a different one. That is attracting customers by offering high returns and convincing them they have the skills to avoid high risk. If we are in this second category there is no need to tell customers that we are not actually in the first category. The large fees and/or percentages we charge will seem to be only reasonable. They assume we have a deep understanding of financial markets, high skills in risk analysis and rigorous investment evaluation criteria.

We may not actually have these skills but if we can make the customers think we have then for this purpose that can be just as good. If we can attract these customers we can make billions over a period. Customers here may be lenders or investors in our fund.

The risk analysis and investment evaluation criteria we offer may not be in the elite class. However, it will probably be adequate at the early stage of an economic growth phase or an asset price bubble of some type or other. Default risks are lower in a riding market. We can apply our filtering processes to cut out the bad risks and still have plenty of low risk opportunities to invest funds.

Towards the end of a growth period or bubble, finding safe investments becomes more difficult. Our customers seek high returns but safe investments and suitable loans may be much harder to find. If we resist temptation we will not be able to place the customer funds and earn those fees and percentages. So we may be tempted to lower the high standards of risk analysis that we claim to use if we want those fees.

Typically these other people's money types of killings are slower than the ones mentioned above. They are more slow bleeds than sudden deaths. Timing is not so critical. Providing we are positioned well in the timing of customer gullibility, we can sell our services for years. If things finally do come to a crashing halt, we will hopefully have made high profits for those years. After the crash, we can keep a low profile for a few years, living off our gains. We can then reinvent ourselves in a few years when new products and systems catch the imagination of the market.

This is an area where display of the high life is an advantage. People look for signs of success when they invest their money. They follow the logic that if financial firms have made money up to now, and avoided losing it all, they are more likely to keep making it. The houses, cars, boats, restaurants and other displays of affluence reinforce the appearance.

What is important in all of these is the impression that our skills are similar to those who successfully risk their own money and consistently win. Customers will then believe that although we are paying a higher interest rate than regulated banks, we have the skills to correctly what is safe and what is not safe. They will believe that the securities we create are as secure. They will believe that if the derivatives we design are particularly incomprehensible that is only because our designers are particularly brilliant. They will believe that the collateral we rely on in our shadow banking activities is safe from disastrous losses in value. Our visible success to date proves to them that we are the financial elite.

9. Risking Customers' Money - Understating Loan Risk

Our financial firm raises money to invest in property developments, offering securities at higher interest rates than banks. Investors flock to buy our securities. This is particularly attractive in a low interest rate era as has applied for the last two decades or more. People seeking income from securities look for alternatives to traditional offerings whose returns have declined. We take advantage of the fact that there has been a boom in price of real estate assets and investors think this will continue into the future.

We lend the funds to real estate development companies knowing they may not be able to repay the loans. This is because the property market has reached its peak and demand is likely to diminish, causing a collapse in price for new properties. Based on large projected profits and not accounting for potential losses due to non-repayment of loans, we pay ourselves large dividends and/or bonuses as we go. We do not account for potential losses due to non-repayment of loans at their true level.

All going well, the developments are successful, with the real estate being sold at good profit margins for the developers. They pay us back and borrow more for the next development.

However, eventually every locality reaches a saturation point for construction of new real estate in a certain price range. With a decline in demand for new houses, our developers fail to sell building lots and/or houses or apartments. They cannot repay the loans. When the non-repayment occurs, the losses to our financial firm become apparent. After delaying as long as possible while our managers collect salaries and bonuses, we declare bankruptcy blaming unforeseen economic conditions. We keep the salaries and bonuses that we have been paid. The same approach works for commercial real estate.

Our investors do not see that the conditions were completely foreseeable by parties with an understanding of business cycles and sadly accept their losses.

The cycles that we take advantage of include:
- Market expectation of real estate prices – this strategy requires expectation of prices to be in the rising phase.
- The Risk Perception Cycle – this strategy works when investors' confidence that past instabilities in the financial system will not recur is in the rising phase.
- The Interest Rate cycle – this strategy is enhanced with low interest rates, so investors seek rates better than banks offer. Risky real estate mortgages offer such rates.
- Political cycle – this strategy is enhanced when the legislators and regulators in power are those who believe that regulation of the financial sector should be minimized.

The above general strategies can also apply to loans in other business sectors where there is rising confidence and the companies we lend to can pay a premium. This allows us in turn to pay a return to our investors that attracts them in large numbers. This happens right up until the time our lenders cannot pay back the money.

10. Risking Customers' Money - Understating Securities Risk

We (typically investment banks) assemble thousands of mortgage loans acquired from mortgage originators into bonds. The bonds do not depend on one particular house which may default and incur losses for the lender. Risk is spread over a number of loans. So far this is sound logic.

The mortgage originators do not have to spend much time checking the creditworthiness of the borrowers as they can pass the risk of default off onto us. We can then pass it off onto the owners of the securities. This means originators can lend to borrowers who would have once been considered too risky, increasing their business volume.

We group the securities by degree of riskiness into graded tiers and sell the tiers as separate securities. The lowest risk security is the highest grade tier, which pays the least interest. The higher risk securities are the lower tiers, which pay higher rates of interest. Then we sell the higher risk tiers at higher interest rates to less risk-averse parties and the low risk tiers at lower interest rates to more risk-averse parties. We also have a real estate market which in many areas is enjoying rising prices year after year.

As long as the real estate price rises continue, if a loan does go bad, the increasing value of the real estate will mean the losses are small. Most parties in the market believe real estate prices will only go up so that even if some buyers do default, other buyers will buy them. Why do most people believe this? There are various reasons: *Because land is finite and people's needs for it are growing. Because the deregulation of markets will mean business and jobs will grow, liberated from the crushing effects of government. Because whatever.*

It actually does not matter why people believe during this period that real estate prices will rise forever. The important thing is that for a period they do and their belief creates opportunities for financial killings. And buyers of securities believe that the risk-spreading of the security will protect them. This is because credit rating agencies, whom we pay to check the creditworthiness of the securities, say they are AAA quality.

If this belief does turn out to be incorrect, we need to make sure we do not have a big inventory of unsold securities. If that occurs, it will not be our customers who have a problem but our stockholders (see Example 14 below). But for the bottom tiers with highest risk where we may struggle to find buyers, we have another cunning plan (see Example 11 below).

We can make hundreds of millions of US$ per year and make it year after year with senior staff collecting tens of those millions per year.

The cycles involved here are:
- Technology cycle – belief that the new technology changes everything, bringing more efficient markets.
- Political cycle – support for liberation of business from regulations.
- Real Estate cycle – a rising market reassures investors that mortgage default levels should be relatively low.
- Financial Risk Perception cycle that general financial risk is low.
- Interest Rate cycle – it is not essential but where rates are at a low phase in their cycle there are a lot of lenders looking for a better return than banks offer.

11   Risking Customers' Money - Understating Resecuritization Risk

The asset-based collateral that was shorted in Example 2 was created in large volumes by investment banks.

As mentioned above, with the ability for mortgage originators to offload mortgages to bond creators, there is less caution in issuing mortgages in first place.
- Whereas mortgage providers such as banks would traditionally require some kind of deposit to provide equity, the new originators would offer 100% financing or even 100% plus extra financing for purchases to celebrate the new home.
- Whereas mortgage providers would traditionally require pay records to prove that the buyers had income to pay the

mortgage, these originators would not require proof of income.
- Whereas mortgage providers would traditionally require a good credit record, these originators did not.

The consequence of these reductions in safeguards was a significant level of risk in the in the lower tiers that made it difficult to sell these bonds.

The solution was to take the lower tiers of the bonds and bundle them again. These are Collateralized Debt Obligations (CDOs), which can be used as collateral for commercial loans. The logic here in the case of mortgage-based securities is that not all different regions will suffer price reductions at the same time because different regions have different local economies. When Detroit is declining, Dallas, Daytona or Denver will be rising. This was true for many years until it stopped being true. It stopped because too many regional markets were over-supplied with buyers who borrowed more than they could afford to repay.

An option here is to select the worst of the bad bonds and CDOs, then buy credit default swaps (see Big Short above) against their failure. This prepares us for a downturn in the economy.

The cycles involved here are:
- Financial Risk Perception cycle - people are much more likely to believe our theories of effective risk spreading if there has not been a big collapse for some years.
- Real Estate cycle – if the asset-based securities are mortgages then we are aided by a general belief in the market that risk of a big downturn in real estate values is low.
- Product cycle – a new type of derivative needs analysis, design and implementation. Analysis that is based in inadequate data can lead to an unsound product.

- Interest Rate cycle – it is not essential but being at a low point in this cycle provides a lot of lenders looking for a better return than banks can provide.

12 Risking Stockholder's Money - Understating Risk to Overstate Profitability

If we produce more securities than we can quickly sell to our customers above, we take on a risk for our stockholders.

We claim revenues and/or profits that assume a lower level of risk than actually applies. The revenues and/or profits claimed are justification for far higher bonuses than would be the case if risk was properly assessed. If the events do materialize, the owners of the company lose. They may lose a portion of their investment, which would normally be covered by an allowance for bad debts. In this case it is an inadequate provision because management bonuses have consumed much of it. Or the losses may be much more than any normal high provision would cover because the real risks are much higher than such provisions would cover.

We could reduce the risk using credit default swaps, and some financial firms do this, but they cost money and reduce profits.

When we do get the risk assessment wrong and an asset we have invested in loses a lot of value, we may still be able to keep profits (and thus bonuses) looking healthy for a while. For assets that do not trade on a regular and high volume basis, book values can be out of step with what they could be actually sold for. We can then avoid taking write-downs which would greatly lower claimed profits. Asset value reductions are to be expected in many businesses alongside asset value increases. But if we only show the positive changes and hide the negatives we can present high levels of profitability and justify high bonuses.

The cycles involved here are:

- Technology Platform cycle (if applicable) – stockholders believe management is being exceptionally successful due to its implementation of new technology.
- Product Development cycle (if applicable) – stockholders believe management is being exceptionally successful due to its development of new financial products.
- Financial Risk Perception cycle – stockholders are not expecting big losses to occur so buy into the process.
- Leverage cycle – this cycle works in our favor up until the time that the leverage ratio suddenly plummets.
- Interest rate cycle – it is not essential but a low rate phase in the cycle provides a lot of lenders looking for a better return.

13   Risking Government Money – Too Big to Fail

Banks which take deposits are usually subject to restrictions on the portion of those deposits that can be loaned out via fractional reserve banking. They are also subject to requirements for the minimum amount of capital required by the banks. These restrictions allow commercial banks to handle liquidity crises and to handle losses due to bad debts. The problem with capital requirements, from a profitability perspective, is that the banks need to increase their capital if they are to lend more once they reach a limit. More capital means less dividends per dollar invested.

Shadow banks are financial intermediaries such as investment banks, hedge funds, money market funds and others which provide commercial bank-like activity. However, they are not regulated as commercial banks. They can have much smaller capital than commercial banks, allowing more loans to be earning interest. This means less sharing of dividends.

This does incur risks for their lenders. In the US they cannot offer deposit insurance from the Federal Deposit Insurance Corporation (FDIC) for smaller deposits as commercial banks do. However, their customers typically rely on collateral typically provided by securities.

One of the problems contributing to the Global Financial Crisis was that a number of large US shadow banks used asset-backed securities as collateral for commercial loans. This was fine as long as the securities held their value. When the value of the securities plummeted due to their riskiness becoming apparent (see Example 11) they were no longer acceptable as collateral for their full face value. Investment banks who created the securities and still held too many were exposed but so were any firms using them as collateral.

Lenders demanded a haircut - an allowance for the lower value of the collateral - or their money back. Once haircuts started, firms would need to sell off securities to top up the cash and this would lower the price of those assets. A price collapse was under away.

This created a liquidity crisis in the short term and doubts on the long term solvency of those firms holding a lot of these securities. Financial firms could not count on collateral provided by other firms so the shadow banks' commercial banking activities threatened to grind to a halt.

Many politicians initially refused to support financial firms who they believed had gotten themselves into difficulties and should therefore suffer the consequences. This would happen to businesses in other sectors, and to small financial firms whose failure would not create havoc across the financial sector. Why should large financial firms be different? However, their supporters from other business sectors, not just financial, told the politicians that they had better save the shadow banks or the economy would crash. The politicians approved the money. The US Treasury and Federal Reserve worked together to provide a funding package to protect lenders by providing hundreds of billions of US$ of capital to the major banks to keep the financial liquid.

This was a great solution for our risk takers because it was not the lenders or stockholders who lost their money but the government (at least in the short term). Most of the managers of the financial firms not only kept their past bonuses but their jobs and future bonuses as well..

Key cycles involved in this type of killing are:
- Political cycle – at the right time in the cycle, legislators and regulators will provide the environment for us to take the risks and step in to pay for the losses if things go wrong.
- Financial Risk Perception cycle – A perception of low financial risk set up the environment that allowed the risks to be taken. A perception of very high financial risk led to the government paying to fill the losses.
- Real Estate cycle – its instability destabilized the securities markets
- Interest Rate cycle – low rates make buyouts less expensive.

General

Often the methods above for profiting by risking other people's money have dramatic consequences when things go wrong: Retired people lose their life savings. Governments spend hundreds of billions of taxpayer's keeping the economy moving. The financial industry gets bad headlines. People protest in the street.

After these events, there may be new regulations to prevent some financial practices. There may also be changes in awareness by investors of risk. It may be harder to convince people to invest.

However, a decade or two later with new business environments, this changes:
- There are new markets, locally and globally.
- There are new technologies and processes used to optimize activities in the new markets. They may be stimulated and financed by the new markets. They also may make the new markets possible.
- There is new terminology to describe the markets, technology and processes.

- Previously understood risks appear to no longer apply. New types of risks have not been experienced.
- The financial firms talk the new terminology, appear to really understand the new markets, the technology, the processes, and the risks and how to avoid the risks..

Even if the old generation remains cautious, new investors come along who are keen to get in on the action. New politicians with funding needs and new regulators with career advancement needs replace the old ones. Regulations get relaxed to make it easier for business. New products avoid the restrictions on old ones and seem to have low risk levels. The cycle repeats itself but with a new style, new terminology and new story.

1C Having It Both Ways

There is no reason that we cannot risk our own money (if we are smart enough) and risk other people's money at the same time in a related area that we know it is a high risk.

14 Make it, Sell it and Bet on its Failure

If we are developing a risky financial product, and selling it to the market, it is only responsible to cover our risks while we still have it in stock. Then once we sell the product we keep the protection for use as a financial killing tool.

We can create CDOs and while we are selling them to the market we buy CDSs on them in case they fail before they are sold. Then just in case they fail after we have sold them, we keep the CDSs in the anticipation of that happy (for us) event. We can also buy CDSs on similar CDOs issued by other firms where we think it would be a good bet that they will fail. And we can buy them on the firms themselves which we know carry a lot of CDOs with good failure potential.

PART 2: KEY COMPONENTS OF KILLINGS

"Remember, there's no such thing as an unrealistic goal--just unrealistic time frames."
Donald Trump

We have mentioned the involvement of various specific business cycles with particular examples of financial killings. We need to understand the nature of cycles and their interactions so as to appreciate their contribution to financial killings. The time we start something, the time we have to ensure all its key components are in place, and the time that key external events occur are all critical to its success. Some of these we can control. Some of these can only be prepared for when a favorable combination of cyclical and one-off events occurs.

2.1 Business Cycles

Cycles are fundamental to generation of wealth and sustained business growth. They are also fundamental to creating the opportunities for the large transfers of that wealth that take place in financial killings. The players who make killings understand these cycles and how to exploit them.

To understand how cycles work to support killings, we need to understand the nature of various business investment cycles, how different cycles interact and how those interactions can lead to spikes and collapses in prices of interest. Those prices include various designed products, commodities, physical assets and financial securities.

We also need to understand how certain variables go through cycles that reflect investment cycles and tell us about conditions for that investment and returns from it.

Some business investment cycles are better known than others. They all share an investment phase and a return on investment phase.

If the return is less than the investment is, they may or may not keep recurring. This depends on expectations of returns improving over time and the financial ability to sustain an operation until improvement. If these are not present the recurring investment will likely cease. If the return is greater than the investment, the cycles will normally keep recurring indefinitely. All of these cyclical investments involve financing by sellers, buyers or third parties (usually the financial sector).

The timing of some of these cycles is applicable to the general economy. The timing of some is applicable only to a specific industry sector. Individual sectors can be rising or falling at different times from the general economy. But in general if enough sectors are moving together at the same time, so will the general economy.

These cycles in different sectors and the wider economy are not necessarily regular. They are each combinations of many cycles at the individual company level, which combine to create diverse cyclical patterns (see Appendix 1). However, this does not affect their underlying mathematical behavior, nor does it affect how the different cycle types combine with other cycles types.

Investment Cycles

Working Capital Cycle

This is the fundamental cycle of business, involving buying supplies, paying operational staff, preparing the product, delivering the product to the customer and getting paid for it. The costs need to be financed until the payment comes in.

The working capital cycle is one of the best known cycles. It covers the time that elapses between investment in such things as raw materials, components, hiring of people, purchase of services to produce a product, whether good or service, and when we receive payment for that product. With sustained profitability, it is a self-regenerating cycle that can continue indefinitely unless demand or supply conditions change.

The interaction of the working capital cycle with longer term investment cycles is very important. It feeds them and they feed it. The sustained viability the working capital cycle is critical to any business. It is of particular interest when it comes to economic stability as this cycle ultimately collapses when developments in the longer cycles lead to its destabilization. The length of this cycle can vary enormously. It can be as low as minutes for some electronically traded securities and, for certain types of projects, it can last years. A 30 day cycle is very common.

The mathematics of failure of the working capital cycle due to price collapse is dealt with in Appendix 3.

Kitchin (Inventory) Cycle

The Kitchin or Inventory cycle is the fluctuation of GDP caused by the accumulation and the selling of inventories. This is not to be confused with an individual business's inventory cycle which is a term related to inventory management. It is influenced by companies' activities to increase or reduce throughput, and it influences their plans to increase or reduce throughput.

If production is greater than demand, GDP will rise but companies will also accumulate unsold stocks. This will encourage some to scale back production, cutting GDP even if demand remains constant. An economic cycle is created and normally the inventory cycle amplifies the existing economic cycle as stocks are accumulated in good times and production is reduced in bad times

In a rising market, we increase inventory to capture a share of increasing demand. This may involve working longer hours, hiring additional staff, running plant harder and if necessarily less efficiently if that produces more output and bringing on less efficient plant if it is available.

When demand is saturated, companies have excess inventories and have to drop prices if they need to clear those inventories. If some companies have cash flow problems, a price collapse can occur.

The Inventory cycle typically lasts 3 – 5 years.

Fixed Investment Cycle

This cycle typically works in conjunction with the inventory cycle. When inventory cannot catch up with demand on an upturn, people invest in fixed assets such as industrial plant to increase supply capacity. They make the judgement that there will be enough time with a period of increased demand to utilize the additional supply capacity long enough to gain enough return on the investment to pay it back.

The Fixed Investment cycle is also valuable for financial killings that involve price collapses. Usually Fixed Investment price collapses are significantly larger than those associated with an Inventory cycle on its own as the downturn is longer and deeper.

The Fixed Investment cycle at the GDP level typically lasts seven to eleven year years. It includes either two or three inventory cycles.

For further information see Appendix 5.

Infrastructural Investment Cycle

This is a type of fixed investment cycle relating to infrastructure such as roads, ports, water supply, power and telecommunications networks. It is influenced by the multiple industry sectors which share infrastructure. Transport infrastructure is of particular interest to us here because it affects the supply chain. It can have a large impact on geoeconomic linkages between regions connected by road, ail, sea or air.

The Infrastructural Investment cycle typically lasts fifteen to twenty years.

For further information see Appendix 5.

Real Estate Cycles

Real estate follows cycles where initially a shortage of housing or commercial buildings leads to rising prices. This in turn leads to developers opening up land, infilling existing land or reusing existing land and constructing buildings. While the prices hold, profits for developers can be good. Eventually supply catches up with demand for any of many reasons: Improved transport links make more land available out of the area or the region's economy slows down attracting less new businesses and workers.

When supply catches up with demand, developers with projects under away may keep building, hoping to sell before the price drops too far. Soon there is a saturation of the market at a particular price point. The price drops. People who need to sell in the short term for whatever reason find few buyers, and the price drops further. Mortgages stop being paid, mortgagee sales drive prices down further until we eventually reach a relatively stable lower price level. If the downturn is severe, houses become homes for squatters who wreck them over a period, diminishing the availability of housing stock.

The Real Estate cycle typically lasts eighteen years.

There is an associated real estate cycle which relates to changes in relative value of localities. This can compound with the primary real estate cycle to create opportunities for particularly large gains in value as it often appears suddenly after a long period of stagnation.

These cycles affect residential real estate as well as commercial and industrial real estate. They can have a large impact on the wider economy because people use land as collateral for loans for business investments and consumer spending.

For further information see Appendices 5 and 6.

New Product Version Cycle and New Process Cycle

These are the cycles involved in building a new product version, product variation or supply process using a proven technology platform. The application of the technology may be a little different from the previous one, but does not require a new technology platform to be developed. Any recent minor upgrades that happen to have been made to the technology platform (see below) can be used for such product and process developments.

These cycles often work in conjunction with minor technology upgrades and may influence their direction. When we develop a new product or process we use the most up-to-date version of the technology platform, using the learning gained from its use in previous applications.

Cycle life is typically 1-2 years. This may be much shorter with internet apps.

For further information see Appendix 5.

New Technology Platform Cycle – Major Upgrade

The underlying technology platform our products use periodically gets upgraded. Computers shift platforms from valves to transistors, from transistors to integrated circuits, from integrated circuits to microprocessors, from single processor chips to multiprocessor chips. Telecommunications data services switch platforms from dial up modem to ISDN, from ISDN to DSL, from DSL to HDSL, from HDSL to fiber. Auto engines switch from gasoline carburetors to fuel injectors, then to higher efficiency diesel, then to electric motors. Each of these stages will have several platform changes with significant improvements.

The new platform will be superior to the old because it is faster, lighter, stronger, uses lower cost raw materials or services, is easier to build, more flexible to design, less expensive to maintain or more able to be controlled from the other side of the planet.

Cycle life is typically 5-10 years.

For further information see Appendix 5.

New Technology Platform Cycle – Minor Upgrade

We change some parameter or other of a technology platform. We might increase the clock speed of a microprocessor, add more memory, add hard disk with more storage, add a faster graphics chip, etc. We might change the mixture ratio of an alloy or increase the compression ratio of an engine. We reuse code modules developed in various developments during the last minor upgrade cycle of a software product. These minor upgrades improve the performance/cost ratio in some way or other. Eventually diminishing returns reduce their impact and we need a new major upgrade. Cycle life is typically one to two years.

For further information see Appendix 5.

Geoeconomic Cycles

In a global economy, markets and production sources for one region may be located in other regions. Markets in our region may be significantly impacted by expansion of production capacity in other regions. That production might be of oil, minerals, grain, timber, fish, meat, vehicles, machine tools, semiconductors, computers systems, software, or services in many sectors. When we invest in production capacity, our markets for the products we produce may be located in any of the continents around the globe and on many of the islands.

Transport costs may be a major component of final price. Transport facilities (road, rail, ports, trucks, trains, ships, planes) have their own construction cycle, which interacts with demand causing transport price cycles..

For commodities such as oil, minerals and grain, price is determined by production costs, transport costs and taxes of the supply source at the margin. For non-commodity products, those designed and produced for a particular purpose, there can be large variations in market demands. These demands depend on confidence in the perceived quality and usability of those products. Lack of familiarity with such products due to regional separation can be a large barrier. There is a cycle of increasing familiarity and increasing market uptake across regional separations. This can take decades or weeks depending on the type of product and means of information spreading.

For further information see Appendices 5 and 6.

Extractive Cycles

Extraction industries such as mining, forestry and intensive fishing involve a period, usually years or decades, of extracting a product from its source. This typically runs until the product is depleted to the point of being uneconomic given the initial processing plant capability and/or market price levels. The cycle involves finding the resource, installing the production plant and running it until the source is depleted to the economic limit. Often, if it is in a remote location, it may also involve building transportation infrastructure facilities such as railways, roads and/or wharves.

Extractive cycles are different from the other cycles in that they do not generally recur after the initial exploitation unless conditions change. The cycle finishes because the markets and/or resources that generated have been depleted. But they are similar to other investment cycles in that they feed to and from these other cycles and add to other cycles in terms of combined economic activity.

The cycle recurs if processing capability improves, e.g. new technology allowing economic extraction from lower density sources. And it can recur if the market price rises to the point the process becomes economic again, even with old processing capacity.

We cover more of this in Combinations of Cycles below and in Appendix 5.

Indicator Cycles

The cycles above are investment cycles. In addition we have cycles that indicate the combined effects of investment cycles.

Leverage Cycle

The ratio of an asset value to the cash required to purchase it (with remainder being debt) is the leverage ratio. The leverage cycle is the cycle followed over time by the leverage ratio. The cycle starts with only low risk loans getting made. Those loans go to buyers and investors having plenty of cash and moderate requirement for debt. Risk is low because if the buyers or investors default on the loan, even with a significant drop in resale price, the lender will probably get all or most of their funds back.

As financing gets easier with rising market confidence, the leverage ratio gets higher and higher. As the ratio gets higher, there is less room for a price drop in the event that the borrower cannot repay the loan. This is fine as long as asset prices are rising but if prices level off, or drop by even a moderate amount, some loans will not get fully repaid.

The leverage ratio reaches a point when more and more borrowers cannot repay their loans. Then a price drop in the product or asset means that not all the loan gets repaid. If enough loans fail to be repaid by significant amounts, caution (or panic) sets in. Lenders reduce the leverage ratio to a safer level, reducing the number of buyers. This can of course reduce prices further. This can cause more loans to not be fully repaid leading to further reductions in the leverage ration.

The price plummets until at some point buyers who do not need high leverage come into the market and leverage bottoms out. Eventually price bottoms out and the cycle starts again.

The leverage ratio has particular significance for banks in terms of the stresses they can impose on their borrowers and their own survival. It has a large significance for financial killings

For further information see Appendix 5.

Political Cycle
"A tax loophole is something that benefits the other guy. If it benefits you, it is tax reform"
Russell B. Long, United States Senator from Louisiana from 1948 until 1987 and chairman of the Senate Finance Committee for fifteen years from 1966 to 1981.

This cycle covers the back-and-forth movements in power between political parties or factions, or between ideologies which may straddle parties or factions. The parties in power legislate, regulate and enforce rules to give advantage to their supporters. The economic changes resulting can aid or impede opportunities for killings in specific sectors and in the economy generally.

In addition to improving the environment for such opportunities, the political party or faction in power can help ensure that their supporters get the best access to those opportunities.

Parties, or factions, group into alliances and then break up and regroup when the alliance does not deliver what they hoped for. A big factor in the maneuvers of parties or factions is their respective leaders' hunger for power and wealth.

Political cycles can take from months to decades, from when a faction goes into power through to it losing power until it returns again. The timing of the phases depends on how quickly people in outer factions become disappointed in with the behavior of the inner factions.

Depending on where things are in the political cycle, we as investors will get greater or lesser assistance from government to make financial killings of various types. If another faction is in power there may still be opportunities for us. They may implement policies that are targeted for their supporters but which overflow into areas where we can benefit. They may throw opportunities our way to keep our factions causing problems at a sensitive time. They may make occasional deals with our faction when their own grouping is split.

For further information see Appendix 5.

Interest Rate Cycle

Interest rates are affected by demand for money and by risk. If there are more borrowers than lenders, the price for the use of money (the interest rate) goes up. If lenders perceive more risk the price goes up. Demand and risk perception sometimes rise together and sometimes one is rising while the other is falling. The relationship between these drivers creates cycles. See Appendix 5.

Generally business loan interest rates follow inventory and fixed investment cycles. When demand is rising and inventory is building, businesses are confident. They borrow more in anticipation of good profits on the supply side and an expectation that prices will firm on the demand side. When the inventory cycle and fixed investment cycles catch up with demand, prices soften. Inventory reduces and supply facilities are operated at lower percentages of full capacity. However, there is increased debt in the system and it takes some time before this is run down. Interest rates lag behind the drop in inventory/capacity until debt is reduced.

In 2017, much of the world is in a long term recession. Employment is depressed. 20% of the US working population is on low wages or working part time and members of another 50% is scared that it might happen to them. This is good for business cost containment. But lower income consumers do not have the capacity to borrow at the level they would have done 30 years ago. Meanwhile higher income classes are earning more and keeping more with lower tax levels. In the absence of investment opportunities they save more of their money.

This availability of savings for investment is good for economic development when opportunities come along. And there is an unexpected side benefit for those seeking certain types of financial killing. Higher supply and lower demand drives down the price (interest rates) of borrowing. Combined with actions by central banks to keep the economy from stalling, this is creating a period of very low interest rates.

This is part of a pattern where rates fluctuate with inventory and fixed investment cycles about a long term cycle. If we look at 10 Year US Treasury rates, this wave declined through the Great Depression, rose after World War II to a peak in the early 1980's, then declined since then. In the absence of a major war to create demand, central banks have attempted to stimulate demand by monetary methods – reducing interest rates.

For further information see Appendix 5.

Currency Value Cycle

Currency values rise with increasing sales of products to other countries and with increasing investment from other countries. They fall with increasing purchase of products from other countries and with increasing investment into other countries. These rises and falls follow cycles. Some cycles are short term, activated by individual large sales or investments. For example the government buys a new weapon system or the national airline buys a new fleet of planes. Some cycles are longer term, activated by longer term changes in balance of sales and investment between countries.

For further information see Appendix 5.

Financial Risk Perception Cycle

This cycle reflects the market perception that financial risk is generally high or low. After a big financial crash with a lot of unpaid loans throughout the financial sector, people tend to believe that financial risk is high. As time goes by bad debts get written off, many dubious debts actually get repaid and people start to forget the pain. Better still new people come into business who have never experienced a big crash. Confidence builds and it becomes easier and easier to borrow money on risky loans until eventually another crash occurs.

This also has an effect on the regulatory environment. After a crash politicians are keen to be seen regulating so as to prevent a similar collapse recurring. As the memories of the crash diminish, politicians are keen to be seen deregulating so as to liberate the market from the heavy hand of unnecessary regulation and bureaucracy. This can be good if they are our politicians easing the way for us to make killings.

For further information see Appendix 5.

Shocks

Economic shocks can be stimulated by many events: Sudden failures of production capacity or transport links can lead to shortages of supply. Unexpectedly large crops due to unusual weather can collapse prices. Technology changes can have sudden impacts such as large cost savings and/or unforeseen boosts in supply capacity. Wars and natural disasters produce big expenditure and big damage. Someone discovers gold, setting off a gold rush, where a lot of money pours into an area as prospectors race to find more gold. After they have gone, the long term miners invest in heavy equipment and a long term extractive cycle gets under away.

The effect of such a shock is a sudden surge of demand which adds to the other demands, or a sudden drop in demand, which subtracts from other demands. It may dissipate (see Appendix 5) but, in that first surge or slump, it may have a big impact.

Shocks generate cycles but these cycles dissipate over time unless self-generating forces come into play. If we imagine a tsunami generated by a seismic event sending a big wave across the ocean there will probably be a number of surges after the big wave. These dissipate. By contrast if we have wind effects creating waves, due to a sustained atmospheric pressure situation, these waves will keep on generating as long as the energy provided by the wind is available.

The wind is equivalent to the profit we get from a recurring investment, such as in working capital, fixed capital for facilities, technology or product development investment. As long as the profit keeps coming at a sufficient level we keep investing.

2.2 Combinations of Cycles

Synchronization

Some of the above cycles synchronize with others or are led or followed by them with some consistent time gap. This may apply at the individual industry sector level or for the economy as a whole. Other cycles operate relatively independently of one and other. They may add or subtract from each other as regards total business volume but otherwise they pass through each other.

Composite Volume

Cycles feed into each other. Working capital cycle profits feed investment in associated facilities fixed investment, product development cycles and technology cycles (see Appendix 1). The profit phase of fixed investment production facilities feed infrastructure cycles and technology cycles.

While facilities are being built, staff will spend for their personal needs and for the facility needs, increasing the size of the working capital cycle. Staff working on the infrastructure and technology cycles will also spend, increasing the working capital cycle and the facility fixed investment cycle.

Potentially any individual investment cycle within a sector can provide financial killing opportunities. In addition to feeding each other, cycles add to each other to produce a composite level of business that may contribute to killings.

High or low composites can lead to cash flow and liquidity problems (see Appendix 2), which can also trigger price collapses in the working capital cycle. We also have combinations of the above recurring waves with one-off pulses. See Appendix 4.

It is often difficult to see cyclical patterns clearly until after changes have occurred. It only takes a few types of cycles combining for the pattern to become very unpredictable, assuming that the individual cycles were predictable in the first place. Generally an individual sector cycle will be fed by multiple businesses. They influence each other but are rarely entirely in sync so the cycle they form is uneven.

Combinatorial Innovation

We have talked of the combination interaction of different types of cycles. We also have combinations of technology cycles. Advances in one technology often create an economic environment which triggers advances in another. An agricultural revolution may generate a lower cost crop, which leads to more trade in that crop because it is now cheaper for people to buy the crop than to grow it themselves.

This may be a local effect where one subgroup specializes in growing a crop and sells it to other subgroups. Or it may occur between regions if one region benefits more greatly from the technological advance. An advance in the growing of rice, which requires a lot of water, may not transfer to an arid region. The selling of rice from the wet region to the arid region may become a significant level of trade.

Either way, the increase in local or inter-regional trade may lead to commercial advances as merchants do more and more trade and gain economies of scale in improved processes. Examples are advances in in trade finance and insurance. These advances may then be used in other areas than the original agricultural area.

Conversely it might be that the advances in trade finance make it possible for agricultural producers to find merchants who could buy their produce if they produced more. So they develop technology to produce large crops.

In a similar way advances in shipping could trigger the above agricultural and/or commercial advances in technology. Conversely agricultural or commercial advances could justify the investments to develop shipping technology.

Centuries ago these developments of one technology leading to developments in others might have taken decades or generations for the knowledge about it to spread and then to be acted upon.

Historically these combinations happened over generations. In the 21st Century they can happen in far shorter time frames. In 2017 developers of mobile phone apps can trigger disruptive forces in months that can change markets that were previously stable for years.

For further information see Appendix 5.

2.3 Price Spikes, Collapses and Triggers

If we are seeking quick financial killings, we are generally looking for upward or downward price spikes and price collapses. Spikes generate opportunities on their own and often also trigger price collapses.

These prices can be the prices of financial securities or any other asset or product. If it is a non-financial product there is likely to be an associated financial security which responds with its own spikes and collapses.

If we understand the relationship between price spikes and/or collapses and the sector's cyclical volumes, we can better identify potential opportunities associated with these price disruptions before the rest of market. We do not need to predict future market changes years ahead of other players. We just see their potential before the rest of the market and prepare to take advantage. We watch all the cycles that will impact our product of interest and look for combinations that will lead to price spikes and price collapses.

These combinations will be determined by the impact that product or asset prices have on credit, liquidity, profitability and solvency of companies and sectors. These will affect securities such as securitized receivables, credit default swaps, debt securities and stocks. They will also lead to attempts to sell companies in trouble and to purchase companies having sudden success, each of which provides killing opportunities.

Price Spikes

Upward price spikes occur when increases in demand volume can be met only by using much more expensive supply sources.

Downward price spikes occur when demand volume reduces to the point where demand can be fully met by using much less expensive supply sources.

Price spikes create opportunities for highly profitable short term increases in revenue. They can also trigger price collapses, which can create much larger high profit opportunities, and often longer term ones.

See Appendix 1 for more information.

Price Collapses

While spikes can be very profitable, particularly if we can get them to recur on a regular basis, the key event required for the really large financial killing is the price collapse. A collapse in the price of just one product or asset can lead to many opportunities for financial killings. For example, real estate prices collapsed prior to the Global Financial Crisis. The collapse in price led to mortgages defaulting. This led to mortgage bonds and Collateral Debt Obligation (CDO) securities prices dropping. It led to stock and bond values of banks declining. This single type of price collapse had a multitude of impacts on financial securities and led to multiple types of financial killings:

- Investment banks who were packaging CDOs and had unsold product incurred solvency and liquidity difficulties. This meant their stock prices dropped and risk of bankruptcy rose. Large profits were made by parties who shorted these stocks (Example 2)

- Shadow banks who used the securities as collateral for commercial loans were not able to roll over loans. This led to solvency and liquidity difficulties. This meant their stock prices dropped and risk of bankruptcy rose. Large profits were made by parties who shorted these stocks (Example 2).
- The payment of Credit Default Swaps (CDSs) on loss of CDO values. Large profits were made when CDOs lost value by parties who purchased these CDSs (Example 2).
- Stock prices in banks who owned hedge funds which owned CDOs, or who purchased other financial firms brought down by the CDOs, incurred solvency and liquidity difficulties. This led to low stock prices. Large profits were made by parties who purchased these stocks when their price collapsed before later recovery (Example 3).

The collapse in security prices during the GFC was a particularly significant price collapse, leading to multiple types of financial killings. But price collapses in many other situations led to killings. The killings in examples 4 and 5 specifically benefit from price collapse situations. The killings in examples 6 and 7 are enhanced in price collapse situations. Examples 9 through 14 are all enhanced by an environment where investors instinctively fear collapse and trust those that they believe have the expertise to avoid it.

For those who are interested, we model price collapse processes in Appendix 3. We use complex variable mathematics, used extensively to model cyclical systems in various engineering disciplines, to extend traditional economic techniques. Contrary to the name, complex variable math often actually greatly simplifies certain types of analysis, particularly in the area of cyclical systems.

Events Triggering Price Collapse

Collapses typically occur when some event or series of events in an unstable situation triggers an irrecoverable movement away from equilibrium. The unstable situation is due to a perception in the market that demand and supply are balanced, or that demand exceeds supply. However, in reality there is an underlying excess of supply, hidden because people are buying in expectation of price increases.

The key to triggers are combinations of events that individually may not incur a dramatic change in volume sold of our relevant product but which, as a composite, push volume over a threshold. At that threshold, price changes dramatically. These can be local to a region or can be geoeconomically linked between regions.

The composite volumes, high or low, create environments which ease or aggravate stability problems of the working capital cycle. Collapses can be triggered by both upward price spikes and downward price spikes. An upward price spike can drive customers to seek medium or long term substitute solutions. This can cause a medium/long term reduction in demand. If that reduction in demand takes it significantly below supply capacity, it can activate a price war. A downwards price spike can encourage buyers to hold back buying and see if prices drop again. This can set off a cascade effect of price drops, followed by delays in orders while waiting for further drops then price drop again.

The spike's major value for those seeking large killings here is as a trigger of a price collapse when the system is unstable. This instability is usually due to excessive lending as a portion of product sales and/or asset investment. To make the killing we need to recognize that state to be impending when others do not see it. Then we put mechanisms in place that will capture the money when the gush comes.

Triggers are very hard to predict in terms of timing, due to the complexity of cycles. Short of sabotage missions, we can sometimes activate them by shutting down supply links or cutting production. However in some jurisdictions this exposes us to charges of price manipulation. If this is the case we need to be a bit subtle about the process.

Liquidity demands in one financial market can lead to a need for cash in other financial markets. This is because firms seek to fill a shortage of cash in one area by selling securities in other areas. This can collapse the price in the secondary areas and cause cascading collapse from area to area.

If a liquidity crisis occurs, either because it was due anyway or because the collapse reduced suppliers' cash flow, the collapse will be magnified in size and extended in time. Suppliers will lower their price further and further. They do this trying to win volume before some other seller does the same in an attempt to raise cash to reduce debt.

Given time in a collapsed state, some companies will hemorrhage profits and move into a solvency crisis. See Appendix 2. This creates further opportunities for financial killings.

Generally we need to be aware of the kinds of events that can trigger a favorable situation when the conditions are right and watch out for them. We need to identify the cyclical situation that makes those conditions right and the cyclical situations that create the trigger events. Then we need to put the right financial arrangements in place to capture the money when it flows.

2.4 Complex Variable Analysis

The financial elite pick the cyclical patterns where the herd fails to see them. They understand aspects of the real nature of financial stability that the others do not grasp. They may not talk about these aspects. They may deny them. But they understand and use them.

We use the term financial elite here as meaning people who are very good at doing something which is difficult. They have the ability to see patterns in complicated cyclical processes that other people miss. They understand the factors that may drive a price change pulse in a particular system, based on the forces of supply and demand in that system. They also sense when that pulse is likely to occur. And they can pick the event which creates the big gorilla opportunity for financial killings, the large scale price collapse.

Most people avoid doing the difficult if possible. They can conscientiously and consistently do straightforward tasks. They follow rules of thumb and comply with documented processes. But for them, difficult is risky so best avoided. They follow the crowd or advisers who they believe to be competent.

Others try to do the difficult and fail. They do not have the core skills for more than routine endeavors. Or they do not have the ability to combine diverse tasks in an integrated series, particularly if unexpected events occur on a continuous basis. Or they do not have a sense of timing to identify the critical moments when they must complete certain tasks. Or they simply overestimate their own talents in these areas.

And others claim that they have achieved the difficult when they simply have done the straightforward. But they have made out that it was fraught with problems, magnifying their size and claiming great expertise and innovation in solving them. They succeed because we do not know that they are not exactly telling the truth?

We describe the mathematics of price collapse and the environment that leads to it in Appendix 3. The financial elite do not need to know that theory. What they do need is an intuitive feeling for the dynamics of what is going on based on experience and an understanding of what drives price in a particular sector. What forces in that sector make price rise rapidly and what make it fall rapidly.

This is similar to how surfers do not need to know the mathematics of ocean waves in order to ride them. Surfers leave the mathematics to ocean engineers. They just need to have a feel for the dynamics of waves.

How do surfers get that feel? They get it by riding thousands of waves in different locations and conditions over years. Surfers start with small waves and gradually develop the skills and judgement to handle bigger and less predictable waves. Eventually the surfing elite may not have a acquired a clue about the application of complex variable analysis to ocean waves[1] but they can ride sixty foot high monster waves.

Similarly the members of the financial elite get a feeling for the dynamics of business cycles by observing many situations where prices of financial and non-financial assets have varied through cycles. This involves:
- An understanding of risk transfers through buyers, sellers and third party financers.
- An understanding of the impact of financing on volume, economies of scale, price and on price stability.

In Appendix 3 we talk in detail of the role of buyer's risk in sales and its transfer to seller's risk and financing party's risk. Typically in the economic world, volumes of products sold increase as price is lowered. A few buyers initially get most value out of a product. Possibly it has been designed for their specific needs, and they will pay more than others. Lowering the price attracts other buyers who get some value but not as much value as the first buyers. Then, as the price is progressively lowered further, more buyers come on. They may get only a fraction of the value that the original buyers get but if the price is right, that is fine.

Economies of scale, if applicable, help justify lowering costs. If they are strong enough, we can increase unit profitability as we lower price and attract more customers. If we cannot do that we may still be able to increase overall profitability by putting more product volume though our facilities. There is a point, however, when continuing lowering of price can no longer be justified as economies of scale have diminishing returns.

In a competitive situation, the classic price/volume curve can change dramatically. A point comes where we need to reduce the price a lot to gain new types of buyers. These buyers may get only limited value from the product. If we have no competition, we simply hold the price and let volumes reach a maximum. If we have competition, we usually no longer have this choice. Our competition is likely to compete for the limited volume in a certain price range by reducing price. If we compete on the same basis because we are under pressure to hold volumes, it is easy to get into a downwards spiral.

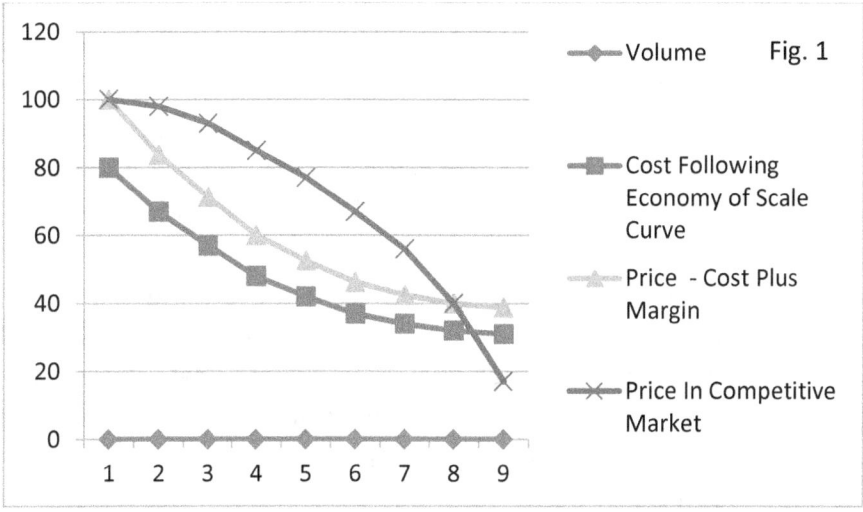

If we sell at prices based on what the market is willing to pay, rather than on a simple cost-plus, following economies of scale, we may initially sell at a higher price. However, as competition increases we may need to lower our price faster than our costs reduce. This applies particularly if there are diminishing returns on the economies of scale. If there is pressure to gain sales volume, prices may collapse past cost and stay down until capacity is withdrawn from the market or market demand expands.

The price/volume curve can change a lot again when we introduce financing. If buyers have to pay in advance then wait for delivery and installation before getting a benefit from the product, they will be a harder sell than buyers who pay only after the product is working for them. There is the cost of money used to pay in advance, doubt about delivery occurring on time, or even ever occurring at all, and doubt about quality of product delivered. All of these to large or small extents erode the price a buyer is willing to pay.

This applies whether the usefulness of a product is very clear or not so clear. If there is also doubt as to how well the product meets customer needs, the impact of financing may be a lot larger. This is because it allows buyers to use it before they have to pay for it. They can confirm that it meets their expected needs. They can also confirm that their expected needs are their real needs if there is doubt here as may be the case with new requirements. Financing, by reducing these buyer's risks, can mean the buyer is willing to pay more for the product than cash-up-front buyers. These buyers are typically at the beginning of the price/volume curve.

In the diagram below we see that the heavily financed variation actually raises price as volume increases. It attracts buyers who would or could not normally buy the product or asset. There can be a potential for greatly enhanced profitability. We do not need huge economies of scale to drive the price down as might apply for cash buyers only.

There is, however, a fine balance between the right amount of financing to support healthy levels of business and levels that can lead to financial collapse.

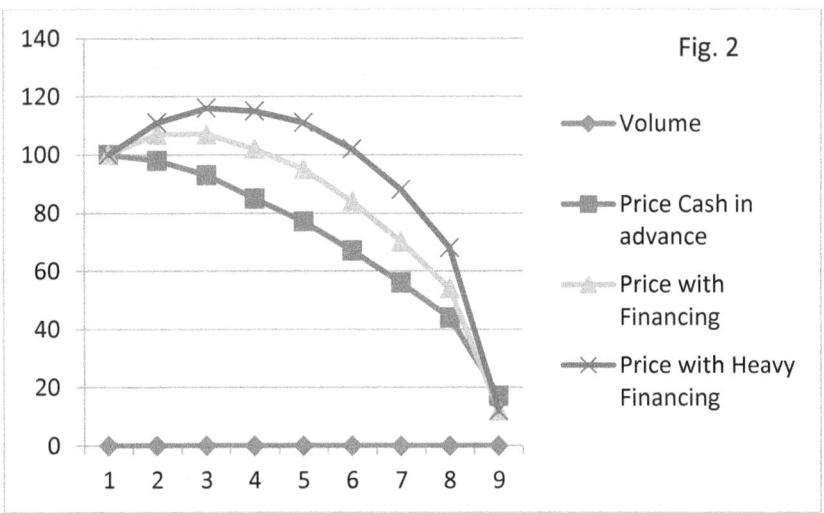

Fig. 2

If the price raising effect is large, we may move into a price bubble situation where buyers anticipate that the product will increase in price with time. They may then start buying, not for expected immediate value, but in anticipation of making a profit should they resell the product in future.

Even without the price bubble, the raising of price due to financing introduces potential instabilities. As the proportion of buyers who are dependent on financing to buy increases, the more sensitive the financial system becomes to any liquidity crisis. If for any reason these buyers cannot get financing, they will stop buying. Sellers then chase the reduced proportion of buyers with cash and these buyers have a lot smaller combined demand than supply capacity. Price will be under severe pressure.

Things may be fine for a long time. If demand is strong, given financing to enable sales, the market will keep growing. However, nothing lasts forever. Something will change. For some reason or other demand will drop if only temporarily. An upwards cost movement somewhere in their supply chain may cause some group of customers to reduce demand. A downwards cost movement somewhere in their demand chain may cause some group of customer to increase demand. These changes in supply cost may be to due to a sudden loss of production capacity or sudden loss of a transport link.

An upwards price spike may drive some of our customers out of the market and they may not come back when the spike is relieved, leading to a demand shortage. A downwards price spike may initiate an expectation of further price reductions. Even when its cause is removed, the expectation of further reductions may have picked up inertia and buyers may hold back from buying.

We can then get into a price collapse situation. Sellers lower their prices to get more sales but it does not add many new buyers. They lower them again to get what new buyers are available in the market but pretty soon buyers see a pattern emerging. That suggests that it pays to hold off from buying if they can because the price will soon come down further. See Appendix 3 for more information.

Buyers who have bought via financing may now see an asset they have purchased being sold new for much less than they still owe. They may default if they need to sell their asset due to difficult circumstances, e.g., loss of job, a struggling company or a need for cash due to liquidity difficulties. The lender can sell the asset but will take a loss and drive down demand for the asset. The price drops further.

Lenders of course allow for a certain level of defaults but, in a price collapse situation, this level may be severely exceeded. With real estate for example, buyers at a mortgage sale will not be feeling the need to pay anywhere near the value of the mortgage if it is a high portion of purchase value. Losses on loans may be large and this can impact on the liquidity of lenders. If severe enough, lenders may need to sell other types of financial assets to raise cash. If really severe, the selling of those financial assets may be widespread and cause a price collapse for those classes of assets in addition to the first class.

Making financial killings from price collapses requires an understanding of the set of conditions under which a sector or subsector will be prone to collapse. It then requires the ability to recognize when those conditions are falling into place. These usually involve multiple cycles so understanding the timing of the different cycles is essential in terms of how they combine to affect that specific sector or subsector. When the collapse scenario is identified, with its potential time frame to occur, the investments can be made that will capture the money flow.

2.5 Analytical Expertise

In an analysis of cyclical factors that can lead to financial killing opportunities we need to consider both microeconomic and macroeconomic factors. Macroeconomic factors apply at the whole economy level and information about them is built using data aggregated and published by government agencies and central banks. Microeconomic factors apply at the individual company and market sector level and tend to be known in detail by parties involved in those companies and sectors.

Macroeconomic Analysis

Government agencies and central banks typically use a range tools and techniques to analyze and forecast economic activity on a macroeconomic scale. An example of macroeconomic information relevant to financial stability is the US Federal Reserve Beige Book. This provides information for each of the Fed's twelve districts on trends in economic areas. These include Employment and Wages, Prices, Consumer Spending, Manufacturing and Distribution, Services, Agriculture and Natural Resources, Real Estate and Construction, Banking and Finance. We can look for conditions at the district level that would have a particular impact on our target business.

The Fed also uses forecasts provided by Board governors and district presidents, based on consultations with staff and external sources in their districts. In addition, Fed staff prepare a range of model-based forecasts.

The Fed's Board of Governors prepares a Monetary Policy Report, which focuses on the Fed's mandate to promote maximum employment, stable prices and moderate long-term interest rates. The report covers leverage in financial, non- financial and consumer sectors as an indication of current financial stability. The report includes a Summary of Economic Projections, which cover the variables above individually for the coming three years and the longer run.

We cover these macroeconomic forecasts in more detail in Appendix 4 because it is important to understand what they can tell us and how reliable that information is. Economic forecasting is difficult and an area of expertize which is subject to continual improvement based on experience. If we can take advantage of both its successes and failures, we can better use our own company-specific information when we target a company for a financial killing.

Appendix 4 discusses types of instability that macro forecasts can identify but also those that they can miss. These macro instabilities need to be considered alongside instability at the individual firm and company level. Even when their economic unit group as a whole is stable, individual financial firms or non-financial companies may be vulnerable to shocks and cyclical stresses. If we understand the limitations and potential errors of a macro forecast, but our competitors do not, we may see killing opportunities that they miss.

Microeconomic Analysis

Macroeconomic information is valuable for background but it is only the beginning of a full analysis. And being public information it is a beginning that is available to potential competitors for financial killings. The financial elite need to know the dynamics of business

cycles relevant to the particular sector applicable to their target assets. These determine how it incurs the kind of sudden price changes that translate into financial killings. Key questions are:
- What are the various components of buyer's risk that affect price in the sector?
- How does some or all buyer's risk transfer into supplier's risk and third party financing risk?
- What are the economies of scale for suppliers to the sector in general and our target business in particular?
- What is the market saturation volume at various price levels?
- What is the potential loss in value of relevant products or assets if market saturation leads to price collapse?
- What financial instruments can be used to best capture value in such a collapse in the expected time frame?

Buyer's risk and its impact on financing risk is the foundation of financial instability. It can change very rapidly and by large quantities. Even moderate changes can translate into large changes in financial stability when thresholds are reached. If we understand it for a given market, and how it translates step by step into instability, we can take advantage of that instability before others see it. Alternatively if we can see beneath the surface that the instability is less of a threat than others think we can exploit that too.

Information of value in understanding price movements in any sector includes:
- Cost structures and economies of scale - operating costs of that sector, its profit margins, its capital costs, its product and process development costs. What happens when a major supply component (materials, parts, services) becomes more or less costly?
- Pricing – the various prices of similar products with greater or less quality, the prices of substitutes, the ability of buyers to move between offerings

- Operational issues - the supply failure points, the maintenance needs, the customer support mechanisms.
- The various business cycles it follows - its working capital cycle, its fixed investment cycle, its product development cycle and its technology cycle. And how these cycles interact with each other and cycles in other sectors.
- The sensitivities of the industry sector where we are going to make our killing. What makes it grow? When did it last collapse? What forces bought it back into healthy prices? What technology platform did new facilities use when it came back? What happened ten, twenty or even thirty years ago that leaves visible signs, the high points of expansion, the low points of recession. Where was the high tide mark - how high did the price get before collapsing? Where is the low tide mark - how low did the price get before offered capacity became less than demand?
- Abandoned buildings and plant. The largest industry structures that were reached in a given expansion? Was the next generation of supply facilities larger or smaller? What brought an expansion phase to an end? What trigger started an expansion? If the technology is completely new and it has no history that far back, what other technology did it replace?
- What schemes to improve the business were offered by suppliers and consultants and how did they fare? What new markets were seen for the product and how did they fare? And if things did not go to plan, what stopped it? Was it internal limitations or was the external view incorrect?
- We also need to know how the sector is normally financed. What methods are used for investment in working capital, investment in supply capacity, investment in product/process developments and in technology platform developments. And we need to know what the sensitivity of its various

financing costs is to upturns and downturns. What is the range of players in the sector? How do the bigger, more established companies compare with the smaller, fringe operators? How hard is it for a bigger competitor to crush a smaller competitor by using its economies of scale to reduce price?

This information helps us understand how a business is likely to respond to changes in macroeconomic conditions and to changes in its specific sector. We can focus on the financial security that reflects those changes in the business in a way which can be suitably exploited. That security might be debt, bonds, stock or derivatives.

If we are seeking to make a killing from a price collapse we need to identify the potential for this chain of events to occur and identify the likely timing. Based on our confidence in the timing, we can select the financial instruments best suited to the task (see below).

We best observe this by working in the sectors whose asset price movements let them make financial killings, or by working as a key supplier to those sectors. A key supplier is one whose inputs have a critical role in profitability. Companies in the sector will typically provide such suppliers with the necessary information to best help them achieve their companies' goals. These include cost structures, customer requirements and technology platforms.

Their financing supplier is ideal in this respect. Financial firms get the information that the companies are willing to share with other key suppliers. They can also insist on getting information that companies might not share with other suppliers. For more information, see Appendix 3, Risk to Financing Party.

We need to be involved with a sector long enough to understand how the sector responds to cyclical changes. We need to understand the progress of multiple inventory cycles, multiple product development cycles and multiple minor technology platform upgrade cycles. We need to understand the progress of a complete fixed investment cycle and a complete major technology platform upgrade cycle.

The Financial vs Non-Financial Sectors

The financial sector, like other sectors, has financial assets with key prices whose movement can lead to financial killings. The sector has multiple sub-sectors within it, such as commercial banking, investment banking, hedge funds, private equity, venture capital and insurance. A holding company may own several different types of these but the operations of each have unique characteristics as well as shared characteristics. If the finance sector itself is where we see the opportunity for a killing, we need to know in depth the sub-sector we are focused on as we would for any other industry.

Commercial banks have particular requirements. Their leverage ratios (see Appendix 5) are usually regulated. This is to ensure that firms have enough capital to pay bad debts. When their capital goes below this they are obliged to raise more or reduce loans to customers.

Other types of financial firms have varying degrees of regulation but a lot more diversity of cost structure.

Non-financial companies, which are usually not subject to any such regulation, are in a different situation. Cost structures can vary enormously. They do not have the same regulatory restrictions placed on them that banks do. They may in fact be restricted most by the financial firms they deal with. If their working capital is financed by commercial banks they will be subjected to lending criteria imposed by those banks. If their fixed investment is financed by finance companies or investment banks they will need to meet the requirements of those firms.

The vulnerability of specific businesses, even when the macro economy is stable, creates many opportunities for financial killings. While a sector may be relatively stable, companies within it may be vulnerable due to cash flow and/or profitability issues. Leveraged buyouts of companies in a short to medium term downturn but with good long term potential can offer big gains. Fire sale buy ups to gain cheap assets and/or to reduce capacity, which is holding prices down, can enhance the value of a sector capacity portfolio for relatively low cost.

Skills of Other Players On The Scene

The fact that we may not have the skills and judgement of the financial elite does not mean we cannot make financial killings of a different kind. We need only to appear to have the capabilities of the elite and investors will entrust us with their money. We may eventually lose it for them but we can make huge bonuses and salaries in the meantime. With average luck we will get half a decade or more of this remuneration before some financial collapse or other knocks over our edifice.

In any sphere of expertise there are the elite and those who are not elite but who can imitate the elite. They go to the right schools, do the internships, copy the terminology, follow the dress codes, attend the right clubs and charity events. They may be grandchildren of the elite and have inherited the trust fund but not the smarts.

We mentioned the Ferrari fleet, racehorses and superyachts earlier. These things are great for conveying power and influence. They may not fool the elite but they can certainly fool enough of the investment community, especially the public, to help get large quantities of funds to invest. The imitators may then ultimately lose a lot of that money but until they do, things go very well for them. They may personally earn tens of millions of US$ in fees, bonuses and/or dividends, depending on the nature of the firm. A good imitation of competence can be very effective.

2.6 Financial Instruments And Timing

The range of financial instruments available for exploiting events and making financial killings from those events is wide. Our focus is on which classes of financial instruments lend themselves to use when we have different levels of confidence in the timing for various.

There are many books on financial instruments. We do not want to go into the details of financial engineering used to create financial instruments for a particular purpose. For a background on that we would recommend Salih Neftci's Principles of Financial Engineering. It explains how to design a wide range of instruments that capture specific financial rights and obligations and the associated price-setting factors for those instruments. If we can work out the particular combination of financial rights and obligations necessary to exploit an opportunity, we can design an instrument or set of instruments to achieve it.

Our focus here is much more basic. It considers the instrument primarily in terms of the timing of a big price change and how sensitive we are to time variations before that killing event.

- What are the costs of purchasing a particular instrument that will capture our expected flood of money?
- What are our risks if we are wrong about it occurring at all?
- What are our risks if it does occur but we are wrong about *when* it occurs?

We will use examples of how five different types of instruments might be applied to different levels of confidence in timing for the price collapse and to different levels of downside risk.

The Long Position

This is the simplest approach for an expected price rise. We think the price of an asset is going to increase so we buy it. The downside is that we lose all our money but there is no theoretical limit on the upside. We might buy for a dollar and sometime later sell for one hundred dollars. We can take as long a time as necessary for the price to rise. If it drops in the mean time we have lost money on paper but providing we keep our nerve and do not need the cash elsewhere we can just wait for the rise to come.

This particularly lends itself to distressed assets (see Example 3 above) where the buy price starts low. But we need to understand how to assess the value in these because they very often go to zero value and stay there.

The Short Position

The short is the simplest approach to win on an expected price drop such as the UK currency short of Example 1. This was not the first big killing made with shorts. One investor made $100 million shorting stocks before the 1929 stock market crash. A $100 million killing in 1929 was equivalent to a multibillion dollar killing today.

Our plan when we go short is that price will drop from the initial price and we will make a gain. But shorts incur a big risk if the asset price we are shorting is likely to rise before it drops.

If the price rises, we owe money. We will then get a margin call by our counterparty to top up the difference. We need to pay this immediately even if the price drops back again later. We may factor this expenditure into the plan but we must put the money aside for it or be forced to sell out at a loss.

The gain, if we do make a gain, is limited to the initial price, which is the value of the drop to zero, as in the case of bankruptcy. However, the potential loss if price rises has no limit. In theory the loss could increase to many, many times the potential gain.

So the problem with shorts is that there is a limited maximum profit but an unlimited maximum loss. They offer a great way to make money in a price collapse situation. But we need to be very sure that the price will actually collapse and not rise too much before it does so. Those margin calls made on us if the price rises may quickly add up to a lot of money. Had the UK government in our example been successful in driving up the value of the Pound, the hedge funds would have lost money, possibly a lot.

We need to be confident that the price of our asset is going to go down and go down soon, before unplanned price increases occur. Or we need a big bank balance to pay out on margin calls for those increases prior to the ultimate price drop. Shorting has a big downside risk. We really need a combination of forces working in our favor to ensure the right outcome.

Options – The Long Call

Options allow us to greatly reduce our downside risk. For a fee we buy the option to profit from an anticipated price change if it eventuates, as for a long or short. However, if the price goes the wrong way we can choose not to take the loss. All it costs us is the option fee.

We can remove the major risk of going long by using a Call option. Then we pay a fee to buy the right to buy at a certain price any time before a specified time when the option finishes. If the price of our asset goes below that price we can choose not to exercise the option. If it goes above we can exercise it and make money. This removes the huge risk of a short.

If the price drops, the loss is much less than it would be for a short – just the option fee. However, when the price does rise as planned, depending on strike price (see above), we get most of the short's profit.

Options - The Short Put

We can remove the major risk of going short by using a Put option instead of a short. Then we pay a fee to buy the right to sell at a certain price any time before a specified time.

If the price of our asset goes above that price we can choose not to exercise the option. If it goes below we can exercise it and make money. This removes the huge risk of a short.

If the price rises, the loss is much less than it would be for a short. However, when the price does collapse as planned, depending on strike price (see below), we get most of the short's profit.

Volatility and strike price

Options greatly reduce our downside risk but they can be expensive. Normally a major impact on the price of an option is the effect of volatility. Volatility increases the risk to the party selling us the option. If the price drops in a random fluctuation, we can exercise the option and make money. The price might rise the next day but that is too late for seller of the option. So the seller prices the option as a function of the volatility. This is over and above the price puts on relating to the risk of an asset price drop occurring for some longer term reason like a price collapse.

The higher is the volatility, the more likely it is that price will drop to a point where the buyer of the option can put the option and make money. The average movement over time may be very small but may move around this average by significant amounts. This means it will cost more to buy options for assets with highly volatile prices than assets with low price volatility. The volatility may have nothing to do with the price collapse we are anticipating but we have to pay for it.

A typical put option might cost 8% per month of current asset price when the strike price is the same as current price. But when the strike price is twenty percent below the current value the put option might cost just 1.6% of asset price.

This price difference between the two strike prices recognizes the role of volatility. A fluctuation down in price of 15% would not incur any payoff for the lower cost option, a much lower risk for the counterparty. Volatility is the major influencing factor on price for options as high volatility could cause a payoff even when there little long term price movement.

A put option will be attractive from a financial killing perspective if we expect the anticipated price drop to be a lot larger than the volatility range. In the example above, if we can take a strike price at 20% below current asset price because we are expecting a 50% drop then the option cost is moderate but the payoff is still large. But if we are expecting just a 25% drop then we could make nothing even if it eventually occurs but takes several months. The amount we have paid out over those months is greater than the gain.

The Credit Default Swap

The Credit Default Swap (CDS) allows us to short certain types of price collapse but without the risk of a short and at a lower cost than via a put option. This is because the CDS only pays out when a specific credit failure event occurs. The seller of the CDS does not need to worry about the asset price dropping as it does not directly depend on the price of the reference asset.

For a CDS, volatility generally has no direct impact on price. There is no payout for small and moderate drops in price as for there is for shorts and put options so the provider does not need to charge us for this risk. A default event either occurs or does not occur and its occurrence will be defined by specific rules. Sellers do not have to pay for partial events as they would have to pay for small price reductions with a short or put option. A typical fee for a CDS, the spread, is 1% or 100 basis points for a year. This is far less than the equivalent put option.

One big consideration with a CDS is that we need to be confident our counterparty can pay us in the event there is a default. If we are paying millions to get billions in return we want to be sure the counterparty will have the billions to pay.

Selection of Instruments

In selecting financial instruments for a killing we need to assess the time frames we are dealing with, the various cycles involved and the movement left in a particular cycle before it hits a critical limit which will force events in our favor.

If we can be confident that the asset price will not go strongly in the wrong direction, or that if it does we have financial resources to hold our position, we can use a short. If we are confident that although the asset price may go in the wrong direction initially, it will not take too long before going back in the right direction, the put option might be effective. If we have a clearly defined credit default event, we are confident that the counterparty will actually be able to pay us and we have relatively limited funds, the credit default swap is the best instrument.

If we do not have to borrow to buy assets and we can sit on a position for a period without needing the funds elsewhere, a simple long position is the least cost approach. If we cannot afford to wait out a price drop that may occur before the expected rise, the call option might be preferable, bearing in mind that every month incurs a significant cost.

In all of these situations, we rarely know the timing of the top of the market or the bottom. People were forecasting a real estate crash years before one happened and triggered the global financial crisis. People were forecasting a large financial crisis years before the GFC and not necessarily one caused by a real estate collapse. There are many potential triggers for a general financial crisis.

What matters is identifying the tipping factor. This is the event that in combination with the other cyclical conditions will initiate the dynamics that lead to change in direction, the point of inflection. The price may continue to rise or fall significantly before it starts to change but the key factors are in place for that change.

PART 3: NEW KILLING OPPORTUNITIES

"I don't play the game by a particular set of rules; I look for changes in the rules of the game."
George Soros

The methods of making financial killings are diverse. When one method becomes less effective, due to changes in economic confidence or regulatory changes, another will become effective. We just need to know where to look. There are always opportunities for those who understand business cycles, sudden price changes, and the financial instruments available to exploit those price changes.

In addition to using killing methods for the established opportunities, we are in a period when new opportunities are multiplying at an explosive rate. They are coming faster than any regulator could anticipate and even begin to restrict.

3.1 Technology

Technology changes have always disrupted business both on the demand side and the supply side. New technology can increase outputs, reduce costs or make it possible to develop entirely new products.

An early example is the improvements in shipping that meant grain could be moved at low cost from high growth areas to poor growth areas. This undercut producers in the poor growth areas. Their revenues could fall rapidly once this occurred.

The shipping advance itself might take a long time to be taken up. The sailors and shipbuilders would need to jointly understand how it would provide an advantage. This might take a lot more time than baking a loaf of bread with the new grain to test its flavor.

Historically many of these technology changes happened over decades, even generations. Travelling merchants and seamen observed innovations in one area and transferred the knowledge to their own. Or they may have picked up just fragments of knowledge if the changes were kept secret.

In the twenty first century we have technologies that have also taken decades to evolve but which have the ability to enjoy rapid advances in much shorter periods

We will look at just five example technologies that can cause rapid changes in economics and lead to convulsions in price, with associated financial killing opportunities.

The Cloud

The internet evolved from technology developed in the US defense and research sectors fifty years ago. It now allows data to flow freely between devices and computers over global communications networks for analysis and action by diverse software programs. It offers new tools for corporate efficiency, new ways of social interaction and machine to machine communications. Its impact on spatial economics significantly increases the frequency of events that provide opportunities for killings.

The Cloud is a vast global network of computers, collecting, processing, storing and transporting data. It delivers the services of global corporations like Google, Facebook, Amazon, eBay and Alibaba. It operates information systems for corporations and government agencies, which would once have been provided from within their own walls. It supports hundreds of thousands of mobile phone apps, used by billions of people.

We build an app which pulls some information from one or more other computers over a network, combines that information in some new form. This is a new product, which can run on a desktop computer, laptop, some hand-held device or even a wrist device. This product might take a month to build. With mass access to the product over the internet, that product can be spread virally and in another two months be used by millions of customers. The development cycle is a quarter or less of the traditional technology sector application development cycle.

Our focus here is not on the development of Cloud technology. But we will look at how the Cloud impacts cost structures, market demand, buyer's risk and financial risk in the wider economic and business environment. We do not have to specialize in Cloud-based products or technology to be heavily impacted by the Cloud. If our business is in the areas of agriculture or aerospace, banking or building, chemicals or communications, diesels or derivatives, engineering or entertainment, it will be likely impacted for better and/or worse by the Cloud.

An example of Cloud technology transforming industries is the energy industry. Historically fossil fuels have held off the rise of renewable energy because fossil fuels can be burnt to produce electricity or transport wherever and whenever people required them. They work when required, not just when the rain is filling rivers and lakes, the sun is out or when the wind is blowing. But fossil fuels increase the portion of CO_2 in the atmosphere.

People have different theories on global warming caused by the burning of fossil fuels. Some anticipate the Greenland and the Antarctic ice packs melting, increasing the oceans' water level by thirty meters. This would drown New York, London, Hamburg, Shanghai, and other great coastal cities, not to mention much of Bangladesh and all of many islands around the earth's oceans. Others believe this is a baseless theory designed to enhance the careers of scientists specializing in it. Others believe the theory is true but see it as a better alternative to an ice age which could freeze and starve billions of people.

Whichever of these is true, renewable energy will increasingly rapidly replace fossil-fuel based energy because technological and economic forces are in its favor, regardless of the politics. We are told China has already started to reduce fossil fuel consumption, in spite of huge increases over previous decades, because of its rapid uptake in renewables. Businesses dependent on fossil fuel-produced energy will be at risk of periodic price collapses. This offers excellent opportunities for parties who time these correctly to make financial killings.

The economic use of renewable energy requires a high level of coordination between systems. With fossil fuels-based energy production we produce when load demands. Renewable energy is available when nature makes it available, which may be very different from the timing for our needs for energy.

To balance these supply and demand with renewable energy we need to be able to burn fossil fuels to fill the remaining gaps and/or use storage systems. This means a very large amount of intelligent control at the physical level and the market level. Cloud technology will make this control increasingly cheaper and more extensive with time.

The renewable energy technology is supported by an emerging ability of electricity networks and markets to respond to changes in types of generation. In a similar way to new product designs being implemented quickly, new types of technology can be inserted into a grid or microgrid. Older technologies can be suddenly made unprofitable. Again, if we have invested in suitable financial instruments, we can benefit from that sudden reduction in profitability.

An accelerating factor here is the arrival of autonomous vehicles. When these achieve legitimacy, they can transform the role of the automobile. By being usable by anyone they can have a utilization rate ten times that of self-drive autos. This provides them with a huge financing cost advantage over vehicles that need human drivers as less vehicles need to be bought. This cost advantage is over and above advantages offered by not having to worry about parking and being able to spend travel time reading, sleeping, working at a computer screen of some type or talking on video connections.

In addition to general change across most if not all markets and industries, the potentially destabilizing factors of the Cloud offer the potential for the suitably prepared to make financial killings such as never seen before. Combinations of cyclical and geospatial factors can lead to events that provide opportunities for large financial gains, often with small investment and relatively low risk.

Robotics

Robots are becoming very common in a range of areas, offering economic ways to cay out more and more tasks:

Industrial robots operate in hazardous environments. They:
- Handle heavy, hot, toxic parts
- Weld materials
- Assemble parts
- Dispense glues and paints
- Cut materials
- Work in into atmospheres like mines

Military robots carry out tasks such as
- Defuse bombs
- Search for hazardous objects
- Spy on the battlefield
- Track and fire on incoming missiles

Medical robots carry out tasks such as:
- Assist with surgery
- Assist with rehabilitation, helping patients exercise

Home robots carry out tasks such as:
- Vacuum floors
- Mow lawns
- Clean pools
- Provide company for less mobile people

Autonomous autos (see above in relation to renewable energy), which effectively have a robot absorbed into the controls, will soon take us where we need to go when the traffic becomes:
- Too difficult for us if we are handicapped by age or medical condition.
- Too time wasting if we could be working or being entertained rather than concentrating on the road.

The high utilization rate of autonomous vehicles could mean far fewer autos are built, offering excellent financial killing opportunities from stock price collapse in those auto companies who suffer from this.

Robots are doing more and more tasks, previously only doable by people. They can work in most manufacturing sectors and in more and more service sectors. They can aid humans to do dangerous, heavy, highly precise tasks or replace the humans entirely. They initially do not seem to be capable of doing certain tasks requiring human intelligence and then suddenly they can. They are great for unexpected step changes which collapse revenues in previously successful companies.

We do not need a sudden great revolution across industry where suddenly the robots rule the world for robots to have a major financial impact. We just need periodic smaller revolutions, subsector by subsector. Each smaller revolution creates opportunities for financial killings as the previously successful supply technology becomes less profitable. The rest of the economy carries on as before.

Opportunities for great wealth will obviously come to some developers of robotics. These are those who have great talent in mechatronics and machine communications can develop products worth hundreds of billions. But there will also be opportunities for financial killings that occur when companies are put out of business by competitors who are stronger in robotics.

Incidentally this is not all bad news for the poor workers being made unemployed. Robots will make possible tasks too difficult or dangerous for humans and generate new jobs maintaining and sometimes controlling the robots. Mining in poisonous, explosive and collapsing underground locations; developing new materials in hazardous conditions; processing toxic and radioactive waste can all expand industries and produce inputs to new products that do need humans in their supply chain.

Additive Manufacturing

Additive manufacturing at the manual level has been around for millennia. Ceramics, some of the earliest manufactured products, have involved build-up of products by adding more clay to enlarge an item such as a pot or add components, such as pot handles.

Sintering of metals is a 20th Century industrial process where a powder was heated until it is soft, but not melting, and compressed into a shape. The shape of the component was defined by the shape of the mold. A small change in shape required a new mold.

3D printing allows a three dimensional product to be designed on a computer and have instructions sent to a printer. The printers can be the liquid resin-based systems used in the home. These repeatedly squirt out a liquid material in thin flat shapes. These build up a 3D shape by solidifying on top of the previous layer. The printers can also be the sintering type used in industrial environments. Here a layer of powder is deposited and selectively fused onto the previous layer with a laser taking its instructions for the shape of the layer.

The key thing about modern additive manufacturing is that our products can be defined and analyzed in software and the 3D printer takes over from there. No building of molds, typically a labor-intensive process, is required. And shapes which are too complex to mold can be built up lay by layer.

The Internet of Things

The Internet of Things involves the use of cloud technology for machines to talk to each other instead of via people. They cut out the middle man. This is good when it saves people the time and effort of talking to one machine and then passing on information from that machine (or several machines) to another machine (or several). People get the benefit of the work carried out by the machines. It may not be so good when people get cut out of the process entirely and no longer get rewarded for their efforts in managing these various machines.

Biochemistry

Biochemistry using cell manipulation allows the enhancement of food crops, nutients and medicines. This can lead to large and rapid revenue growth for products in these areas. It can also lead to massive declines in the fortunes of businesses and sectors supplying previous alternative products.

General

What these technologies all share is an ability to support sudden changes in product design and to switch production from earlier versions. If the market likes a new product, the supplier can respond very rapidly. If it is taking market share off another supplier, that supplier may incur rapid reduction in revenue and profitability. If we have invested in suitable financial instruments, we can benefit from that rapid reduction in profitability.

These are just a few technologies that will have large impacts and create great financial killing opportunities. There will be shorting opportunities when the market does not see an impending collapse. There will be opportunities to go long when the market does not see how a particular combination of technologies will push a sector past a tipping point with massive gains for the winners.

3.2 Geoeconomic Changes

The Impact of the Cloud on Supply Chain Costs

The supply chain is undergoing continuous cost reduction due to the Cloud. The Cloud supports global logistics systems which allow bigger container ships to be packed, gaining reductions per ton mile of freight to be made due to reduced and manning fuel costs. It coordinates factory production with port operations, with ship load and discharge, with distribution warehouses.

The reducing transport costs level costs make the differences in production location less important. Suppliers in other parts of the world can offer products at prices where their own local production costs become the dominant factor rather than transport costs. This puts more and more pressure on a local supplier in a country where local production costs are relatively high.

What often protects the local supplier or established foreign supplier from increasingly challenging competition is buyer's risk. The established foreign product is one that has proven itself over years, possibly decades, and been enhanced to meet our local needs over those years. It acquires the value of a valued local product. When lower cost products from new sources arrive on the scene, buyers often simply do not believe these new poducts have the qualities that they require. There may be a number of factors in this. Design for purpose, ease of use, safety, reliability, attractiveness of design, support, economy in use of consumables are all qualities that may make the local product or established foreign product more desirable.

The Impact of the Cloud on Buyer's Risk Between Regions

The Cloud can change buyer's risk rapidly and substantially.

In the early days of online purchasing of books from sites such as Amazon, we could not browse through a physical copy as we could at our local bookshop. We would be relying on a description or review which might tell us very little that we really needed to know.

For a technical book in a particular specialty this could be a problem. It might be a professionally written book helping the reader with various technical problems but they might not be the particular problems that we needed to solve. If we were on the other side of the world from the online supplier, sending it back might not be a quick or cheap option.

Suppose the price of the local book was $100 and we could buy it online unseen for $70. We might have thought the $30 saving was not enough to risk buying a book that we discovered on arrival offered little benefit. The buyer's risk of getting it wrong might be significantly more than that $30.

A tool like Amazon's Look Inside, however, when introduced a few years after the online sales service started, changed things. It allowed readers to get a much better idea of how relevant the book was to their own requirements. So buyer's risk for online sales of books was greatly reduced.

Now buying such a book through our local bookshop may carry the bigger risk. The local bookshop is unlikely to stock it for us to browse through unless it is a big seller. A specialist technical book is likely to be something they can order for us but it will be sight unseen unless we use Amazon to look inside. Then we might as well just buy it online. Not so good for the book shop.

Instruction on how to use products is enhanced with dynamic visualizations of product operation.

Social media allows us to hear from knowledgeable colleagues, friends and friends of friends on the other side of the world on how some new product works. We may have never met physically these people but the social fabric created by the people we jointly know gives us confidence they know what they are talking about and share common values with us.

On certain subjects we may have far more confidence in the advice of someone ten thousand miles away than that of that nice sales person who lives next door. The foreigner may speak a different first language, have a different religion and work in a different legal system. But on this subject we have a high level of confidence in their expertise and trustworthiness.

The other way to reduce buyer's risk with a product built on the other side of the world is to design the product locally to meet local market conditions. We then use the ability of the Cloud to control the processing of materials, components, assemblies, software code modules and applications. These processes may not be located only in the location sending the final product to us but may be operate in various locations around the world.

The effect of these changes can cause sudden growth in markets for product from foreign suppliers. Market uptake can move from years to months. This can mean suppliers of competitive products that previously dominated a market can suddenly lose significant sales revenue very rapidly. These suppliers may be local or supplied from overseas.

Many products will not respond this way, or at least not as quickly. If buyers require some machinery for work in the Arctic, and are assessing something built in South America designed for the tropics, they may be very cautious. Whatever the supplier says about factory testing in chilled environments, buyers will have their doubts. But suppose they hear on LinkedIn from a colleague who knows their technical issues that the colleague used it in ice fields in Southern Chile, near Cape Horn and it worked perfectly. They might then have a lot of confidence that it might work well in the Artic.

The effect of this is that buyer's risk can rapidly drop in size and products can make rapid inroads into previously difficult markets. This may occur alongside a continued squeezing out of transport cost in supply chains, accelerated by economies of scale as market growth occurs.

In such cases companies with a previously strong market share, built on local confidence in product and supplier expertise, can suddenly plummet in revenue and/or margins. If they have high fixed investment servicing costs, profitability can drop even faster. This may lead to excellent stock shorting opportunities.

Robotics and Geoeconomics

A key thing about robotics from a geoeconomic perspective is that it allows us to reduce labor costs, without having to export production to low wage labor cost regions. This means we can simplify our transport arrangements where this offers a benefit. There will be products that benefit from this just as some products benefit from more connections in supply chain at the expense of complexity.

Long supply chains and high economies of scale derived from very large container ships could incur losses if those huge ships cannot be filled and/or price competition increases. The ships will still be there, and they will still have low ton-mile costs but the shipping companies may not earn enough to pay the capital charges. This could lead to collapses in stock value of shipping companies and offer associated financial killings. A year or two later the ships may have products and materials for new markets but a shot term drop in demand can have large effects on price.

Additive Manufacturing and Geoeconomics

As with robotics, we do not need to outsource to foreign places to gain low labor costs. The 3D design instructs the 3D printer what to do, bypassing the human manual input. Where low cost labor has previously offered a competitive advantage, this advantage may suddenly be lost. Again there will be products that benefit from simpler supply chains just as some products benefit from more connections in supply chain.

Renewable Energy and Geoeconomics

Oil has played a big role in geoeconomics for a long time. The price varies widely over cycles and has a big impact on the economies of supplies and consumers as it does. Renewable energy is likely to be similar. As Middle Eastern and North African regions produce less oil they are likely to become big producers of solar energy with their high levels of sun and low levels of cloud cover.

Losses of electrical energy over long distance are greater than energy losses incurred oil and gas tankers. A significant portion of electric power would be lost transporting it from Saudi Arabia, for example, to Europe. However, electricity markets change prices far faster than oil and gas markets. Oil and gas prices can increase by 100% over a few months. Some electricity markets can increase by 1000% in an hour when loads increase and there is a limit to available generation capacity. It might be well worth losing a big chunk of energy in losses to transporting power thousands of miles gain a 1000% better price for an hour or two. There is great potential for large transfers of wealth to occur that are only foreseen by those who make a point of analyzing them.

The Internet of Things and Geoeconomics

We can only imagine the limit of what happens as machines increasingly talk to each other. But in the medium term there is likely to be an impact on business as we know it.

There will be operational gains made by distributing supply facilities around the globe as discussed earlier. The other benefit is reduction of buyer's risk though interregional communications between machines. Machines can check highly detailed specifications and quality control data for materials, components and products as they constantly search for better prices. They can do this much more quickly than people so can work at a much finer granularity of transaction.

Biochemistry and Geoeconomics

In the case of food crops, entire regions can be affected, with roll-on effects in real estate prices, financial securities prices and currency prices. If the new crop thives in one region but not others, that region may undergo a boom and othe egions may undego a collapse.

General

Some forms of manufacturing will continue to expand with multi-nodal production. This is likely for types of production where very large scale production has significant economies of scale. These economies are not necessarily related to low cost labor but to high capital cost facilities. Conversely some production will move away from regions whose historic competitive advantage was low cost manual activities towards robotics and/or additive manufacturing.

At the same time, buyer's risk should continue to decline as information about products' design, construction, usage and maintenance spreads faster and in greater volume than before.

For established companies, competitors with new products will appear rapidly and take market share without the slow buildup as customers cautiously build up confidence in those products. Economies of scale will continue to be essential for survival so companies will need to invest in large capacity facilities as in the past. But they may not enjoy markets long enough to pay back the investments. This will mean rapid loss in value of company stocks and bonds. Companies who have dominated markets for decades will not be safe from this.

These changes do not necessarily happen in a linear or predictable manner. As sales volumes drop off, companies have different options for reducing costs. The attractiveness of these varies with circumstances. They can refocus their marketing into areas where the new competition is still weak. They can reduce costly extended hour operations. They can mothball old inefficient plant. They can sell off underutilized land and buildings.

Such actions can buy time and reposition companies for sustained success or just defer the inevitable decline. From their public relations statements we may not know which of these scenarios applies. We need to read between the lines and study the underlying cyclical changes.

The speed of change will increase killing opportunities. We do not need to wait for the Mexicans or Chinese to build a factory for a traditional US factory to close. A software upgrade to a competitor's robotics software will achieve the same result in far less time. The managers of the old factory may have no warning and the company's stock price will collapse with associated shorting opportunities.

The good news for US workers is that the robots may located in the US and supported by US mechatronics engineers. That is provided they are not located in the IS but supported remotely across the Cloud by Japanese, Korean or German engineers.

3.3 The Twenty to Fifty Billion Dollar Financial Killing

The global financial crisis produced some exceptional financial killing opportunities. Tens of billions of dollars were made from shorting opportunities. A single firm made more than US$15 billion from a set of short positions. Long opportunities were not so extensive, as making money out of going long in a financial collapse is a very specialized art. But one firm made more than US$5 billion from a set of long positions.

The GFC occurred after a period of relative stability and a widely held belief that deregulation would allow markets to relieve imbalances. When problems did occur, central banks would inject liquidity into markets which looked like freezing up. The GFC was not supposed to occur.

Since the GFC, government agencies and central banks have acted to help prevent such an event recurring. One might expect that these actions will reduce the potential size of financial killings associated with financial instability. However, the signs are that coming instability will be larger than ever due to regional instabilities and technological disruption. Potentially even bigger killings will be available than during the GFC.

Regional Stability

Geopolitically speaking at the time of the GFC, the US dominated the world economy just as its military ruled the waves and the skies for much of the world. Europe was integrating its economy and government deeper and wider. China's economy was growing rapidly due to its ability to supply low cost manufactured goods to the world, especially Europe and the US. India's economy was also growing rapidly but from well behind China. Russia was earning big oil revenues to help pay for the protection of its vast territory. Technology was transforming business communications, transport linkages, financial systems and markets. Economic cyclical factors were perceived to be moderate and manageable.

When the GFC did occur many would see it as a once in a lifetime event. Increased financial regulations would be put in place to stop a repeat. The expectation was that after central banks injected liquidity into the financial sector, the global economy would return to growth. Financial killings could be reasonably be expected to be more moderate.

However, a decade on, the global economy still suffers the repercussions of the GFC. .
- Russia is suffering a sustained depression due to long term low oil revenues.
- Middle East oil exporting countries are suffering long term low oil revenues.
- China is struggling with its transition from a high export focus to a greater consumption as.

- Southern Europe countries are in a long depression caused by high values of the Euro with the potential for wide scale banking failures.
- Germany is under threat of a decline in its economy due to its high level of exports shrink as other countries can no longer afford to trade with it.
- The US economy has come out of recession but the middle class has shrunk and the lower income sector has a significantly smaller share of the economy than before. This provides a continuing downwards pressure on interest rates (see Appendix 5), which has potential destabilizing factors.

These regional weaknesses have potential for instabilities that could lead to continued large scale disruptions. We do not know if any particular one of these regions will incur a major economic disruption and financial disruption. They may navigate their way through the difficulties, find new markets, find lower cost suppliers and develop other ways of moving into more stable situations. However, some probably will not be so successful. We should not assume that the global economic system is more stable than at the time of the GFC.

Technology and Stability

The other factor for instability is technology. Technology changes comparative advantage and economies of scale, the driving forces behind economic success for the diverse regions of the world.

Technology may fail with catastrophic results for business. This may be due to simply not delivering the hoped for capability and being rejected by the customers. It may be due to delivering the hoped for capability and being taken up by the customers but doing it badly and then being rejected by the customers.

Or it may succeed but only to a limited degree and divert resources and focus from other areas which would have produced better results. And the technology business fails or at least loses a lot of its market share because those results were essential to success.

Or it may succeed but with growth in its use being too rapid to build the experience necessary to identify less obvious risks. That can lead to major failures in function if widespread use occurs before design flaws can be identified and corrected.

Or it may succeed on a large and rapid scale with catastrophic results for competing businesses or subsectors. This is of course the outcome that technology developers and their financing parties love.

All of these outcomes can lead to big losses by some party or other and create opportunities for financial killings. The killings could be by shorting the companies' stock or buying up the companies or their assets at fire sale prices and then using them as part of a more successful regime.

The scope for these technology success/failure impacts is large on global business and finance. Supply chains and associated financial systems will become increasingly extended and complex as physical product supply is increasingly controlled by the internet of machines. Communications will occur between robots in mines and agriculture, transport systems (trucks, cars, drones), manufacturing robots, additive manufacturing systems, biochemical process controls, field implementation robots and testing systems. At every step there will be financing activities linking undeployed funds with the need for funds to pay for steps in the supply chain. Regulation of trade and finance by government agencies will become more difficult.

This supports rapid change of geographic deployment of supply facilities. Traditional competitive advantages for geographic locations such as low wages, tolerance for hazardous working environments and acceptance of ecological damage, become less valuable. Manufacturers can move production much more easily. Production can be rapidly deployed in a region and just as rapidly shut down. This rapid change on the supply side is in addition to rapid change on the market demand side as buyer's risk factors change faster and faster. This change in buyer's risk is inevitable with increasing information flow about product function, ease of use, ease of integration into processes, quality, ease of reliability and serviceability.

This environment of increasingly rapid change has large implications for financial assets. Companies supplying products can suffer sudden and major losses of sales as competing products and substitutes for their type of product gain rapid global acceptance. This can lead to sudden loss of stock values. Currency values for a country can rapidly rise when capital pours into a region to support a successful new industry. They can rapidly change after decline in a local industry's ability to compete with other regions. Real estate values for localities can change rapidly as people move to or from those localities to follow rapid business growth or decline for a particular sector.

These changes are not new. People have migrated into and out of localities for millennia. What has changed is the speed of establishment of industries and markets. Faster change means a greater portion of the total global economy is in transition at any time. Combinations of transitional portions involve smoothing each other out because the ups will often neutralize the downs. They can also occasionally lead to the ups or downs adding to each other and creating really big events with large scale, multi-sector changes in financial assets. Every decade has significantly faster technological advancement than the previous one.

The net effect of ever faster technology advances, geoeconomic development and political change is ever-increasing potential for price instability. This leads to price spikes and collapses with associated opportunities for financial killings. As economic conditions and regulatory actions restrict some opportunities, others will open. We would expect the rate of technology and geoeconomic developments to exceed the rate of regulatory changes. The details of financial killings keep changing but the principles do not.

The other factor in economies and financial markets that continues from the time of the GFC is low interest rates. The low rates and high savings levels mean vast amounts of money are swirling around the globe looking for a good return. That return could be a high but risky interest rate or a dividend stream, which might turn into a bad debt or a failed company. Alternatively the high return might be a high capital gain but perhaps one associated with an asset price bubble.

Either way, sustained low interest rates are likely to feed risky investments with a portion of large failures. If we can get sector-wide failure, or just large corporate failure, we have good potential for large financial killings. Even when risky investment produces positive results it usually means some kind of disruptive change is occurring. This is good for the companies enjoying the success but not so good for the ones they displace. It can lead to sudden collapses first in stock values, and in debt instrument values.

Essentially these developments in regional stability and technology mean that the next big event could involve more financial asset value going through sudden changes of price than occurred with the GFC.

The regulators may have currently stabilized the global financial system after the experience of the global financial crisis. They may have ensured that there is adequate capital in system-critical banks to keep leverage ratios at safe levels. They may have restricted bank's involvement in speculative trading, hedge funds and private equity activities. They may have more effectively regulated derivatives and improved disclosure of swaps trading. This should help ensure that counterparties can actually pay on their commitments and not set off cascading defaults though financial markets.

Or maybe they have not sufficiently reduced risk through these rules and the system is exposed to some unforeseen risk. Or maybe they have reduced risk now but politicians will feel safe to reduce stabilization in the future. This might be after a sufficient period of economic calm. Or it might be after a sufficient number of successfully managed financial crises to build confidence.

We cannot tell when the next big event will happen. The financial elite will see the signs when cycles combine to produce potentially instable situations and position themselves to be ready. They will not know exactly when a killing event, or series of events, will occur. So they will select the financial tools required to capture the money flow whenever it occurs over the period they have identified as being likely for that event or series of events.

We will not know the specifics of a major killing until its time is close enough to identify the imbalances of capacity and demand that produce large changes prices of products and assets. These imbalances depend on interactions of the various cycles that respectively affect supply capacity and market demand. Working capital, inventory, fixed investment, product development, process development, technology platform development and transport linkage cycles all add or subtract from each other to produce unpredictable sales volumes.

What we can tell though is that the potential for disruption is increasing. The coming years should see bigger killings because the energy of change in the global economy has grown continuously over the last decade and will accelerate. If we could make a fifteen billion dollar killing during the GFC it seems entirely reasonable to make a twenty, thirty or even fifty billion dollar killing during the next major convulsion. The opportunities are there for those with the experience, the understanding, the connections and the imagination to make it happen.

APPENDIX 1: BUSINESS CYCLE GENERATION

Business cycles do follow very logical, albeit highly complex, patterns of behavior. The math behind them is well understood, being based on fundamental day-to-day business mechanisms in the working capital cycle. It can be displayed as graphical outputs which business people can grasp intuitively even if they are not math enthusiasts. This Appendix describes and illustrates some of those mechanisms.

Some of the aspects covered include:
- The multiplicity of business cycles
- Combinations of cycles
- Difficult of identifying trends
- Inter-temporal financial flows – maturity transformation
- Generation of cycles
- Growth of cycles
- Price spikes

Multiplicity of Cycles or Waves

There are many business cycles or waves, each driven by their own economic logic and associated investment/return timing. We have cycles of investment in:
- Working capital - materials, staffing, services consumed
- Inventory – materials stocks
- Fixed investment (Supply facility capacity) – factories, warehouses, trucks, ships, planes
- Product development – new functions, new interfaces, more speed, additional reliability
- Process development – new production and delivery components, sequences, automation and integration
- Technology development – new materials, new architectures

Working capital cycles vary widely between industries, from minutes for purchase and resale of financial securities to years for major construction projects. This means that there are many different cycle wavelengths.

This diversity means that the cycles aggregate in diverse ways. Sometimes they cancel each other to varying degrees but they also naturally align themselves with each other because of grouping effects due to economies of scale. The factors that affect individual businesses also affect industry sectors, market sectors and entire economies. So in addition to the behavior of individual waves at the individual business unit level, we have much larger waves caused by the grouping effect. The aggregation of these is visible if not very predictable.

This should not be a surprise. If we study normal ocean waves we see that they start as ripples generated by local wind forces. These are not like ripples in a still pond which occur when a stone is thrown into it, and which disappear soon after the impact of the stone has gone and equilibrium returns. The ocean waves can continue to be generated for hours or days, as long as the wind feeds them. They steadily build in size and energy as they group together and get larger and larger. Eventually they gain enough energy to travel hundreds of miles beyond the area where the wind originally generated them. They finally collapse on a beach or reef when the depth of the water becomes insufficient to support the wave. The mechanisms and mathematics of business waves are not identical to those of ocean waves but they have certain common characteristics in terms of generation, growth, dissipation and collapse.

Note: We use the terms *cycle* and *wave* interchangeably for this purpose as they describe the same entity. When we use the term *cycle* we are focusing a little more on numerical values at recurring points in the cycle, key indicators such as interest rates, employment levels, book-to-bill ratios for electronic devices, durable goods orders and housing starts. When we use the term *wave* we are focusing a little more on its shape as well as the mechanisms and associated mathematics that define that shape and change it through time.

Combinations of Cycles or Waves

When different sized waves combine we get more complex shapes. One relationship between waves in business and economics is that one wave adds to the other, as in ocean waves. In the charts below we show cash flow on the vertical axis and time on the horizontal axis. Flows below the x-axis show outgoings and flows above it show revenues.

We start with one cycle frequency in Fig. 1. This could be a working capital cycle for a business, where the business invests in working capital, produces its product, sells it. It could be monthly or it could be a shorter or longer period. Other related cycles include profits earned, liquidity and solvency but we will not deal with them here.

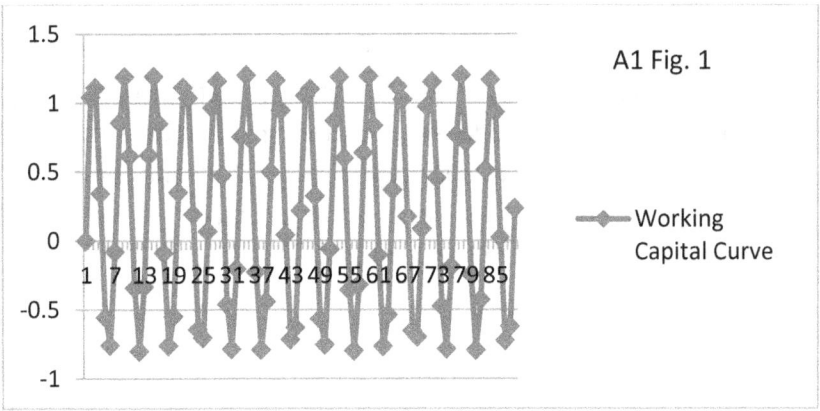

A1 Fig. 1

In Fig. 2 we overlay a longer term cycle, which will vary volumes by adding a delta to demand. The positive delta could be due to a sustained period of additional money in the hands of buyers or lower cost money for them to borrow to assist with purchasing. It also could be due to accumulated profits making it possible to improve operations and/or product functionality and thus attract more sales. The negative delta could be due to less purchasing power in the hands of buyers or higher interest rates. It could also be due to a decline in attractiveness of the product relative to competing products as those products enjoy the benefits of investment in function and delivery. The curve shown is a simple sine curve but it could follow a wide range of shapes.

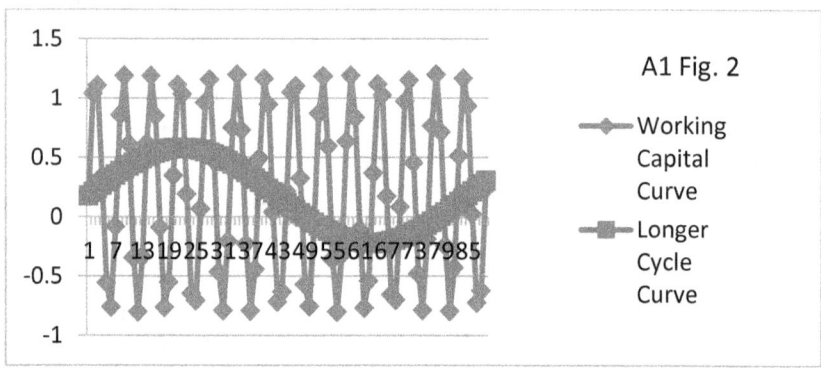

The composite in Fig. 3 below shows the net effect on cash flow when the longer cycle is added. The situation with just a short cycle and one longer cycle produces a relatively predictable shape to the wave. The peak of each short cycle is a little higher than the preceding one when coming out of a trough or a little lower than the preceding one when going into a trough.

A1 Fig. 3

Of course this has just one longer term cycle added to the short cycle. We know there are other long term cycles which can and will have a significant impact. When we start adding them the composite shape gets more complex. The chart in Fig. 4 below shows the overlay of another cycle, longer than the short cycle but not as long as the first long one.

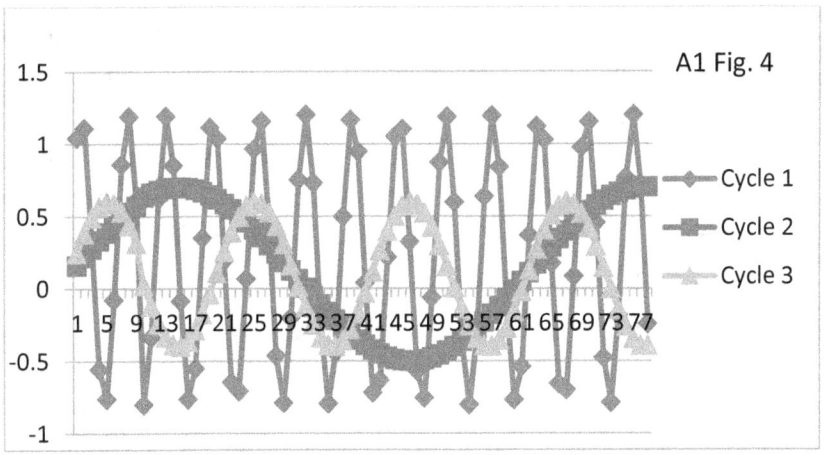

A1 Fig. 4

Whereas the first composite above followed a simple visible pattern the one in Fig. 5 below is a lot more complex and unpredictable. There seems to be some kind of pattern going on but it is hard to pick it. With just one additional wave added to the initial two, consistency and predictability seems to be much less clear.

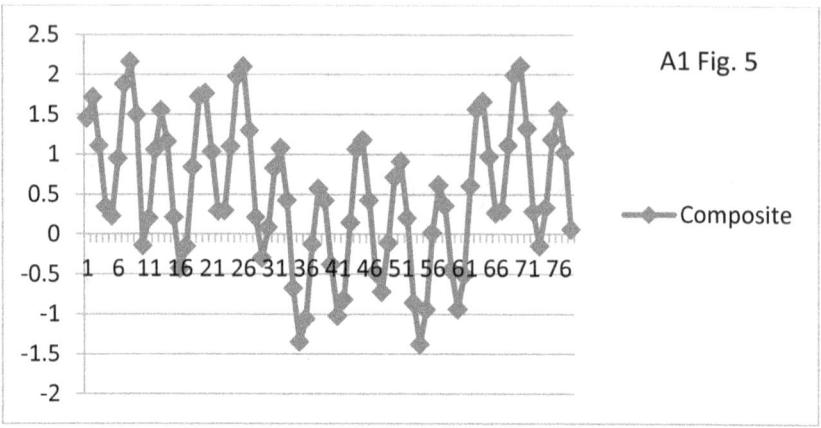

In Fig. 5 above if we look at the peak between points 43 and 46 along the horizontal axis we seem to be coming out of the previous trough but then we drop back again. If we were investors working in a particular market we might be struggling to work out where the market is going. If we were economists advising on whether the economy was emerging from a recession or about to go into a deeper one we might also be struggling.

We should also note that components of composite waves drop in and out of the mix. Cost structures change with changes in suppliers. New customers come on stream. A composite wave may never actually recur in identical form to its previous cycle. But the underlying mathematics do not change.

The fact that wave patterns rapidly become complex and hard to predict does not mean the composite waves are not present. It just means they may be hidden. They are just as powerful as if they were visible to all. Their difficulty to be seen makes it even more critical that we understand them. By doing so, we can better prepare ourselves both for great opportunity and great risk. To understand more about these waves, we need to look at what generates them in the first place.

A preliminary to that is to understand how waves of different frequencies feed each other, over and above their ability to add and subtract from each other in real time.

Inter-temporal Flows

As a business consistently generates operating profits in its working capital cycle it can pay back debt and accumulate funds for future investment. The short term cyclical profits are feeding the negative cash flow phase of a longer cycle investment wave.

Fig. 6 shows operating cash flows from Fig. 1 in a situation where net profits were all saved and accumulated as reserves in the operating account. More likely there would be transfers such as debt repayments to long term lenders, dividends to equity holders and transfers into accounts for future investments in various amounts depending on financial structuring.

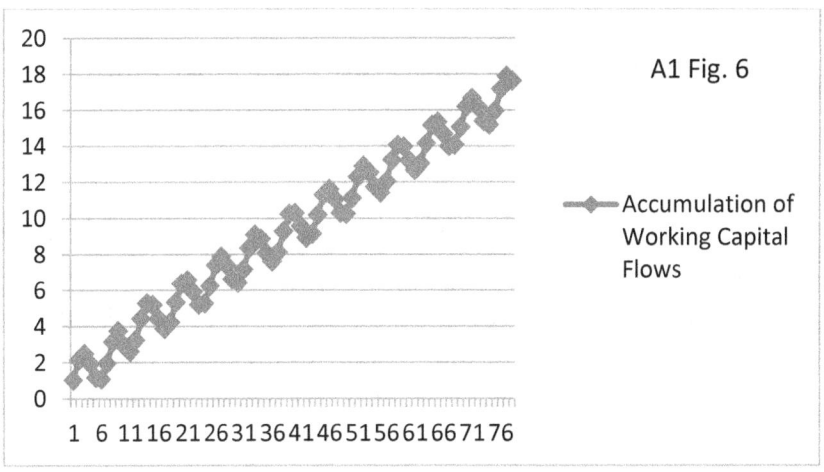

We will show in Fig. 7 below just one of these potential transfers, a debt payment to a long term lender below. We pick this because it shows the inter-temporal transfer between a short cycle, in this case the working capital cycle, and a longer cycle, say financing of supply facilities via debt. Every three short cycles we will make a financing charge payment. These might be quarterly payments if the working capital cycle was monthly in length. For simplicity's sake we assume our lender has financially engineered a fixed payment covering principle repayments and interest over the period of the loan.

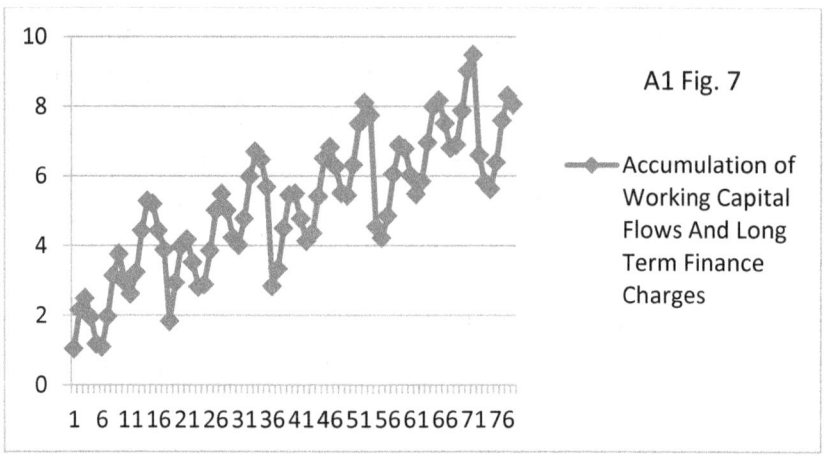

A1 Fig. 7

Accumulation of Working Capital Flows And Long Term Finance Charges

This shows a less steep accumulation than in Fig. 6 but still leaves potential for periodic transfers into a long term fund for future equity investments to supplement future borrowings.

Financial firms dealing with these various cash flows with different cycle frequencies need to be able to balance the different inputs and outputs. This is a complex and risky process involving many financial firms of various types, If flawed, it has potential for financial failure of the firm with potential disaster for the firm's creditors. Capital and reserve requirements imposed on commercial banks are designed to protect depositors from high levels of bad debts.

Generation of Business Cycles

Cycles/waves can be generated by a single one-off event. For example, a stone can be thrown in a pool causing a single primary ripple to spread out across the pool. A similar situation applies for business and economics. An event such as a mineral discovery, a war, a natural disaster, a sudden advance in technology, a sudden change in central banking activities, a sudden change in taxation, a collapse or a boom in a market are examples. The event can be positive with a burst of new revenue or negative with a sudden reduction in revenue.

The direct effects of these tend to dissipate fairly rapidly once the initial energy has gone. Fig. 8 shows a large positive initial net cash flow, perhaps the exploitation of a natural resource. After the initial surge, net cash flows go negative as revenues drop. Perhaps this is because diminishing quantities are extracted, but costs do not drop off as rapidly. Then there is a surge back into profit as costs are cut by reducing capacity to match the new, smaller volumes. Then there is continued decline and ultimately (out of the picture) there will be dying spasms.

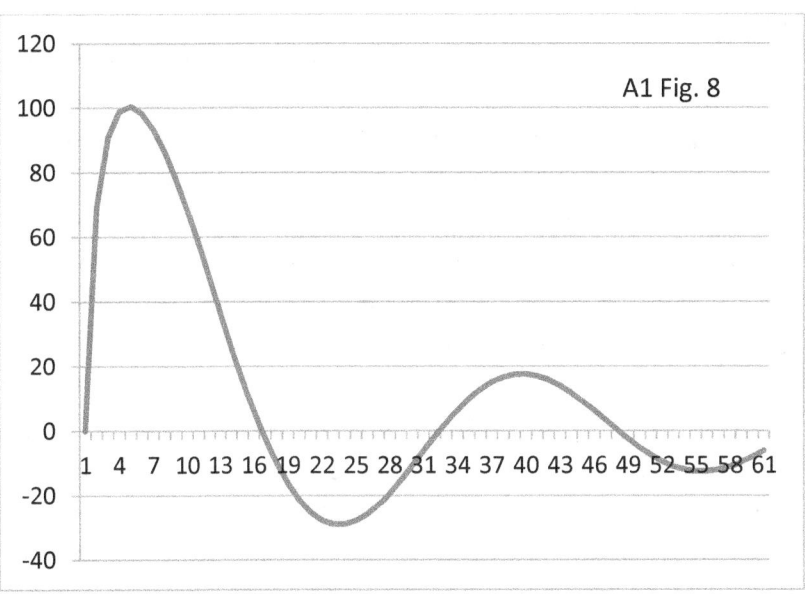

A1 Fig. 8

These kinds of wave dissipate, usually rapidly as above, unless they have a source to re-activate them. A new tract of forest, a new seam of minerals, a new reservoir of oil might all apply. Alternatively we might have steady volumes able to be extracted over a long period of time but we might have big surges and declines in price due to market shortages and saturations, which lead to large cash flow surges and drop-offs.

If they are large enough and, even if they soon disappear, these waves can have a long term impact. A pebble thrown into a lake will cause a ripple which may have disappeared from the water at the point of entry long before the ripples reach the edge of the lake. But a mountainside collapsing into the lake may cause a 700 foot high wave. This not only creates a lot of havoc as it moves through the water and surges around the edge of the lake but may remove much of the water from the lake.

Similarly a large shock can cause damage to parts of the economy while causing long term stimulation to other parts. A war may suck money out of the economy, starving parts of it and causing long term decline. It can also develop certain technologies much more rapidly with ongoing peace time benefits. A price shock such as oil in the 1970s can cause a lot of damage throughout the global economy but it may also help justify investment in more fuel-efficient engines. And a positive shock can leave residual assets after it dissipates. Major extractive industries may boom and die but leave behind ports, railways and roads which reduce the costs of other industries so that these other industries become viable where they would otherwise never get established.

However, the great majority of waves in business and economics, like those earlier mentioned wind-generated waves on the ocean, are generated by a sustained economic driving force that may last for many cycles before dissipating. When we understand the nature of that force we will better understand the forces that expand business and the forces that contract it. To do this we need to understand what happens with cash flow through the cycle of interest. This in turn depends on sales price and costs as they vary with volumes sold through the cycle.

There are many, many price/volume curves or cost/volume curves in business and economics but we see three again and again.

Typically prospective customers can be split into a spectrum of groups along lines like these:
1. Would not buy the offered product unless at a very low price.
2. Would buy if the price was low enough and they could be quickly convinced of value.
3. Can already see significant value and would buy if the price was low enough to match that value for them.
4. Would pay more than for Case 3 if they could be quickly convinced that the product had some advantages over similar ones.
5. Would pay more again if they could be convinced, perhaps during in-depth information exchange and analysis, that product met very specific requirements of high value to them.
6. Would buy at price asked without further question.

When demand is price-sensitive, as we reduce price we increase sales volume when buyers who previously did not see sufficient value in the product now buy it.

A1 Fig. 9

This dotted curve is very similar to a cost volume curve driven by economies of scale (see Fig. 11 below). The business sector is full of these. Price volume curves often follow cost volume curves when suppliers share cost savings with customers to attract more business, particularly those ones whose sales volume helps move the volume down the curve. This curve applies when continued lowering of price expands the market on an indefinite basis.

But there is another price volume curve that appears when competition is strong and the market is prone to saturation.

The curve may take many variations within its general downward movement with volume.

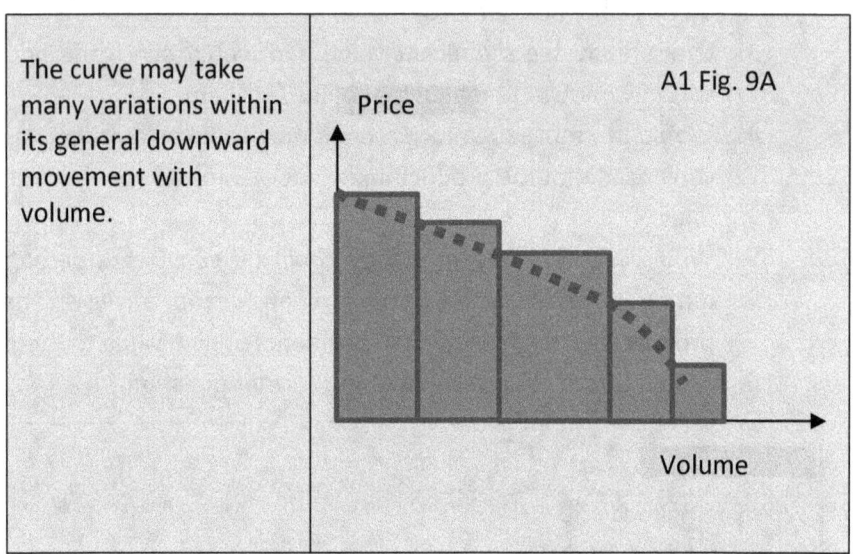

A1 Fig. 9A

The shape of the curve will depend on the populations of buyers in the various categories. Some curves may start as concave like the one in Fig. 9 and move to the convex like the one in Fig. 9A.

Conversely when demand is strong and supply is limited, price tends to rise with demand. The extreme case of this is a price spike (see Fig. 18 below) but the general case is more gradual.

When demand increases, due to a lowering of external cost or an increase in customers due to better access, while supply capacity is unchanged we see price increasing as volume increases.	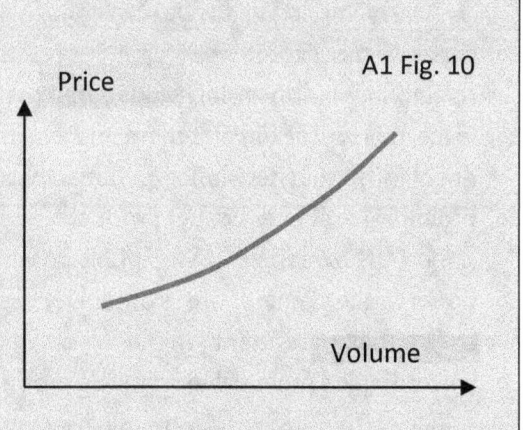 A1 Fig. 10

We first consider the working capital cycle. The same patterns apply for longer cycles but the working capital cycle is something we all deal with and see many more of than the longer cycles.

The curves above make no reference to the variation of cost of supply with sales volume, only to valuation of product by customers. Economies of scale allow us to increase our gross margin, or to lower price to customer, as volumes increase because our costs reduce. This may be simply due to working existing supply facilities harder – longer working hours for staff, extra shifts – and/or due to using larger scale facilities.

The economy of scale curve shows how unit cost of a product typically reduces with volume produced.	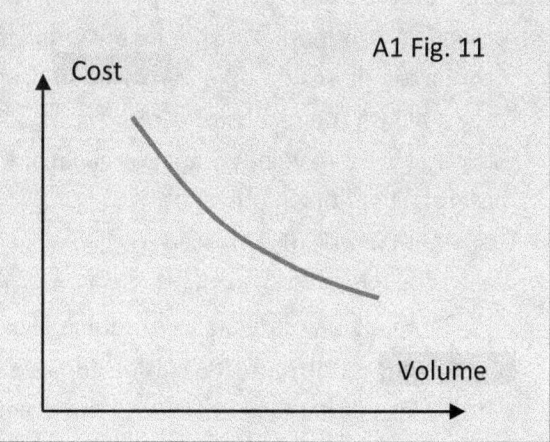 A1 Fig. 11

A very important special case of the economy of scale cost/volume curve is the experience curve. Here, as time spent working with a technology platform increases, the cost of production reduces. This leads to cyclical development of new technology and new products enabled by that technology. Initially a new technology platform will probably produce costly products and may require an extended period of investment before unit cost reduces. Then unit costs get down to the point where profitability replaces losses and starts paying back initial investment. Initial buyers in the cycle will usually be those who perceive most value from the product.

All of this applies at the single company level and at the single market sector level. This includes the sectors with high impact on the general economy such as the financial and real estate sectors.

Economies of scale are fundamental to the development and success of business. The driving force behind the cyclical nature of the business operations is based on them. Beyond what might be available to a specific business at a specific time is an entire business environment. That environment is built upon layer after layer of economies of scale amongst numerous companies and sectors.

We can be tempted to focus on a particular development when we think of economies of scale but across a global economy they are occurring continuously and in millions of businesses at any time. Economies of scale come in waves and if they have staying power they build on the results of earlier waves. There are many types, all of which can be developed again and again and success in one feeds potential benefits in the next:

- Marketization – We trade what we can relatively easily produce more than we need for something we find it relatively difficult to produce. For example, we trade olives grown on our dry hillside for rice grown on someone else's wet flatlands. Then we can spend more time on growing

olives rather than spending a great amount of time trying to grow rice in poor conditions.
- Specialization - We develop specific skills to increase productivity for our market of choice. We develop new techniques so we not only spend more time on the most productive produce but we get to produce more for each hour that we do spend on it.
- Organization – We build systems and processes to analyze, plan, coordinate and supervise resources of businesses to produce more product per unit of management resource.
- Mechanization – We use machines to magnify human force, control sizes, quantities and shapes with repeatability and consistency to allow more physical production per hour of staff input.
- Financing – We expand to a larger scale than we have cash to implement and support, to a scale that repays the financing and hopefully much more.
- Exchange Marketization - We invest in market systems so that we are no longer limited to bilateral deals between market participants. We can offer more choice in customers and buyers with multiple bidders for every bid and multiple bidders for every offer.
- Automation – We remove the need for a human to operate a machine process, to feed it, activate its mechanisms, clear its out feed, to control its speed
- Production Integration – We chain together multiple production processes. Some or all of these may be automated as individual sub-systems. They can then be managed from a single point further reducing the staff input per unit of output.
- Logistics – We integrate firms and transport modes, linking the organization we have performed within those entities.

- And last but not least we acquire facilities that simply have greater physical capacity. An 18 wheel truck might carry 20 times the load of a 4 wheel pickup truck but, like the pickup it only needs one driver at a time. It also does not need an engine that is 20 times as large as the pickup truck.

All of these have potential for generation after generation of improvement in economies of scale. While we develop one of these our customers, suppliers and competitors will likely be developing others.

Of course many expected economies of scale fail to be delivered. Investors can be impractical, commercially naïve, technically incompetent, lazy, ineffective at getting results from others, or just do their sums wrong. People who can see and exploit one wave may not be best at seeing and exploiting the next. Experience of what works well on one technology generation influences perceptions of what will work well with the one which replaces it, possibly quite wrongly. Expected economies of scale may not eventuate and those that finally do eventuate may not justify the investment made to achieve them. And some or all gains can be lost due to unintended consequences in changed processes, increasing costs or losing sales should customers perceive that service levels or product quality are reduced.

But in spite of the failures there are constant successes and these create a net driving force towards continuing increases in economies of scale in our business environment. The result of these is that, over a period, there is an incremental expansion of individual sales volume in working capital cycle. This leads to a sustained increase in volumes, reduction in cost (which supports price reduction and further increase in volume). And fundamental to these is the role of financing, which enables us to achieve the scale necessary to gain the economy before we start making those economies.

Let us look at the consequences of Fig. 11 in terms of profitability and add another curve (dashed line) for price. This assumes we hold price steady. This might apply if we were a small seller in a large market and our additional capacity did not require price reductions. As volume increases, costs reduce and profitability increases. We also now introduce a new value, Cost+, which is the Cost plus the profit margin at low volume. The reason we do this is that it highlights how margin increases with volume.

For a given price, as costs drop with volume, profit margins increase.

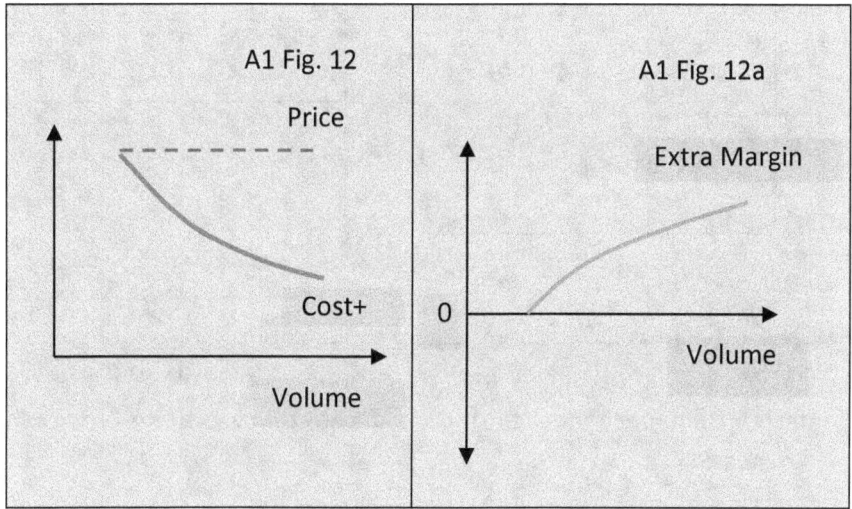

But of course this situation is not the general case. In addition to our economies of scale reducing cost of sale we usually need to reduce sales price to attract customers gain and gain this additional volume. This is our Fig. 9 situation. This may apply when we are the sole supplier to a particular market or if we have significant market share and want to maintain that market share.

We now have a number of possibilities:

The first possibility is that economies of scale reduce cost slower than price needs to be reduced, to gain the extra volume. This generates a smaller extra margin than before. This is not a healthy environment for growth, especially not growth requiring capital investment. This applies whether it is working capital, fixed investment for facilities with more capacity, or capital for development of new products and new technology. If price drops faster than cost with increasing volume, incremental margins drop.

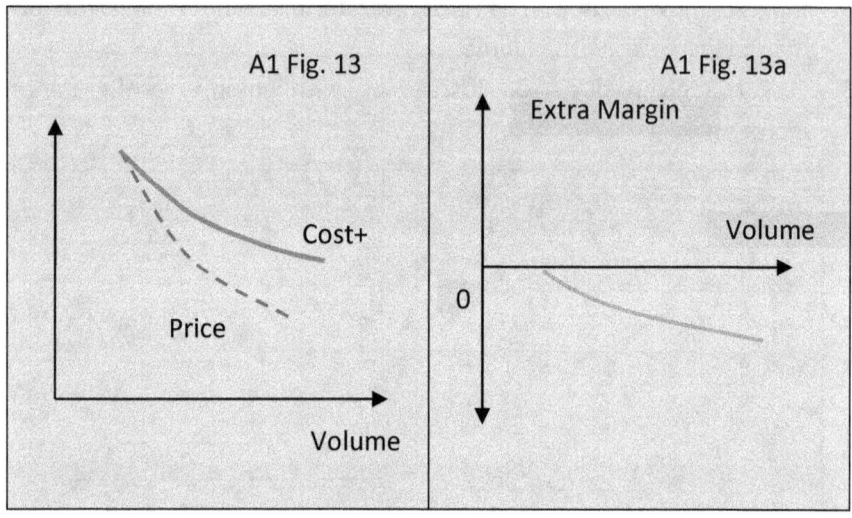

The second possibility involves economies of scale reducing cost faster than price needs to be reduced to absorb the additional volume.

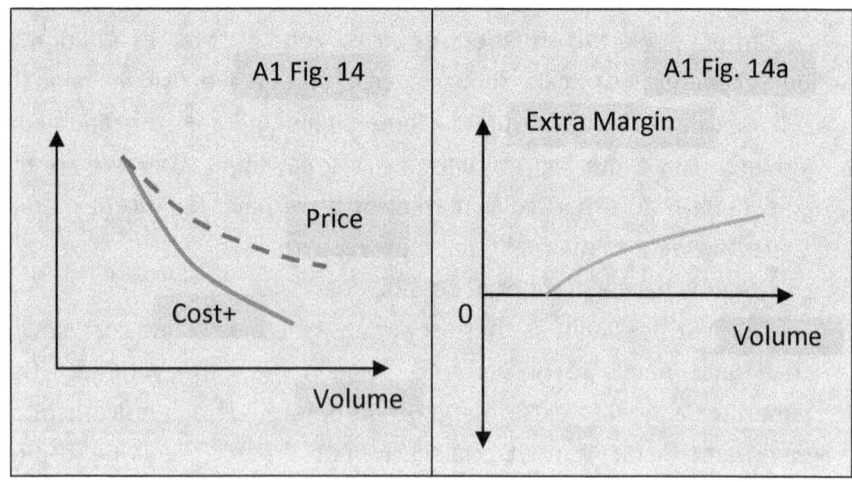

This is a much more attractive environment for growing volume and investing if necessary.

The third possibility starts as the second case and transitions to the first. This is quite common because it typically involves either or both diminishing returns for economies of scale or saturation of the market (our Fig. 9A situation. Given that, for a given level of technology, economies of scale usually do eventually diminish and markets often saturate, this is a common pattern.

We start with costs reducing faster than costs, with rapidly growing economies of scale early in the growth phase. Then, as economies of scale incur diminishing returns, price reductions become counter-productive and may require reversing to some extent.

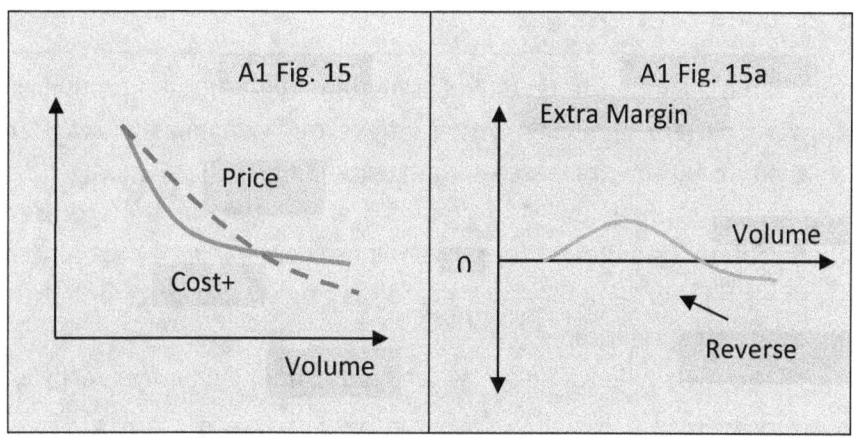

Ideally we would never lower price below Cost+ because we then start losing the benefits of economies of scale. But in practice, with costs and prices fluctuating, this may not be easy. If we can at least minimize the negative dip by stopping, or even reversing, price cuts when they cross the line we can minimize this erosion of margin.

We replace Volume on the x axis in the Extra Margin chart above with a Time axis, the little dashed curve represents the backup path.

The Margin/Time curve initially follows the Margin/Volume curve but the backup curve continues to the right with time on the dotted line rather than to the left with volume. There may still be some profit margin remaining but less than the low volume level.

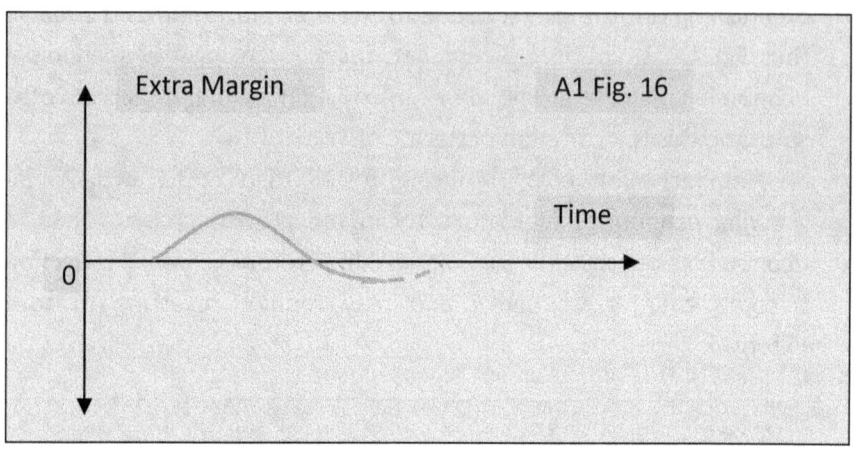

A1 Fig. 16

Squashing up the time dimension a bit, we can see a profitability wave pattern emerging. Here intra cycle economies of scale are encouraged by increased profitability and then discouraged by negative profitability. This creates a wave effect as the process is repeated indefinitely. The pulses will not necessarily be neat replicas of each other. The negative phase may be smaller or zero, but the basic pattern will apply.

We see a series of pulses, which feeds continued business activity.

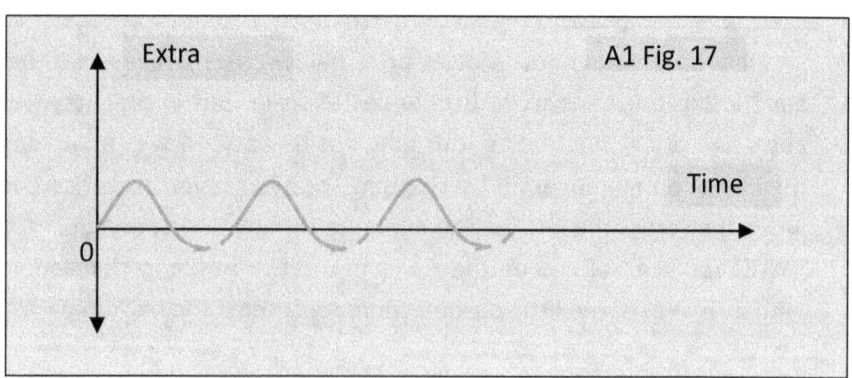

A1 Fig. 17

These pulses of extra profitability, over and above the minimal volume level, motivate us to act to get their full benefit. We build up stock, take on more staff, rent larger premises, buy new equipment, build new facilities. All of these are commitments which require some form of additional financing. It might be trade finance, supply facility capacity product capability or market development finance.

So, while many external factors may stimulate wave behavior, they are not essential for it to occur. As business people, we create wave behavior simply by carrying out the essential activity of seeking profitable recurring business. And if we are to be successful we must seek it repeatedly.

Longer Cycles

In business we are familiar with working capital cycles because we see many of them. So the patterns here of pulsing economies of scale are ones we can see daily, weekly or monthly as the case may be. However, longer types of cycles have the same driving force provided by economies of scale. The product development cycle is one example. Here we invest to enhance in new product capabilities on a regular basis based on successes gained with previous enhancements. The production capacity cycle is another. Here we re-invest in capacity after earlier capacity reaches end of life and when we believe we will get a similar return on investment in its replacement. These are routine cyclical re-investments for many industries.

Longer cycles have of course much more potential for the environment to change during the cycle than short cycles. Demand may increase or decay as buyer populations change and usage patterns change. Supply capacity may increase or decline as resources are depleted or substituted. Constraints to flow may tighten or loosen. This may mean there is more or less likelihood of conditions for repeated pulses of investment to be favorable than is the case for a shorter cycle. We also have more time to deal with longer cycles. If things go wrong over a longer cycle we have time to look in the environment for things going well and to tap into them before things become catastrophic. This is a luxury we may not have over the shorter cycle.

Given time, we can refinance, liquidate assets at reasonable prices, reduce operating costs, develop new markets, negotiate lower costs from our suppliers, reorganize our business processes and introduce new technologies. An example of adapting to changes over a much longer cycle is handing technology change over to the next generation. If we have worked with and profited from a major technology development over our business life and see it being replaced by new ones we may choose to take this approach.

Having refined one technology platform to the point where it is easy to use, standardized and reliable we may find the early years of a newer technology platform extremely irritating. The younger generation may find it fun to embrace the new technology when it is fragmented in function, constantly changing in methods of use and unreliable. Conversely the young may see opportunities that an earlier generation cannot see because the older people are so accustomed to technologies that they worked with in their earlier career stages. They do not see how the constantly changing combinations of technology and application may provide particular mixes that offer large economies of scale.

Longer cycles also feed back into the behavior of short cycles. Funds accumulated on the upside of a longer cycle become available to invest and finance the shorter cycle more freely. Investors then also feel more confident about investing longer term in facilities and developments. Optimism, developed by having accumulated those funds, makes us think those investments will be profitable and easily repaid. And we fear losing our relative share of assets when asset values are rising. We fear that we do not buy now when we do buy they will be a lot more expensive. These are some of the factors that encourage us to remove constraints that protect us from instability and price collapse.

Price Spike Generation

Price spikes are caused by changes in supply capacity and demand. Upward spikes can be caused by supply capacity being reduced - a production plant breakdown or a transport link from production capacity is blocked. Downward spikes can occur by demand being reduced – a major customer stops ordering, a transport link to demand is blocked. Or, in either case, combinations of demand cycles can aggregate to move demand over high or low thresholds that activate the particular type of spike.

Typically in any market there will be a range of suppliers of comparable products who have different economies of scale or different component supply costs. For commodities, these determine what price companies can supply at. There is usually a range of prices with some profitable at the lowest level and others profitable only when the price is much higher.

For non-commodities, there may be suppliers of substitute products which require additional effort to use, or consume more costly resources in production or usage. They may thus be significantly cheaper because the market will not pay the same price for them. Or they may be products which are richer in capability or consume less costly resources in production or usage, and thus can normally gain a significantly higher price.

The effect of these factors is that generally, as demand volumes rise in a market, more costly supply sources need to be bought into production. This drives up price and if some of the sources are very expensive, and all the lower cost sources have reached their capacity limits, the market price will spike upwards.

The reverse effect is that as consumption volumes fall in a market, more costly supply sources stop supplying and when all the low cost sources have spare capacity, the market price spike downwards.

A supply capacity problem may last longer if it is not quickly repairable. A collapsed bridge, a washed out railway or highway, a wave-damaged wharf or a landslide across a road may take weeks or months to repair. This may force supply to be met from another otherwise more expensive location without the bottleneck. Our spike may come and go over an extensive period, possibly cutting in or out during peak and low demand periods.

We can make significant financial killings from price spikes, especially recurring ones. The upward price spike is the classical killing, going back to medieval times and before. We have berths to sell on the ship escaping a city under invasion from army or plague. We have grain to sell in a land in famine. The price we get is far more than the normal rate and we make a small fortune. If the spikes recur over a period we can make multiple small fortunes. The downward spike emerges when there is a sudden surplus on the market, a bumper crop for example.

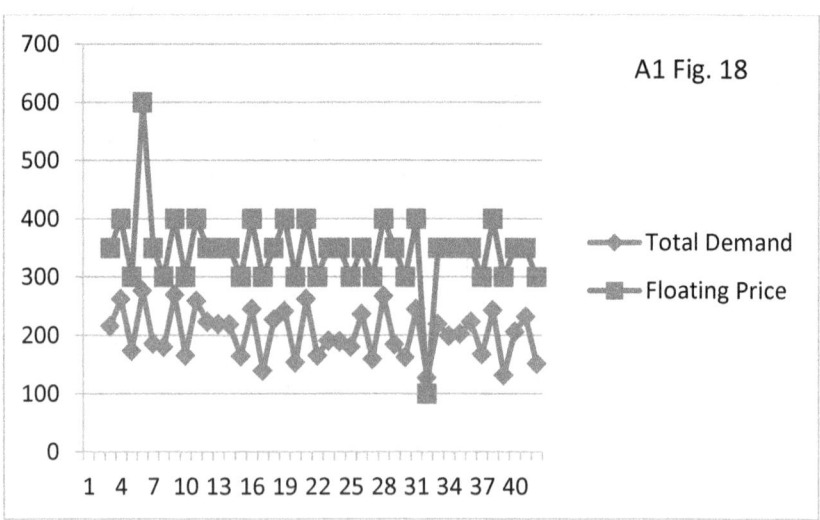

A1 Fig. 18

We see two spikes here, an upward one early on and a downward one. The only thing that is changing is demand, which is a composite of several cycles.

Spikes tend to be self-relieving when the system is stable so they often only last for a relatively short period. Customers will try to cut purchases where possible. Inactive potential suppliers may see the price and start producing. The price differential is high but the volume of product sold at the high or low price tends to be moderate. Spikes may recur but each time total money flow is relatively moderate.

The exception is when some supply outage is not only long lasting but makes up a large portion of total supply. If we could take out a big production facility transport link for a long period at a planned moment we could set up the financial instruments in advance to collect the money. However, it is hard to plan these things unless we have a high level of control of production capacity at critical times.

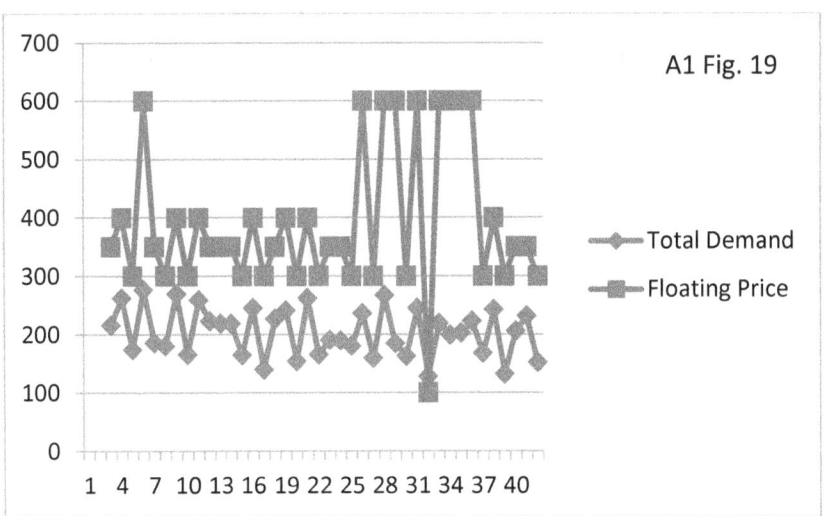

A1 Fig. 19

In the diagram above, Total Demand and Floating Price are the same as the previous diagram but an item of supply capacity is removed at Point 24. This leads to repeated upward spikes until capacity is restored at Point 34. Coincidentally there is also a downward spike when cyclical demand happens to drop at Point 30.

Price spikes, up or down have a big impact on businesses. They may be predictable for those who are familiar with a particular market but can still catch businesses off guard. In the case of an upward spike they can severely impact cash flow, liquidity and even solvency for buyers. This is because of their generation of a need for much larger payments than usual, even for a limited period. In the case of downward spikes, they can do the same for sellers.

Of course price spikes also occur due to the application or release of external bottlenecks. Natural disasters, accidents and acts of war can all remove supply capacity. External bottlenecks can also create good opportunities for killings from price spikes if we know they are coming before others in the market. However, as their effects are usually physically obvious they can often be more quickly moved than ones caused by market cyclical combination. Governments can also gain votes by helping fix problems after disasters. By contrast, fixing some peculiarity of the market may be much more difficult and time-consuming.

APPENDIX 2: LIQUIDITY, SOLVENCY AND CREDIT FAILURE

Financing Business

Agreeing on a price in a contract, delivery of the product and payment for it are activities that can occur at three distinct times. Each can also occur in multiple steps.

Generally price acceptance leads cash flow. As suppliers we usually need to set a price at which we will commit to deliver product before buyers can commit to purchase. They may negotiate it downwards of course, but they need a price that they can agree on before the delivery process starts. There are exceptions. Some buyers will risk a high variance of cost over typical costs for some type of product if circumstances are sufficiently urgent but these buyers do not come along every day.

This usual lead of price acceptance over cash flow applies to all investment cycles, short and long. Before investment in supply facilities and working capital is made, the supplier will want to know that the market will buy at a particular price if it is product that is used by multiple parties. There is always room for individual negotiation around that price, and things can go wrong resulting in a lower price even below that negotiated but that is another story (see Contingent Price in Appendix 3).

On the supply side, there is almost always some time spent between investment of funds in resources and delivery of finished product. This covers activities like purchasing or hiring resources, awaiting delivery, converting the inputs, assembling the product, holding and transporting (or vice versa) for delivery. The time spent involves a period of exposure to risk and is thus a deterrent to supply. Some degree of confidence in some level of expected price is required to invest for this period. Confidence in price expectation can be increased with a customer contract or a known market price for similar products supplied by other suppliers for other customers. Price leads supply.

There are exceptions to this. Sometimes customers will ask suppliers to build something and agree to pay whatever it costs.

Winning markets when time is critical can be such an incentive if the first mover shuts out latecomers who do not comply with the standards it creates. Wars and natural disasters are examples where normal economies for such a task are set aside. The cost in life or property of not dealing with a problem is so high compared with the cost of the task that this is justified.

However, even then we usually agree to a charging rate or set of rates in advance - per hour, per day, per mile, per ton, etc. Or we provide an estimate, which may not be binding but is an indication.

Here much higher risk falls on the buyer than when price is agreed in advance. This risk can be reduced with detailed design and specifications but sometimes time to prepare these is limited under these circumstances.

Remembering seller's and buyer's risk:
- The seller ideally wants to receive the cash before creating the product. Next best is cash at delivery time. Next best is cash soon after delivery. This relieves the risk of not getting paid at all, which often increases once the product has been consumed or used. Next best is getting paid as the buyer uses it.
- The buyer would ideally have the product delivering its benefits before paying for it to confirm its performance (the longer it does this the better). The next best is to pay for it when it is delivered. Next best is to pay in advance but on milestones that relate to visible activities that reduce the probability of the product not performing when it arrives or never arriving at all.

Either buyer or seller can perceive the greater risk from the deal. There is a spectrum of payment timing arrangements from full payment in advance, partial payment in advance, cash on delivery or collection, to payment on invoice, payment after use and variations of each of these. The payment time relative to delivery will tend to be negotiated according to which party feels the highest risk.

The effect of this is that if, as a supplier, we want to increase sales by reducing buyer's risk we need to inject finance into the working capital cycle. This allows deferred payment by buyers until their risk level is reduced.

This financing allows customers who cannot pay the required price with the funds that they have available now, but who believe that they will be able to pay it at some future time, to buy now. There are multiple types of buyers who may have this belief but they can be combined into two classes.

One class includes the buyers who are expecting income earned or savings made by the use of our product during the loan to be sufficient for the loan to be amortized. The other class includes buyers who anticipate that, while the asset they invest in may not earn enough or save enough to pay back the financing during its use, the funds will become available when it is due for repayment. This availability could be due to a capital gain in the asset's market value or to its use generating value in some kind of development. The risk here is that, we are requiring an improvement future that comes into effect in possible future conditions. We are not basing the repayment on revenue or cost savings under today's known conditions.

Financing has an impact on price. Many customers will be willing to pay a higher price through added financing costs than they could pay without it. The value of having the product now, rather than waiting, is worth paying a higher price. The first class of borrowers will push the price over the levels that cash-only buyers will pay and increase total sales volume. The second class will push the price higher again and increase total sales further. Conversely if we have a situation where buyers have to pay in advance of production, those buyers who need the product ready to use immediately they pay will miss this benefit. This reduces the price they would be willing to pay for that benefit and reduces total sales.

In Fig. 1 below, the lower curve shows sales volume increasing as buyers who pay in advance have the price is reduced and we attract more of them. Buyers here are providing the working capital of the supply process.

The next curve up shows sales volume increasing if we add buyers who won't pay in advance but will pay cash on delivery. The supplier is now paying working capital of the supply process. The price is still reduced to capture more buyers but not by as much as for the lower curve.

The next curve up shows sales volume increasing if we add buyers who won't pay in advance or on delivery but will pay as they gain a benefit from using the product. The supplier is paying working capital of supply and also financing the usage of product by the buyer. The price may be increased by a moderate amount and then decreased as economies of scale improve.

The top curve shows sales volume increasing if we add buyers who won't pay in advance or on delivery, or even pay off the financing as they gain a benefit from using the product. They anticipate that what they invest in will increase in value sufficiently to pay it back after the financing period. It may even pay accumulated interest charges.

Curves rise as we add increasing levels of financing by the supplier.

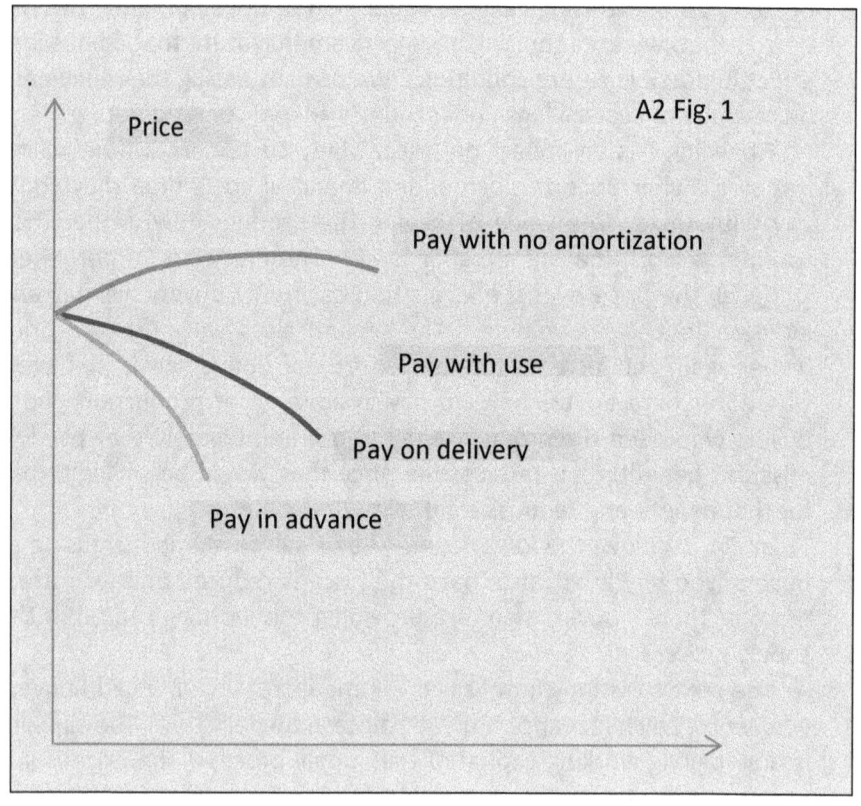

A2 Fig. 1

So as the supplier increases its financing of supply and use of the product it attracts new types of customers who previously would not have purchased and increases sales volume.

Economies of scale described in Appendix 1 work in conjunction with financing to increase sales volumes and supply more product to more people at lower cost.

PRICE COLLAPSE

Price collapse occurs when suppliers have more product volume to sell than customers want to buy and the suppliers. Suppliers repeatedly reduce price, hoping to attract new types of buyers and/or undercut their competition. The suppliers' hope is that, before prices get too low to be profitable, their price reductions attract new customers into the market, and win competed sales with existing customers. If these extra sales are enough it will restore their balance of supply and demand, albeit at a lower price level.

However, excess capacity may exceed the extra customer demand attracted by the lower price level. Then suppliers and their competitors may feel the need to reduce price further, particularly if some have cash shortages. This starts a series of competing price reductions. It may continue until enough new customers re brought into the market to balance the supply/demand of the whole market, not just individuals.

The suppliers' predicament may be further aggravated if buyers who would buy at that new lower price level anticipate further reductions. If they are in a position to wait, they may hold back until those continued reductions occur. They are more likely to do this if they anticipate the capacity surplus will last longer. If it is a short term inventory excess and it is expected to clear quickly, this is less likely. If it is a long term supply capacity excess, the customers learn from repeated price reductions that they can afford to wait. If it is a supply capacity excess those suppliers with high variable costs have will usually stop supplying first. When only those with lower variable costs are supplying, and there is still excess capacity, there will be little to stop a continued decline. The lowered price will not be able to cover the fixed costs of some suppliers and those ones will go out of business.

The price collapse curve follows the pattern of Fig. 2 below:

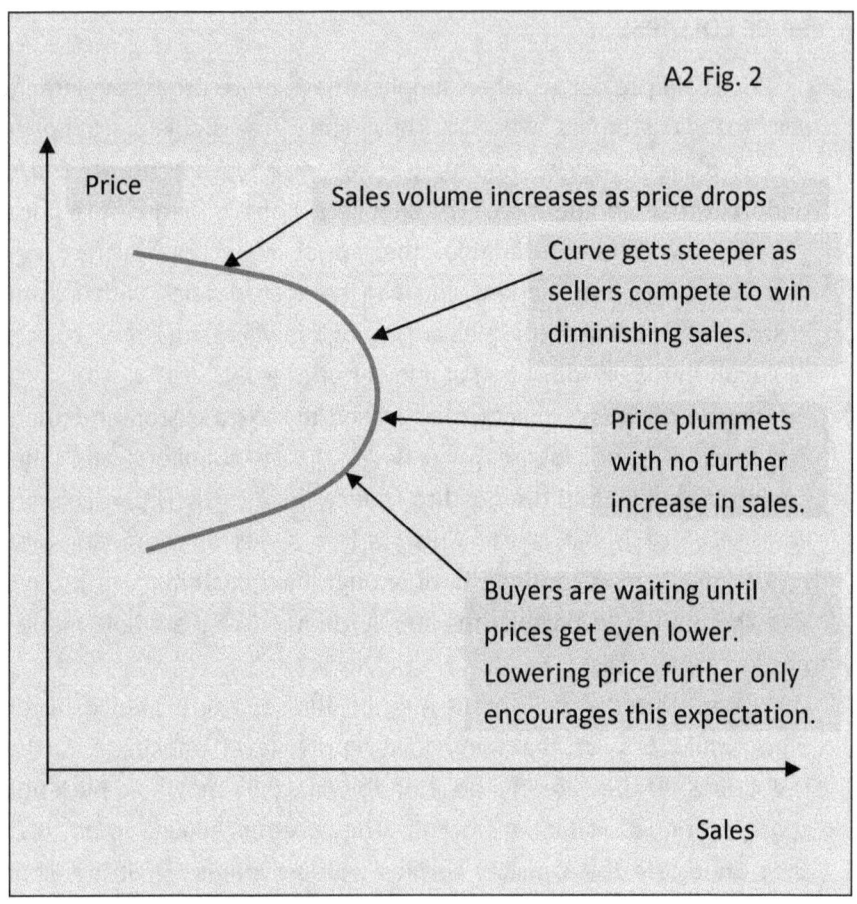

A2 Fig. 2

Individual suppliers cannot prevent price collapse from occurring in any market where we have multiple suppliers. They may withdraw from a market and leave it to other suppliers to continue to sell.

However, price will continue to collapse as long as there are plenty of suppliers and an excess supply of product.

The other behavior that is shown by the curve is that the price/volume curve after collapse is quite different from the one before collapse. This is not necessarily obvious. We might expect that if demand at a given price drops for any reason, we simply move back along the price volume curve to a lower volume at the higher price. But increasing price while competitors are reducing theirs may reduce our sales to near zero. Conversely reducing price will also reduce sales as customers see this as a sign of further price reductions if they wait for them.

Impact of Financing on Sales and on Price Collapse

The chart in Fig. 4 below shows peak price and maximum sales volume that will be achieve as each class of buyer participates. The mathematical analysis that shows how these curves are generated is described in Appendix 3.

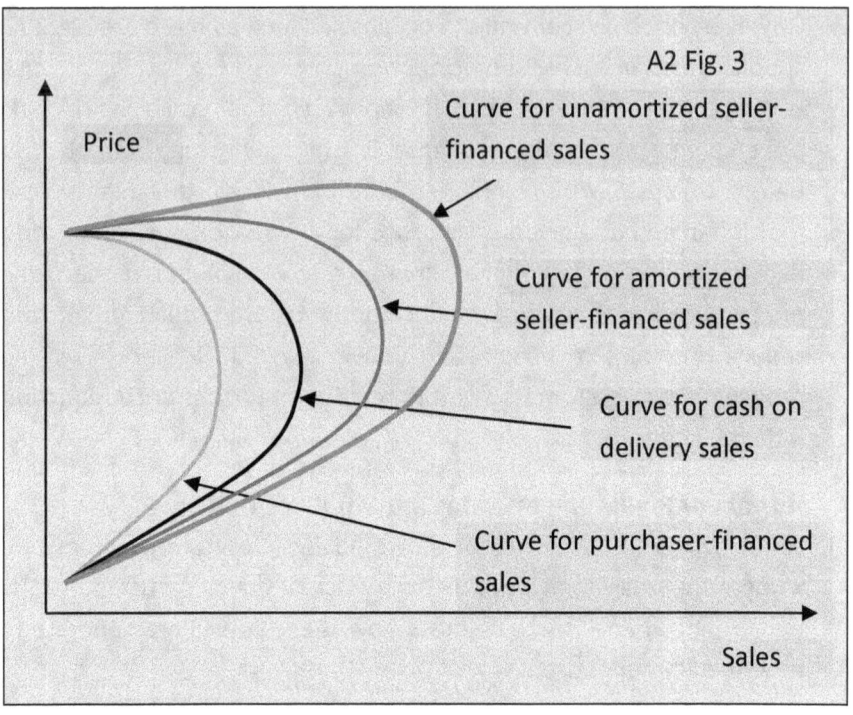

A2 Fig. 3

Curve for unamortized seller-financed sales

Curve for amortized seller-financed sales

Curve for cash on delivery sales

Curve for purchaser-financed sales

There are significant points to note here:
- Until the point of collapse, price obtained with financing is generally consistently higher than without financing. It is higher than for the situation when buyers must finance the working capital. It may even exceed the normal maximum price point achievable at low sales volume as the portion of financed sales increases relative to cash sales.
- The nose of the curve, indicating final point in collapse, is higher with financing.

When the curve reaches its lowest point after collapse, spare stock or spare capacity needs to be consumed before we can return to a higher price/volume curve. We might note that although we have drawn a smooth curve below the point of collapse, the consequences of collapse tend to be chaotic. So while the curve indicates the general direction, the actual price path may be highly erratic.

Common to the curves in Fig. 3 is the nose portion on the far right of the curves, which indicates the price collapse zone. All the curves can go into collapse mode. What differs between them is the sensitivity that the various curves have to disturbances such as sudden price fluctuations and cost spikes. The curves further to the right have less distance downwards to the nose. What this means is that when some disturbance creates a short term price reduction, it pushes price over the nose where it plummets with no gain in sales. The price reduction can be triggered by a price spike caused by some shock event or a supply constraint. The temporary price spike causes a short term reduction in demand and the price correction overshoots downwards, pushing the price over the nose.

Impact of Financing on Financial Stability

The curves above show how increasing levels of financing increase sales volume but eventually price collapses and sales plummet if we go past a certain point. It is also useful to understand how sensitive the system is to routine business fluctuations. We might want to provide financing to a high level to have high sales volumes but keep volumes just below the point of collapse. Stability now becomes a very important issue. If volumes safely stay close to the limit, but not actually reach it, economies of scale are at a maximum. But if some small event would push us over the limit then we might want to keep a bit further away. The question is how stable is the system in the event of relatively small disruptions? How close can we get to the limit before instability becomes a high risk?

When an increasing portion of sales becomes dependent on financing, sales volume can dry up quickly should some external event occur. Highly financed buyers are sensitive to increasing interest rates and are prone to default payment in the event of a market turndown, even a short one. If many buyers are depending on future income and that income does not materialize, defaults are inevitable.

As the top of the curve gets higher, the nose also gets higher and approaches the height of the low volume cash sale price. Head room required to reduce price prior to collapse is thus reduced. Relatively small reductions in price can then push it to the point of collapse. Often a triggering event may push other costs up temporarily, which impacts on price. For example, a spike in the price of oil caused by a war, a storm, an earthquake, a tsunami, a terrorist event, may momentarily chill price rises in real estate in suburbs or satellite towns that require long commutes. These may lead to people, who needed increasing house prices to maintain positive equity, defaulting on their mortgage This leads to mortgage sales, which causes house prices to drop, which encourages more to sell, driving prices down further.

This slowdown would normally be just a blip followed by a return to previous conditions, but not now. Some suppliers get nervous and reduce prices. Others follow and soon all are reducing prices if they wish to maintain market share. Sooner or later buyers figure that if they wait prices will come down further. The additional reduction in demand panics sellers so they drop prices further. A downwards spiral continues until demand balances supply.

Who do the borrowers sell to if they all need liquidity? The cash buyer is the ultimate fall back. But the cash buyers will not buy until the price is down to their normal cash buy price, or less. The more borrowers there are looking for a buyer, the greater will be the discount compared to normal. And if the price curve has its nose sufficiently close to that cash buy price, by the time the price is low enough for the cash buyer to step in and buy, the system will be at the point of collapse.

The effect of financing is to initially add stability to price but to eventually destabilize price if expanded too far. Too much financing, based on underestimation of real risk, creates a price bubble. Financing risk can be underestimated for a number of reasons. The classic bubble occurs when lenders think asset prices can only go up so their borrowers will always be able to sell assets and pay them back if they need to.

Impact of Market Collapses on the General Economy and Financial Sector

The observations above apply to any market sector. And one market sector can suffer a collapse on its own without necessarily having a major impact on the rest of the economy. It may even suffer an irrecoverable collapse and shrink to a fraction of its former self. Or it may disappear entirely, without much impact on the rest of the economy. Collapse of one market does not automatically spread more widely.

Recessions and depressions are a consequence of sustained price collapse in a sufficiently large market sector, or group of sectors, to have an impact on the overall economy. The collapse will reduce personal equity by dampening real estate prices, causing losses in the financial sector and reducing tax revenues. These are all areas that have impacts across the whole economy.

In themselves these flow-on effects do not necessarily have long term impacts. The various parts of the market affected will usually adjust to new market conditions and return to a new normal not very different from their previous state.

However, each of these can have deeper and long term impacts if certain pre-conditions are present:
- If the real estate market has been through a boom phase, a reduction of buyers and/or a surge of sellers, may cause a price collapse the real estate market. The surge of sellers may be created by a price collapse in another market. This may lead to people needing to raise cash or reduce mortgage payments.

- If the financial sector has financing levels close to stability limits, the impact of credit failures in the industry initially affected by the price collapse in another market may be enough to trigger a price collapse in the financial sector. Firms may have enough reserves to ride out a limited collapse but if they do not, and start selling other financial assets to fill gaps, the price of those assets will also collapse and a domino effect will occur.
- If there is already a high level of government debt present, governments may be reluctant to incur more if tax revenues drop so they reduce spending. This can have a chilling effect on people's consumption behavior across the economy and on some investments, leading to a price collapses in other sectors.

In essence, if the financial system is at or near its stability limits for lending, a relatively small and short term setback in one market sector can collapse it and cause long term decline across the wider economy.

All of the above conditions were present prior to the 2007/2008 financial crisis and the financial system was roaring along but approaching stability limits. It did not need a major event to push it into collapse.

Financial Institutions

Financial institutions have a need to track cash flow and profit like any other business, but they also have a particular need to focus on liquidity and solvency. The panic of 2007/2008 showed that financial firms can be highly profitable right up until the moment that there is a liquidity crisis and then their profitability cannot save them from a collapse in asset values. Even if their cash flow position is also strong, large changes in mark to market values of financial assets will lead to hemorrhaging of cash.

Credit rating agencies and economists did not see the 2007/08 crisis coming in spite of their supposed expertise[1]. In relation to liquidity and solvency, some particular patterns are consistent though all banking eras in the US, including the Charter Banking, Free Banking, National Banking and Federal Reserve eras[1]:

Unless financing is constrained, crises occur with regularity, regardless of the financial regulatory environment. Instability is systemic, not limited to a particular regulatory environment.

- If financing is constrained, stability can continue indefinitely, as in the Quiet Period. This applies until financial firms find ways to circumvent regulations or until they persuade politicians to remove those regulations.
- If financial asset price collapse is threatened, regulators have historically found ways to release banks of legal obligations until the crisis is over. This is regardless of previous positions on moral hazard. Letting incompetent operators fail, as is usually permitted in non-financial markets to the advantage of competitors, can lead to a downward spiral in asset values. This can annihilate the most competent and cautious operators.

The consequence of these systemic crises have been that when the system is at risk of collapse, regulators/central banks will always relieve solvent (but illiquid) banks of legal obligations, or lend them the money to meet them. The alternative is to face a financial collapse and, regardless of previous positions on moral hazard, governments and regulators avoid financial collapse at great cost. But those firms who do not qualify for assistance may come to a rapid end.

A full collapse could lead to a death spiral for the wider economy. When politicians and regulators have the collapse scenario detailed to them they have invariably chosen to save the financial system. Political postures and ideology are pushed aside by systemic forces threatening the economy and the personal future of the regulators and politicians.

Our wave model described in Appendix 3 predicts the potential for product price collapse and asset price collapse: Unless financing is constrained, product price collapse is likely to occur and reoccur on a regular basis. It can be avoided but as long as financing is unconstrained it will almost certainly occur. However, the price collapse analysis in Appendix 3 does not directly focus on wave patterns in liquidity and solvency. It is worth considering how these relate to cash flow and profit.

The Particular Sensitivity of Financial Firms

All businesses need to be conscious of liquidity and solvency but they may not have the risk exposure of financial firms. If a construction company cannot pay its creditors in full they may choose to give it relief for a while if they believe will return to liquidity in due course. If a factory suddenly loses 20% of its asset value in the market, but can continue to produce saleable products at a profit, it does not usually have the same problems as a bank losing asset value. Loss of market value for the factory may end up with its owners losing the business if they need its collateral value to satisfy lenders, but the factory retains its ability to function.

If a non-financial industry sector suffers a major price collapse, many of its members may go out of business but the rest of the sector will continue on. At some stage the economy will probably create demand to reactivate the supply capacity of the suffering sector. This involves reusing shut down assets provided they have not deteriorated though lack of care or become obsolete. This is not necessarily the case with the financial sector. A bank needs its financial assets to hold their value in order to borrow and lend. And if these are perceived as having lost value, creditors may force it to sell assets to meet cash demands, and ultimately destroying the value of these assets.

A financial firm can be solvent but illiquid if it has lent out money on fixed term to companies, who will pay it back at the end of the term, but it cannot access that money to cover cash shortages now. Conversely a firm can be liquid but insolvent if it has borrowed money via long term instruments that it will not be able repay in future but has cash or liquid assets now to meet immediate demands.

A commercial bank's leverage ratio (see Appendices 4 and 5) is critical to the survival of a bank if it suffers losses through unpaid loans. Losses that are greater than a percentage put aside for this purpose need to come out of the bank's capital, which usually must be kept above a regulated level as a percentage of assets. If it goes below that figure the bank must add new capital or reduce assets – typically cut back on loans to customers.

When a financial crisis occurs and solvent firms do not have enough cash to pay back short term loans, so that they are illiquid, bank regulators/central banks can save the day. They can suspend the firms' legal obligation to repay loans or lend them cash to meet their short term obligations. When the crisis is over, the suspension can be removed or the firms repay the money loaned by the regulator.

If a firm is also insolvent the regulator/central bank risks not being paid back so they may choose not to lend money to these firms and thus let them fail. However, it may be very hard to identify which firms are solvent when asset values are in a state of uncertainty. And if letting possibly insolvent firms fail will lead to an uncontrollable spiral of declining financial asset values, then the regulator/central bank may choose to lend to these firms as well as the solvent ones to avoid a systemic collapse.

The question arises, how does our analysis of collapse in product prices relate to collapse of financial asset prices? A simplistic answer is that financial assets, in addition to being commitments for future payment and being assets that provide collateral for borrowing, are products like bushels of wheat, barrels of oil, autos, phones, communication network services and restaurant meals. From this point of view their price collapse is just another product price collapse. And in some respects the behavior of financial assets as products demonstrates the growth and instability model more simply than for most other products. For example, reducing interest rates, drives up the price of existing fixed income financial assets.

But while this may deal with the initial sale of a financial product it does not deal with the product's ongoing role as collateral for demand deposits and loans. If its market price diminishes for any reason, specific to the asset in particular, or to its class of assets, that collateral value reduces. This in turn reduces the amount of money that can be borrowed in new loans. It also leads to lenders of existing loans wanting some of their cash back to align the loan value with the collateral backing it. If enough lenders want this, the firm may need to sell financial assets to find the cash.

If firms need to sell assets in a hurry their sales activities may drive down the price of the assets they sell. This reduces the collateral value of these assets, which may lead to more calls by lenders for cash returns to align with the value of the assets. This may lead to more assets sales, further market price reductions, further cash calls, further sales, further price reductions, etc. If multiple firms are involved we may have a panic and then ultimately a death spiral as further asset sales lead to further price reductions, leading to further cash calls, leading to further asset sales across the market.

Establishing the relationship in financial firms between liquidity/solvency and cash flow/profit as they all fluctuate through business cycles is useful. Intuitively we would expect these items to be connected and problems in one pair to relate to problems in the other but how closely is not necessarily obvious.

The Mathematics section below in this appendix describes the underlying cyclical dynamics of asset prices in a model that is focused on liquidity and cash flow. It also describes the underlying cyclical dynamics of product prices in a model that is focused on cash flow and profitability. They are mathematically essentially the same.

From the Mathematics in Appendix 3 we can expect that, in theory, instability in liquidity and solvency will behave like instability in cash flow and profit/loss. Instability in the asset price wave should build steadily if financing is liberal as it does for the product price wave. It should ultimately lead to asset price collapse. The question is does this happen in the real world?

When we model a cycle as a wave we observe the following:

- The model shows that with unconstrained financing a cyclical business will expand to the point of instability and finally to price collapse.
- The model does not specify a time on how long this will take. The progression can pause. It can go backwards along the price/volume curve for a while if financing tightens or confidence weakens. But sooner or later it will resume its path to instability and collapse. If we constrain it, by controlling one critical parameter, the mathematics shows that the system will be much less sensitive to disruptive forces.
- When collapse does occur, the price/volume curve that applied in the expansion phase bifurcates and follows a new curve. Behavior here is very different from previous pre-collapse behavior. Normal market price/volume behavior, which provides for resilience and stability of markets, is replaced by an entirely different mechanism. The mathematics shows that price reductions do not increase sales volume but reduce sales volume. The spiral into price collapse is a logical outcome of the mathematics.

To understand how this applies in the financial sector we need to look at the phases of a longer investment cycle, as shorter cycles within it move to collapse. The key driving factor here is increasing economy of scale in the expansion phase, followed by diseconomies of scale in the post collapse contraction stage.

The Destabilization Phase - Limits

Economies of scale by their nature suffer diminishing returns. As scale increases, the incremental gains get proportionately smaller. They are still occurring but not with the impact of the early phase. Expansions need to be increasingly larger to gain an equivalent unit benefit. We can be tempted to invest in extensions when the returns are simply not good enough. With advances going on all around us it is easy to believe economies will keep on coming, we will get to win or at least share them, and demand will continue to grow. The market may also need continued price reductions to maintain sales growth in line with the increases in scale. Those price reductions may be greater than the cost savings offered by proportionately smaller economies of scale than we have had earlier. Profitability per sale may weaken and/or we may struggle to sell our increased capacity.

When an economy-wide expansion is well established we are less likely to be short of financing sources. Widespread economies of scale can lead to widespread profits and thus generate many sources of funds available for lending. When the expansion is booming, funds available for lending may be at their peak. Lenders may struggle to find sound borrowers and may feel the need to lend to borrowers who might not qualify for financing in tighter times. Risk tends to be underestimated, particularly if new financing instruments are used to put the money to work. These may so complex that they hide their real risks in favorable periods. But in the event of a financial crisis they are likely to be suddenly seen as particularly risky because it will be difficult to calculate their value.

To appreciate how different types of borrowers with different risk levels are handled by the model, we consider one of its key mathematical parameters. That parameter is the time by which the seller's delivery lags or leads the payment from the buyer. This determines the division of risk in the transaction between the parties, specifically risk that the buyer does not get value for money and risk that the seller does not get paid.

In a market we have a spectrum of buyer types, each with different risk sensitivities:

1. There are those that are cash rich enough and confident enough of product capability to pay in advance of production of the product. This is sometimes even in advance of design and development of the product if their need is specific enough, and if they can scope its design.
2. There are those liquid and willing enough to pay on delivery of a working product with known capabilities.
3. There are those who can pay only after achieving expected earnings/cost savings based on current conditions and realistic variations from those conditions. The product needs to save them money, earn them money or deliver some other type of benefit for a period before they can actually pay for it.
4. There are those who can pay only after achieving expected earnings/cost savings plus further increases of asset values. These would be increases based on the economies of scale they have experienced over a high growth period and which they expect to continue; increases based on observation of expected technology developments; increases based on market efficiencies; or increases based on whatever else they see as driving prosperity.

Partial payment arrangements blur the lines between these buyer types but the essential pattern remains. The longer is the lead of delivery over payment, the more exposed is the lender in the event of a business downturn or any other kind of significant setback. If some event occurs, which stops expected growth, even for a short period, those planned revenue growth/cost savings can suddenly fall into a delay from which they may never catch up. Type 4 buyer types, which require increased asset values, not just returns based on existing values, are most vulnerable to such setbacks.

Destabilization occurs because risk is transferred from buyer to seller as sellers increasingly use financing to sell their products. The increasing portion of buyers who have borrowed rather than paying cash on delivery, not to mention cash up front, means that price rises relative to what it would have been had only cash buyers been buying.

Cash buyers, whether paying in advance (Type 1) or on delivery (Type 2) may get a benefit from their product or for some reason they may not. If they do not get the expected benefit they expected, then provided the contractual terms were met and the product has been paid for, the lender has no exposure. But if Type 3 or 4 buyers do not get the benefit they expected they may not be able to repay their financing. And this becomes a particularly high risk with Type 4 buyers whose expectations are based on improved asset values rather than current values.

As more Type 4 buyers enter the mix, sensitivity to risk increases for sellers as does risk of instability for the system as a whole when a lot of sellers and buyers are involved in sales under these conditions. Too many sellers will drive down the asset price, possibly into a spiral. In addition if some Type 3 buyers get their sums wrong they also can become very sensitive to disruptions and contribute to destabilizing the system.

How this equates to financial assets past their initial sale as products, in their role as assets which can earn revenue on a continuing basis, can be seen by evaluating cash flows of financial assets. A financial asset is defined by a set of cash flows covering the principal which deliver the use of money to the customer for a period and a set of cash flows which cover the interest paid. Any fees applying can be included with either set of cash flows. The cash flows for the principal might simply consist of a one-time payment when the customer needs the money to buy some of the supplier's product, or some other asset, and a one-time repayment after the loan period. The interest might be a simple monthly or annual payment throughout the term of the loan.

From this simpler case the options are very diverse and we will consider only a few examples applicable to our immediate subject matter. We look at four types of financial asset that parallel our four buyer types in terms of lead/lag of delivery relative to payment.

An example of a Type 1 financial asset might include a one-off loan to the borrower to buy a non-financial asset with a market value greater than the loan but with the full asset value as collateral. The borrower will need to pay a deposit. The borrower then pays back principal at a steady rate over the loan period plus interest (fixed or floating rate). Many property mortgages work like this, as do loans for autos and industrial/commercial equipment. The financial assets once created can then be on-sold to other investors who gain principal repayment cash flow, interest cash flow and collateral to protect their principal.

An example of a Type 2 financial asset might include a one-off payment to the borrower for full value of the non-financial asset. The borrower than pays back principal at a steady rate during the loan period plus paying interest similarly to Type 1. The lender does not initially have the protection provided by collateral of greater value than the loan as they would for Type 1. But protection starts growing from the first principal repayment and continues to increase until the principal is repaid.

An example of a Type 3 financial asset might include a one-off payment to the borrower for full value of the non-financial asset similarly to Type 2. The borrower than pays interest over the loan period similarly to Type 1 and 2 and pays the principal with recurring repayments smaller than for Type 1 and 2, plus a single balloon payment at the end of the loan period. The extreme case of this is to have just the balloon payment and no recurring repayments though the loan period. The larger the proportion made up of the balloon payment, the greater is the risk carried by the lender.

An example of a Type 4 financial asset I might include a one-off payment to the borrower for full value of the non-financial asset similarly to Type 2 and 3. The borrower pays both principal and accumulated interest in a single balloon payment at the end of the loan period. This borrower does not have to deliver a result at any time until the loan period is up. If collateral does not increase in value during the period of the loan it will be of less value than the accumulated interest and principal, creating a high risk for the lender.

A high proportion of Type 4 borrowers and associated financial assets in a financial firm's loan mix make the firm vulnerable to failures by its borrowers. It also makes it vulnerable to relatively small disruptions, such as short term interest rate rises, short term asset price reductions. These disruptions would normally be routinely handled, which but, in our more fragile state, they may trigger a chain reaction with continuing losses in asset values. And of course it makes us more vulnerable again to bigger disruptions like large storms, wars, droughts and floods. If the financial system as a whole has a high proportion of Type 4 assets it too will be vulnerable to disruptions.

We can also have constraints in our supply chain which can cause delays or product price separation. These are the areas in our supply chain which have not yet been expanded in sync with all the other parts. Perhaps they have been overlooked. Perhaps they are in the process of being expanded but have suffered delays. Perhaps there are real difficulties in expanding them with current technology, current skill limitations, current geographic restraints, current climate conditions, or current political conditions. Whatever the reason we can encounter an unforeseen constraint and suddenly our economies of scale stop increasing when we were counting on them to expand according to plan and repay our investment.

Constraints not only cause supply disruptions but can cause price spikes as prices separate on either side of the constraint. These can be very large in some markets where price elasticity is limited and buyers cannot easily reduce volume to relieve the constraint and associated high prices. And even if we can reduce volume to relieve a price spike, that reduction may destroy the expected economies of scale required for repayment of our financing. The appearance of high product prices, even temporarily, may be enough to dispel the expectation of increasing value in financial assets, and trigger a slide in Type 4 asset prices.

The effect of all these difficulties in the general economy is that our Type 4 buyers, and some of our Type3 buyers, can end up unable to repay their financing. The financial assets, whether direct loans or securities packaged up from loans, based on their financing lose value.

A key requirement of financial firms is to spread risk, by providing diverse loans and/or by using securities that package up diverse loans. Then if some customers do get into difficulty and cannot repay their loans, their number will be relatively small. A small number can be handled by bad debt allowances and reserves. And just as important, we should pick sound borrowers in the first place. Or we should buy securities packaged from multiple loans that do not have too many unsound loans in the mix.

But after a long expansion the portion of Type 4 buyers may be much larger than in early years of an expansion. A lot of buyers presenting themselves as Type 3 buyers may really be Type 4 buyers with optimistic projections of sales growth, cost reductions and lack of pressure from competition. As an expansion ages, all of these factors can deteriorate and once they start deteriorating and do not look like improving, panic can set in. If financial assets lose value, the firm's ability to use them as collateral for routine short term financing purposes will be damaged.

Some financial firms specifically target Type 4 borrowers. For example, private equity financiers may structure buyouts of companies that create Type 4 borrowers. They then seek to systematically work to improve asset values. They do this through cost reduction, productivity gains, anticipation of cyclical market rises and buying cheap assets that have values hidden from other investors. Venture capitalists take another path, typically focusing on large gains in productivity made possible with new technology. The VCs also allow for more half of their investments going bust, with losses paid for with one big success. These are specialist investors who take equity positions as well as providing lending

The diagram in Fig. 4 below shows four different product price/volume curves which correspond to our buyer types in Fig. 3 above, plus to our borrower types when considering financial assets. These curves are defined by the equations in Appendix 3, with the differentiating parameter being lead/lag of delivery over payment.

We start on the left with customers willing to pay cash in advance of delivery. There are always a limited number of customers willing and able to pay on these terms and the furthest left curve indicates these. When terms are tough, many buyers need price reductions to attract them so price needs to drop rapidly to develop more sales.

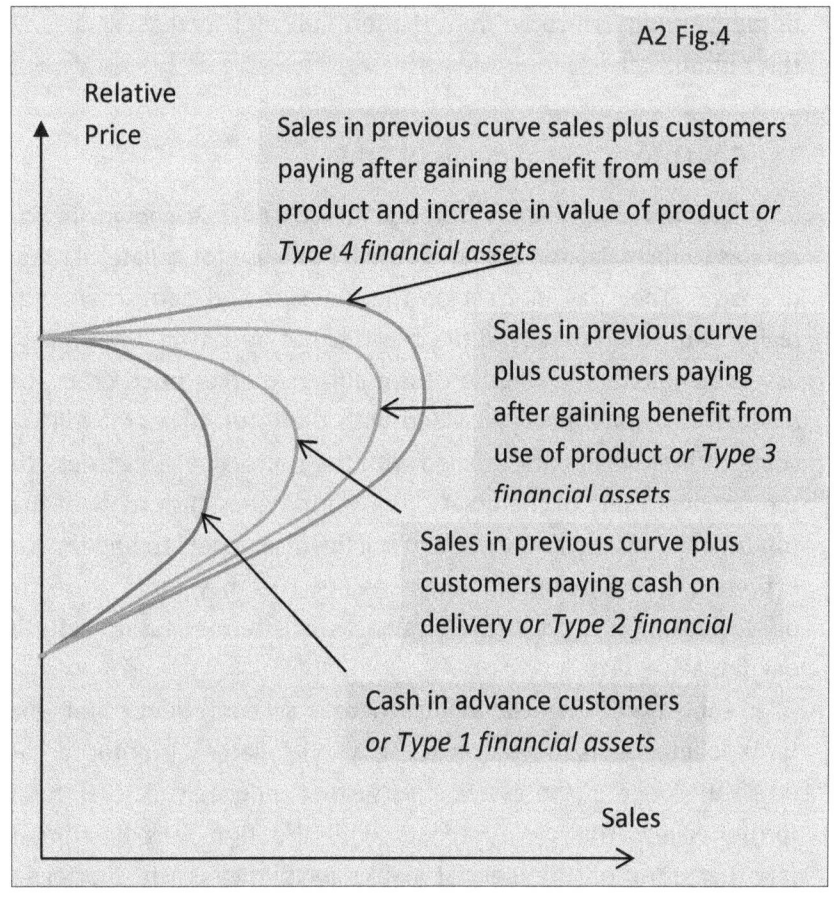

A2 Fig.4

More buyers are willing to pay if cash on delivery is an option and the second curve from the left indicates the increased sales with this option.

More again are willing and able to buy if they do not need to pay until they have used the product for a period and gained an accumulated benefit. The third curve from the left indicates increased sales with this option.

More again are willing and able to pay if they do not need to pay until they have gained some accumulated benefit and the asset they acquire increases in value. Rising markets attract these buyers in hordes. The fourth curve from the left indicates increased sales with this option.

The Collapse - Diseconomies of Scale

A process equivalent to product price collapse shown in Fig. 5 applies to financial assets that financial firms use for collateral to raise deposits. They pay interest on the deposits and earn interest at a higher rate when they lend the deposits out, receiving other financial assets as collateral. When an asset suffers market price drops, cash lenders who have been provided with them for collateral will want some of their cash back to align with the new value. This is less than the nominal value of the asset. If our firm needs cash to meet these top-up obligations, it may need to sell financial assets to find the cash. If there are few buyers for these assets, this may force down their price, causing a drop in their value as collateral, causing a further need to sell assets.

In the case of financial assets, there is an equivalent spiral where firms selling assets to generate cash when collateral is reduced, drive down the price of the assets. This further reduces collateral, forcing further sales. This cycle repeats until the firm fails or someone (another firm or the central bank) pays their cash shortage or suspends their obligation to meet debt obligations.

Cash flow and profit are loosely coupled. Problems with one do not automatically lead to problems with the other, if that one is in a sufficiently healthy state. But if one is already shaky, problems with the other are likely to be dangerous. The same applies to liquidity and solvency. It also applies to the relationship between the two pairs. Cash flow/profit problems may lead to liquidity/solvency problems but do not automatically do so. Product price collapses can last days or years depending on how long it takes for demand to be reestablished. They may be over before asset price has time to be impacted. Or if it is already in a sensitive state, just a short disturbance may be all that is needed to trigger asset price collapse.

If a price collapse in the revenue area does lead to a price collapse in asset value, we would expect from the price collapse mathematics in Appendix 3 that there will be a time delay. Moving into negative cash flow eats up liquidity over a period and moving into losses eats up solvency over a period (probably a different one). This in each case assumes we have some liquidity and solvency to start with. If we do not, the asset price collapse may come very soon after the revenue-related price collapse. But if we have enough liquidity and solvency respectively, we may be able to survive for some time and hopefully ride out a price collapse, as long as it does not last too long.

Conversely we might have an asset price collapse prior to a revenue-related price collapse. Depending on the arrangements we have with our financing parties, we may be able continue in business if cash flow and profits are positive. If we are in the financial sector and we are illiquid and there is a panic, positive cash flow and profitability will not help us. If we are illiquid but solvent we may be helped out by the regulator in some circumstances. If we are illiquid and insolvent we may not be helped out in some circumstances but we might be in others.

Again we should bear in mind that asset price crashes do not occur exactly at the same time as product price collapses. One often leads the other of course, after some time delay. We do not know when a product price collapse occurs when the associated asset price collapse occurs and vice versa. That is if one collapse leads to the other. Depending on severity it may not. But if we have our money at risk we need of course to be aware that it might.

THE UNDERLYING MATHEMATICS OF LIQUIDITY AND SOLVENCY

Mathematically, revenue product price cycles and financial asset cycles have similarities. Both follow some kind of wave behavior in volume and price curves. Their mathematical relationship deserves exploration. Liquid assets, which determine liquidity, can be viewed as an integral over time of cash flow, if we take collateral values and mark to market adjustments into account. Similarly, net capital assets after debts have been subtracted determines solvency. This is an integral over time of initial capital and debt, profit/loss, dividend payments, debt payments and capital injections. Generally integrals of curves do not usually have the same shape and behavior as the curve that is integrated. However, the sine waves we met to model business cycles in Appendix 1 do have the same shape as their integral. The integral of a simple sine wave is a cosine wave, a wave that has very similar characteristics to a sine wave.

Our business waves, working capital and fixed capital investment cycles, are of course not simple sine waves. But, as seen in Appendix 1, we can add waves with different heights and frequencies to form composite waves. The composite wave may have a very different shape from its simple sine wave components and yet it has key properties of those component waves, such as a potential for instability and collapse. If a major component wave is unstable then that component can collapse even if the other components do not. We do not need to worry about every component, only the ones that are critical at a given time. And what applies to the sine wave components of our cash flow/profit-related wave applies equally to the cosine components of our liquidity/solvency-related wave.

To see how very different composite waves can be created by adding a relatively small number of simple sine waves, look at the two composites below in Fig. 7 and 9. The five component waves above each composite in Fig. 6 and 8 respectively are all simple sine waves.

The composite wave is in each case created by aggregating the values of each sine wave. The amplitude and frequency of each component wave are shown on the left.

The first composite wave in Fig. 7 may not have a lot to do with business cycles. It is included to show a distinctive wave shape as a contrast with one which is more business cycle-oriented.

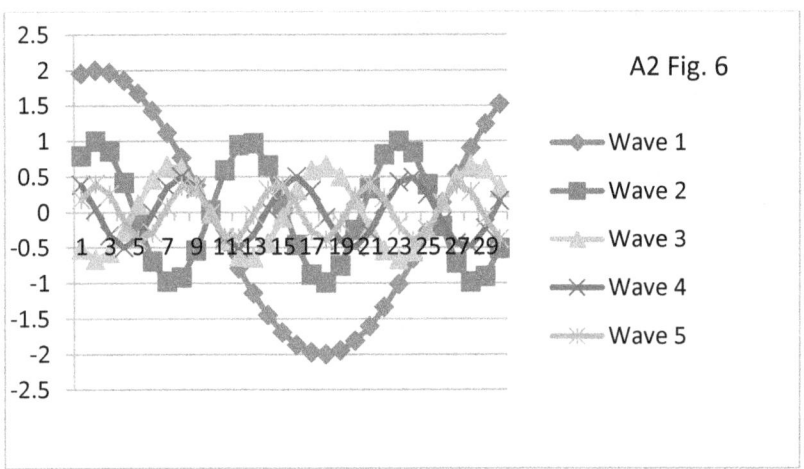

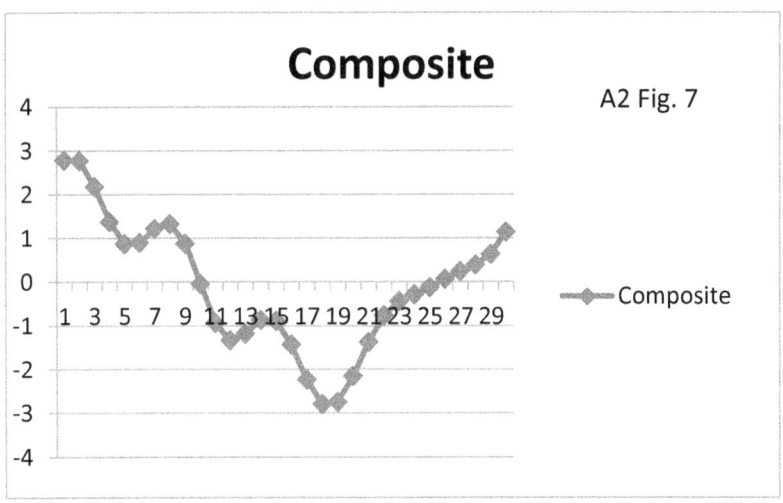

The second composite wave in Fig. 9 is quite different in shape from the first composite in Fig. 7. The Fig. 9 wave might represent cash flow over a month with net costs incurred through the month followed by a burst of revenue at the end of the month. However, the component waves are similar in shape, i.e. simple sine waves, for both composites. The French mathematician Jean-Baptiste Joseph Fourier established in the early nineteenth century that an infinite range of wave shapes can be decomposed into a series of component sine waves[2]. If we can think of the shape of any business cycle we will be likely to find it can be decomposed into a Fourier Series.

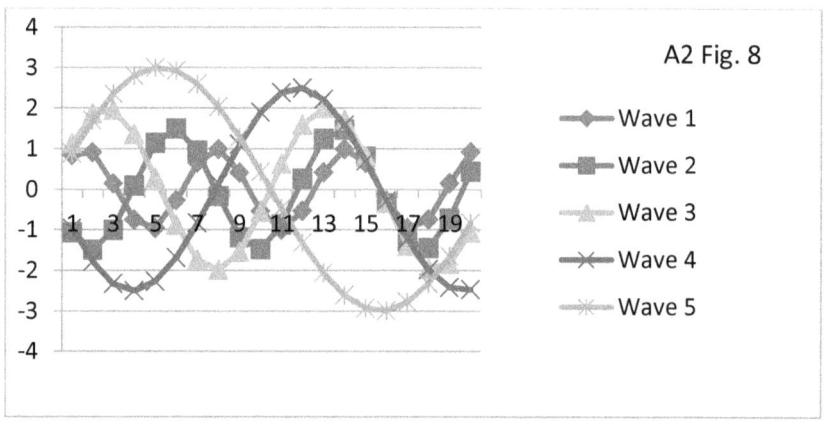

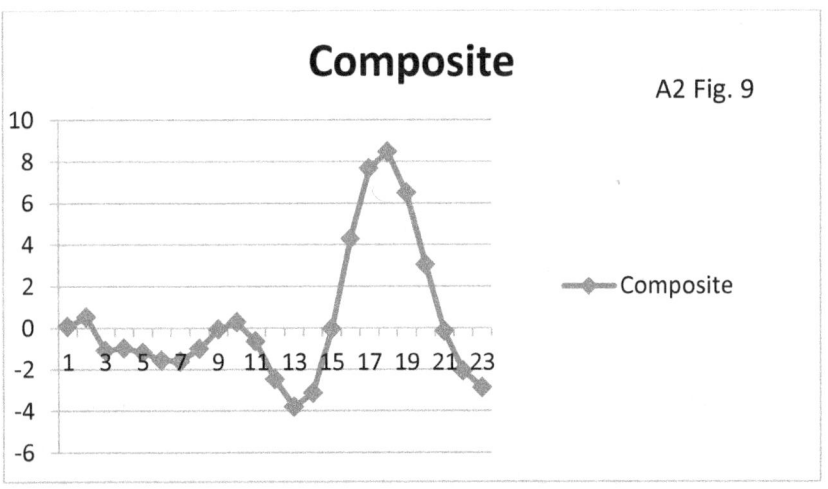

A2 Fig. 9

We may not see a composite wave shape exactly repeat itself in any particular time frame. Some of the component waves may recur at low frequencies. Amplitudes of each component will vary from cycle to cycle changing the composite shape each cycle. This is due to all kinds of factors such as varying suppliers, design changes, market variations, logistics and many other factors.

We should also remember that the components do not last forever. They come and go so the composite shape can change continually. Composite price curves for complex products may include many components and some components may appear only intermittently. Our illustration has just five components but there may be hundreds of components that affect price of a product on a regular or occasional basis. There may also be significant short term components, shocks, which have a dramatic impact for a while but then decay without a continuing force to energize them.

But alongside these shorter term events that add shape to our composite waves, there are the recurring ones that are at the core of business. When a working capital investment is successful, people typically repeat it again and again until it stops being successful. Volume and price waves are generated by fluctuations of economies of scale through the working capital cycle. These fluctuations create a recurring driver for working capital investment. Those repeated investments generate recurring waves which continue when other wave components drop out of the picture for a short term, a long term or permanently.

Fixed capital cycles, including product, process, technology development and facilities, are similar. If an investment is successful and we expect its next generation to be successful, we are likely to repeat it.

In Appendix 3 we see how relationships between volume and price waves, the time lags between the waves and division of risk between buyer and seller, change under the influence of increasing levels of financing to develop instability and ultimately price collapse. There is a level of financing that supports stable growth but which, when exceeded, leads to an inability of the system to ride though small disturbances. Essentially when risk transfer between buyer and seller becomes excessive, prices become unsustainable and collapse. Whatever shape our business cycle may take, hidden inside it are component cycles with a mathematical predisposition for instability and collapse when a critical parameter reaches a certain size.

We mentioned that the integral of simple sine waves are simple cosine waves so that the integral of a wave composed of sine waves will be a wave composed of cosine waves. For those who are interested, the actual value of the integral of $\sin mx$ is:

$$\int \sin mx \ = -(1/m)\cos mx + C$$

where m is frequency, x is angle and C is a constant.

The amplitudes of the component waves thus vary from those of their equivalent sine wave according to the size of the frequency, which can be seen in the curves below. The lower the frequency, the higher is the amplitude relative to that of the sine curve. This is what we would expect if the financial asset logic is sound. Big waves in financial asset values come much less frequently than small ones. Fig. 10 shows cosine waves that are the integral of the sine waves in Fig. 8.

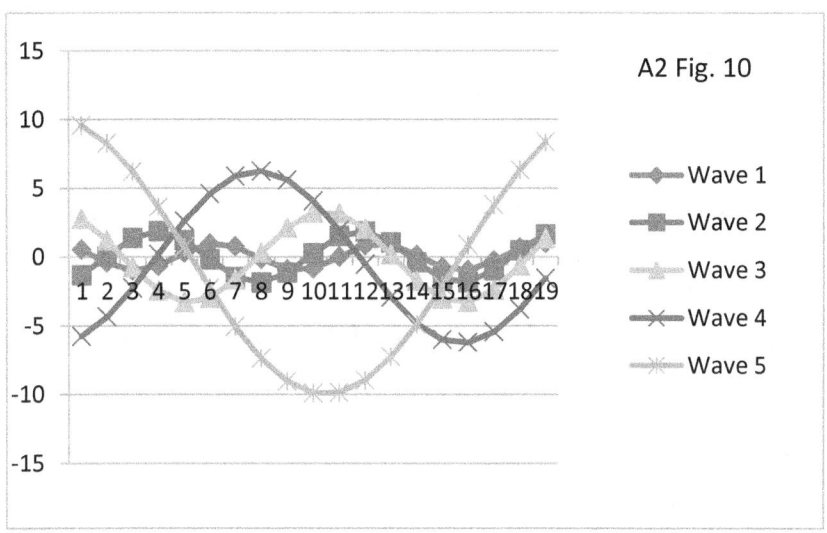

A2 Fig. 10

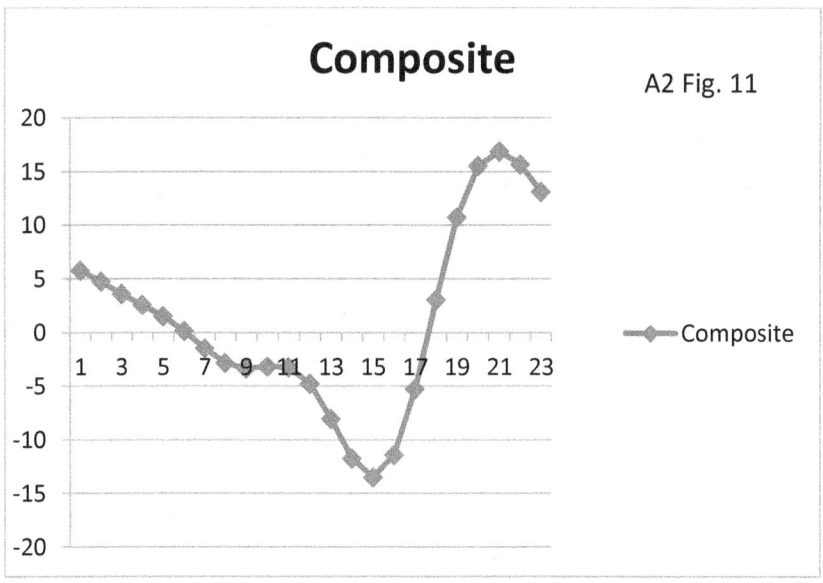

A2 Fig. 11

Fig. 11 looks somewhat like Fig. 9, suggesting some kind of relationship between them. If the Fig. 9 represents cash flow over a month, Fig. 11 shows a steady decline in cash reserves during the net cost phase and then a surge in reserves after the surge in revenues at the end of the month. There is a lag between them.

This is a picture over one working capital cycle. On its own, it does not tell us what happens to the curve over many of these cycles, if for example amplitude steadily increases. The analysis in Appendix 3 does show this but we are not covering that level of detail here. However, it shows that the component cosine curves in Fig. 10 are essentially the same kinds of entity as the component sine curves in Fig. 8, although at a different phase of their respective cycles. We can reasonably expect that if the wave analysis carried out in Appendix 3 is valid as an analysis of product price stability, the analysis should also equally valid for financial asset stability.

This may seem a little abstract. We pay little attention to the shape of cycles, if only because they seem so erratic. But what it shows is that there are forces beneath the surface that have real impacts on business stability.

Cash Flow and Price Stability

Instability results in cash flow failures and price collapses, sometimes separately, sometimes in combination. Either of these on its own is dangerous for individual businesses. Combined, they are very difficult to deal with. And while many risks in business come and go with changing conditions, the risk of these two events is always present. The business operator should understand the underlying forces that drive instability, so as to recognize them early enough to prevent them and even gain when competitors suffer them.

Of the two, cash flow failure is the most widely understood. This can come about in a number of ways:

- Operating profits may be lower than expected due to lower sales, lower prices or higher OPEX than expected. New products may not match the performance projected in their strategic plans. Old products may be killed off by competitors or product substitution earlier than expected. And customers may default in their payments due to fraudulent action or their own inability to manage cash flow.
- Expected capital gains may be lower than expected due to an inability to sell off surplus assets at expected prices. Or it may due to the realization that future income streams will be smaller than expected. The loss of expected capital gain may lead to an inability to refinance, which can be fatal if refinancing was part of our strategy for continued business.
- Higher interest rates than expected may be incurred, consuming operating profits and accumulating debt over time. Highly leveraged operations with little or no pay down of debt are particularly sensitive here.

From a wave perspective, cash flow problems can be seen as a decaying of cycle frequency. If we are late in paying our suppliers they start to delay supply, which in turn delays our ability to deliver to our own customers who delay paying us. This leads us to a downwards spiral of supplier delivery delays, customer payment delays and delays in our paying suppliers.

We can manage this by an injection of funds and the logical source is some party with confidence in our long term ability to pay. If one cycle frequency starts to decay, injection of funds from a longer wavelength cycle is required to prevent failure. For example, if we can't make a required operating profit in the working capital cycle we might need a top up from a capital budget in the fixed investment cycle. This would take into account future income streams.

The misalignments between liquidity problems and solvency problems can create many opportunities for financial killings.

Cash flow problems can be a key tool to enhance liquidity/solvency opportunities.

Price collapse (see Appendix 3) can be just as fatal but is usually less predictable and can be very sudden. Price collapse can occur in specific markets while the general economy is not severely affected. Cash flow failures of large companies can trigger isolated failures in the financial system or widespread failures in the financial system if the system has reached its stability limits.

Financial system failure can then lead to cash flow failures and price collapses in the general economy. Predicting these combinations is not easy. And of course even moderate difficulties in the general economy can trigger an unmanageable event for an individual company if it is getting close to its stability limits. Many otherwise clever business strategies have crashed and burned where, with a little attention to stability, they could have survived and thrived.

Conversely, given sufficient stability of the individual business, a cash flow shortage and/or price collapse in its wider market, or in the general economy, can be to its advantage. Asset values can drop to very low levels in such times. This offers buyers large future capital gains when the market is eventually restored to a healthier level.

In the cyclical nature of business, cash flow and price both follow wave patterns. The wavelength varies dramatically from short term working capital to long term technology development and market development cycles. But the essential properties are the same in terms of their potential for financial failure and price collapse. Some capital costs incurred during the investment phase of business cycles are large and have to be paid over many shorter cycles. The waves of different length influence each other, but coexist.

The price wave in a cycle moves at the same frequency as cash flow but is usually out of phase with cash flow to a degree dependent on buyer's risk and seller's risk. This is very visible in the cycles of the general economy. We see in the financial pages each of employment levels, commodity prices and interest rates moving in cycles. But the risk-influenced component of price is also cyclical right down to the individual business working capital cycle and for is cyclical for products with weaker links to wider market behavior.

In Appendix 3 we analyze how price collapse as a natural consequence of the cyclical nature of business. External disruptions can assist but are not essential.

1. *Misunderstanding Financial Crises,* Professor Gary Gorton
2. *Fourier Series,* Wikipedia

APPENDIX 3: COMPLEX VARIABLES AND PRICE COLLAPSE

Cyclical mechanisms are inherently subject to instability and those in business and economics are no exception. Individual businesses can suffer instability on their own, even when profitable and growing. In fact being profitable and growing can increase their exposure to instability. Businesses can also suffer instability of their market due to the collective behavior of competitors and customers. And, not least, businesses can suffer from instability in the financial markets, which impacts on most other sectors of the wider economy.

If we prepare for instability there are great profits to be made from it.

Modelling cyclical behavior in the business environment is enhanced with the use of wave mechanism mathematics, including use of complex numbers. This allows modelling of the dynamic relationships between cash flow, debt, price and the phase differences between them through the cycle. By using polar views of the cycle as well as time views, the mechanisms leading to cash flow failure and to price collapse can be identified. These include the contribution of financing to sales growth and price buoyancy. This financing is valuable for business at stable levels but can increase instability to dangerously bubble-prone levels if too high.

In Appendix 2 we discussed the mathematics of cash flow. Price collapse is a little trickier. If we are in a market-wide price collapse, we need to ride it out, perhaps sacrificing market share to some degree to reduce erosion of gross margin. Alternatively we follow the price down to hold market share. Whichever strategy we follow, profitability will be impacted and we may start bleeding cash.

Generally, with supportive financing parties, we can survive one or other of cash flow problems or price collapse at a given time:

- We may have temporary cash flow problems but are getting good prices and making good profit margins. These margins indicate an ability to back fill temporary cash shortages with future earnings so our financing parties should support us.
- Or we are experiencing a temporary price collapse leading to reducing price to hold market share, or reducing market share to hold price. But we have enough cash to ride through the situation and survive until prices rise to a healthier level.

However, if we have a cash flow problem pressuring us to seek additional profits, and simultaneously have a price collapse cutting back on those profits, then we are likely to be in a serious predicament.

Wave Patterns in Cash Flow and Price

Observers of the general economy will know that cycles in sales volumes and prices in markets within the general economy follow clear patterns. In the expansion phase of a general business cycle, demand increases relative to available capacity and prices rise. The cause of this for an individual industry could be old capacity reaching the end of its economic life, population growth, new uses for a product being found, reductions in cost of other products used in conjunction with this product, improvements in product making it more attractive or some destructive event removing competitors' supply capacity.

An expansion in the general economy can be a growth factor for a given industry in addition to factors specific to that industry. Here, multiple industries (or one very dominant one in a region) are in expansion mode at the same time, leading to widespread demand for resources such as labor, materials, land, construction services and finance.

Whatever the cause, the increase in relative demand attracts more investment in supply capacity. Eventually demand is saturated and prices drop. Capacity is withdrawn or let fall into disrepair due to being uneconomic at lower prices and eventually excess capacity is used up. Demand increases relative to capacity, starting the cycle again.

This is all normal and healthy. New (hopefully more reliable, more resource-efficient and perhaps even more environmentally friendly) capacity is built when the market requires it. Uneconomic (obsolete, worn out, inefficient, unreliable, and/or incompetent) capacity is removed when no longer required. Average productivity across the industry increases. Customers enjoy lower prices, business staff enjoy higher pay and investors enjoy higher earnings.

However, the cycle does not always match supply capacity and demand in a smooth manner. Companies seek to optimize profits and seek to avoid missing out on potentially profitable opportunities, particularly if others are enjoying them. Even after a sustained growth phase when they might start to expect a decline, they anticipate that price rises will hold or even increase further. Based on this expectation, they invest in more capacity.

If companies produce more capacity than is required to meet demand at a given price, the price will drop to attract new customers. Stability is threatened when there is a lot more capacity put into the system than there is natural demand. There may be some new customers but not enough who are willing to pay at a level that is economically viable for all suppliers. Prices then drop below that economic level until excess capacity is flushed out.

The above applies to cycles within individual industries and to the general economy. The variations of various indicators of the general economy are well documented in economic literature. Each indicator such as job starts/losses, interest rate rises/drops, construction increases/decreases has its own typical role in the cycle.

All of the above involves uncertainties as regards size and timing of excesses and shortages of capacity, and on its impact on price.

Investors are exposed to a high level of risk in their roles as buyers and suppliers.

During the working capital cycle, cash flow is negative in the supply phase as resources are consumed. This negative cash flow is possibly reduced with partial advance payments by customers. On delivery, cost incurrence has largely been completed and positive cash flow of payment takes over. Partial prepayments and delayed payment (financing options) can adjust this by varying degrees. The wave behavior of price deserves particular study because it is this, combined with wave behavior of cash flow, which leads to price collapse.

Economies of Scale and Cycles

Many things can activate waves or cycles in business: Natural events can create shortages and surpluses. New technologies can take over markets or fail to perform as expected; transport links can be overloaded. Wars can disrupt supplies and impoverish regions (but also eliminate competition, generating surges of wealth for the well positioned).

In addition, government expenditure can choke or accelerate growth. Central banks can vary interest rates and inject or extract money from circulation. Bank regulators ease or tighten lending restrictions.

All of these have greater or lesser impacts on markets and industries at various times. Many are beyond the control of individual businesses, which just have to ride out the effects as best as they can.

But if none of these occurred and there was no other reason for wave behavior in business, economies of scale would cause it. This applies at varying cyclical frequencies:

- At the Working Capital cycle level, as sales increase, profitability typically increases at a faster rate than sales. This is due to reducing unit cost with fixed operating expenses and CAPEX being spread over larger sales. Conversely as sales decrease, profitability typically decreases faster than sales. This is due to increased unit cost as less revenue is available to cover fixed costs. The result is alternating pressures to expand and contract sales, resulting in cyclical cash flow and cyclical price levels.

- At the Inventory (Short) cycle level, for given fixed CAPEX, we may increase fixed operating expenses through the cycle to support increased sales. But if we hold CAPEX while sales increase, the share of CAPEX that each unit has to contribute declines, increasing profitability. Again as sales reduce, even if we can reduce operating expense, the share of CAPEX for each unit increases and profitability declines faster than sales.
- At the Manufacturing Capacity or Fixed Investment (Medium) cycle level, economies of scale continue. At a minimum, economies of scale in supply capacity can be gained simply by adding more facilities of the same size. This spreads development capital involved over a larger total capacity. In addition classical physical economies of scale can be gained from larger capacity components that may be faster, deliver more load or move greater volume. Examples are diverse: A 100% increase in capacity of a container ship typically might require an increase fuel consumption of just 70%; a 100% increase in throughput in a power line requires an increase in voltage of just over 40%; for some types of liquid flow in a pipe, a 100% increase throughput will require an increase in pipe diameter of just over 20%.
- At the Technology (Long) cycle level, early applications of a new technology are usually limited in scope and are relatively costly per function delivered. As time goes by, more functions are delivered to enhance initial applications and to add new applications. The cost share of the total development cost gets less for each of these. Profitability

increases with the number of applications using the new functions. Eventually, however, as a new replacement technology platform emerges, functions are progressively replaced by the new technology. Progressively less and less remaining functions are available to contribute to the cost of maintaining the technology. Profitability per unit drops.

All of the above economies of scale involve a pulse in profitability that encourages greater investment to increase volume. This pulse is driven purely by internal cost structures.

The wave effects created by economies of scale in individual businesses, at any of these levels, ripple out from them into their environment. As the businesses grow, they consume more resources and thus contribute to economies of scale of other companies. Similarly they contribute to diseconomies of scale amongst their suppliers when they incur downturns. So the activities of many small companies combine to create market-wide waves. And multiple industries combine to produce waves across the general economy due to their sharing of financial markets and often property markets.

However, while businesses contribute to its stimulation, the cycle in the general economy, or in a market with many suppliers and buyers, is not something that individual businesses control. Initially demand drives prices up. Companies invest in supply capacity to enjoy the prices and demand, often borrowing more than they would normally on the expectations of higher than usual profits. Capacity exceeds demand and the prices level off. As capacity remains above demand, prices start to drop and this continues until capacity is removed from supply or demand increases again for some reason or other.

Often a triggering event may push other costs up temporarily, which impacts on price. A spike in the price of oil caused by a war, a storm, an earthquake, a tsunami, a terrorist event, may increase fuel costs for drivers with long commutes. This may momentarily chill price rises in real estate in suburbs or satellite towns that require such commutes. These may lead to people, who needed increasing house prices to maintain positive equity, defaulting on their mortgage. This in turn leads to mortgage sales, which cause prices to drop, which encourages more to sell, driving prices down further.

This slowdown would something normally be just a blip followed by a return to previous conditions, but not when the market is becoming saturated. Some suppliers get nervous and reduce prices. Others follow and sooner or later buyers figure that, if they wait prices, will come down further. The additional reduction in demand panics sellers so they drop prices further. A downwards spiral continues until demand gets back in balance with supply, when some supply capacity is forced out of the market.

If we are willing to let sales fall faster than our competitors, we may be able to hold our prices to some extent. We might concentrate on the customers who are willing to pay a premium for better service. We might concentrate on the ones who do not have time to find the best deal around. We let other customers go to our competitors. This assumes the numbers of these types of premium customer are large enough to keep us operating. And to do this we need the ability to reduce costs to make up for the loss of some sales and/or have funding to allow us to ride out a period of losses.

If we seek cost reduction this requires time to respond by cutting supply capacity and offering lower product volume to the market. This also assumes reducing capacity means reducing cost, which is not always the case. We are being hurt by lost economies of scale throughout this process.

Having strong financing to survive this difficult period is always a huge advantage for survival during the period and profit when recovery occurs.

Whatever we can manage at the individual company level to hold price, the market will move with the lowest willing seller. The price collapse curve is that of Fig. 2 of Appendix 2:

Businesses with high fixed costs, including interest rates on borrowings and high debt repayment schedules, may have severe cash flow problems when demand drops off. If they also have competitors' prices fall, due to those competitors fighting to gain or hold market share of that market share, they may experience a collapse of their own achievable product price. Lower sales, lower margins and high fixed costs may combine to take the business down. Businesses can, of course attempt to reduce fixed costs by selling supply facilities and thus reducing debt. However, they may find there is also a collapse on the saleable price of such facilities. Other parties may be trying to reduce debt and there may be few new parties coming in to invest.

Eventually excess capacity will be scrapped, abandoned or fall into disrepair. Supply shortages will start to occur, driving up prices and restarting the cycle. However, depending on the severity of the collapse, this may take a short time or a long time. The excess capacity may be flushed out in a one day clearance sale or may take years, even decades.

It should be reiterated here that there is much to be gained for some parties from an economic collapse and an extended period of recovery. Businesses which are positioned to acquire assets at fire sale prices or to gain market share from bankrupt competitors may find it well worth sacrificing their usual economies of scale for a while. The medium and long term gains can be large. If we have enough cash to survive an extended downturn, and have influence over political and regulatory bodies, we can gain much by encouraging these bodies to act in ways that deepen a recession and delay the upturn.

Whether we are in a position to gain from price collapse or whether we just need to minimize damage caused by it, we need to understand the dynamics of instability. We can then see its patterns and take action to best deal with it.

Understanding these patterns helps a company survive long enough to find the next economy of scale that returns it to a healthy profitability. That may simply be the next upturn of the cycle that has just turned down, if the associated period with collapsed price is short. But we should also be constantly looking for new economies of scale. This is the essence of successful business. Sometimes there is an activity that suddenly lends itself to economies of scale precisely because of a downturn in the economy and associated reduction in costs that were previously high. It might be some service that cleans up unused facilities. It might be some budget product that fills the gap left by the premium product. Those who can identify these activities, when others do not see them, may find them particularly profitable.

These activities can be in diverse areas relating to scale in physical production systems, transport networks, administrative processes, skills, technologies, markets served. They do not need to be in the areas where we previously found them. They may also have different cycle frequency. As we constantly search for them and drive to achieve them we need to keep an eye on the inevitable turn down of the associated wave.

Risk For Supplier, Buyer and Financing Party

Supplier Price and Risk

Investment in working capital, supply capacity or product/market development always incurs risk and investors need to expect a certain profit level before taking the risk. That profit level depends on price. All these risks present impediments to investment by the supplier. They require financing, with associated exposure to risk, for the period from the time the supplier identifies a potential revenue stream, sets prices and commits resources to when the money is actually paid back.

We need to be confident (based on some analysis or other) that the price we earn for our product will justify these various risks. The greater the risks, the higher the price needs to be over and above expected actual costs. For the supplier, like the buyer, price is not determined just by actual costs, but by risks. We cover buyer and seller's risk at some length because they each contribute to stability. Each cycle has its own set of risks for buyer and seller and how they pass risks back and forth has a large impact on stability.

We also have a concern as suppliers that we will get paid. Transferring some of the credit risk of a transaction to a party who is skilled at managing and spreading credit risk reduces our overall risk.

Buyer Price and Risk

There are two key components to price from a buyer perspective, the known cost component and the risk component. The known cost component is what we could buy something for as it comes from the supplier but with no certainties that it will work for us to give us full value. The risk component is the cost of the extra resources that need to be provided to make sure the product achieves our needs. The risk component can be small or very large compared to known cost. A large part of the price buyers are willing to pay for a product often relates to the risks associated with non-performance of that product.

Imagine we go to a street stall and buy a takeout meal, a curry for $6, and then walk across the road to the park and eat it in the sun listening to the birds singing in the trees. Alternatively we can eat a curry in the hotel restaurant beside the park for $30. Why would we pay five times as much? It could be very pleasant eating our curry in the park with the birds singing, the sun shining and the leaves gently rustling in a gentle breeze. However, the word is *could* be pleasant not *will* be pleasant. There are many things that can happen in the park that are unlikely to happen in the hotel. It may suddenly rain or the wind may come up and blow dust in our eyes. The park may be littered with rubbish, perhaps putrid rubbish. There may be shrieking babies, loud and annoying people, even violent people there.

These may be risks well worth taking in our private time if we are adventurous people with an eye on cost. However, if we have a business lunch where we want to be comfortable, safe, free of distractions to discuss business worth far more than $30, we will very probably select the hotel.

If we are high profile businesspeople we may be willing to spend yet more on our curry so that we can enjoy it in a private room with our own dedicated service staff. This will avoid us being pestered by other business people who want our attention and might also be willing to pay $30 for their curry. Hotel restaurants will keep out homeless and street hustlers but not well dressed paying customers. These presentable people may want us to buy their products or invest in their schemes. Worse they may want us to pay them back money they think we owe them for some unhappy investment they have made in one of our past ventures. So paying an additional premium for a private room to gain exclusivity may be very worthwhile.

In general there are many threats to getting value from the product purchase that may justify spending a premium to remove them. The premium will depend on the size and number of risk factors. These include:.

- Comfort – avoid cold, rain, hard surfaces and loud noises
- Quality – avoid failure to perform and avoid personal injury
- Availability – avoid delay in commencing use
- Performance – avoid delay during use
- Security – avoid attack

As a buyer we decide a price we are willing to pay based on our assessment of value and risk. We risk not only that the product may not perform fast enough, reliably enough, easily enough, etc, but that even if it does all of those we may not get enough value from it. We may not use it often enough, intensely (in terms of speed, throughput, weight carried, force resisted) enough. We may not use it long enough when we do use it, to get value, even though it may perform perfectly.

Buyer's risk is thus highly context-sensitive. If factors in the environment, other than those unique to the product fill some of these gaps, the risks for the product reduce. If we assess a price premium worth paying to reduce buyer's risk, that premium will decreases as those risks are lowered by external factors.

The lower extreme in the buyer's risk range from a product use perspective is of course commodity pricing. This essentially deals with a product where a large number of the above risks have been removed by production of a product with the same properties by many suppliers.

There is also another risk, which is of particular significance to stability. That is the risk of future price changes. Suppose we believe prices will increase in the near future due to rising demand or shortage in capacity. Provided the intrinsic product performance risk factors outlined above are acceptable, there can be a strong pressure to buy now before the price rise. Conversely if we believe prices will decrease due to falling demand or excess capacity, we will tend to delay purchase if possible. In each case we have to balance the risk of being wrong about the price change assessment against the impact of being wrong about the product availability. If we have good alternatives to using the product, we may not be easily pushed to buy now before a future price rise. If we really need the product, we may not be willing to risk it not being available just for a moderate cost saving.

The importance of risk in buying decisions is important for the seller, not just to adjust its price, but to engage with the buyer throughout the sales process. Readers familiar with person to person sales activities will know that an adept sales person can sense the prospect's concerns. They can then minimize or emphasize risk in such a way as to favor his or her product. The seller analyses the situation based on conversations of a general, personal and product-specific nature. These range from weather, sports, family, shared friends and associates, through logistical issues, efficiencies, quality and budgets to technologies, techniques and processes. Things come to the seller's mind such as:

- *What are they worried about in their current situation? How can we use that to drive a decision to buy?*
- *What have they not thought about that we could draw to their attention to make them worry about their current situation? What would happen if component M failed? What would happen if event Z occurred? Do they understand how the right kind of product (ours) reduces these risks?*
- *How do we secure their trust? What do we need to project to indicate our honesty, reliability and competence? How do we dress, talk, move?*

While considering these the seller seeks to raise perceptions of risk about the competitors' products by asking questions such as:

- *Is that technology really proven?*
- *Is that function really worth the extra cost?*
- *Perhaps you could do without feature A and B but could you really do without C if problems occurred?*
- *That probably works well in an X situation but what if you get a Y situation?*

Understanding buyers in terms of what they perceive as risks can be of great value in winning business. Perception of risk can be a major activator in the decision to buy, a major delay factor, a major influence on the price we are willing to pay, and a key determiner of who we buy from. If we can adjust perceptions of risk held by our customers we automatically adjust perceptions of a reasonable price.

Risk to Financing Party

We have considered seller's risk and buyer's risk but an important third consideration is risk for the financing party. The financing party can be the seller, the buyer via advance payments, or an external direct investor, but often it is a financial intermediary such as a bank. By accepting risk for seller and/or buyer at critical moments the financing party can greatly increase sales volumes and the entire viability of the business. But of course accepting risk is dangerous and requires good understanding of repayment capabilities, collateral and spreading of risk across multiple borrowers.

There are many financing mechanisms and associated instruments, each of which exposes the financing party to different levels and types of risk. Selection of these can be made to match cash flow requirements through the applicable investment cycle, whether trading or longer term investment. The essential function of financing is to transfer money from a party, who is in a cash flow positive phase of their cycle, to a party who is in a cash flow negative phase of their cycle. The financing party's expertise is in judging that the money can be paid back as the borrowing party's cycle goes into a cash flow positive phase.

Lending and borrowing cycles do not need to have the same frequency. We can lend money from the cash flow positive phase of a long cycle to a series of shorter cycle phases. Conversely we can lend from short cash positive phases to much longer ones if the right mechanisms are in place. This allows us to get our money out when we need it and have some other party's money in to replace it.

The demand deposit account of the commercial bank takes a major role in financing business working capital cycles via lines of credit. Readers familiar with fractional reserve banking will know that if Customer 1 deposits $1,000,000 in cash with our bank and we hold back 15% in reserves we can then lend $850,000 to Customer 2. Customer 2 spends it with Customer 3 who deposits it with us and we hold back 15% then lend out the rest to Customer 4. We repeat the exercise again and again. If we are not the only bank in town other banks will get some of the initial million in cash deposited with us but on average we will get a similar amount of theirs. We may use interbank lending to even up short term imbalances.

This allows the initial million deposit to finance five or six million (the theoretical maximum is nearly $6,666,667). If we have a lower reserve requirement, say 10%, we can effectively create more money again (theoretically up to $10 million). Creating even five or six million from one million sounds like easy money but there is a price to be paid. This is a very high one if we do not know what we are doing. The price is that our bank has accepted risk of five or six million but has only one million cash to back it up at any moment. And any of the depositors can request their cash at any moment.

If we are careful and skillful bankers, we will understand what each of those customers is doing with the money and how their working capital cycle will produce a positive cash flow to pay us back. Commercial banks monitor their customers' financial parameters and adjust their customers' lines of credit to minimize the numbers who default. If they do this well, the percentage of defaults will be low and more than covered by the profits made from the rest of the customers. The bank's capital also needs to be sufficient to cover losses that exceed the level met by profits in the short term. The leverage ratio, the ratio of loans to capital is an extremely important number and one subject to much debate in regulatory circles.

And of course the bank requires collateral on many of its loans such as a business owner's residence or securities that can be turned into cash if the customer cannot pay back the loan. These securities might be mortgage-based (prime and/or subprime) securities, commercial bonds or rights to other expected future cash flows. Such cash flows could be business receivables of many types, from record royalties to credit card repayments.

Of course the collateral has its own risk of being worth less than the money borrowed if our quantitative analysis is unsound. So it is wise to have a good understanding of our customers' ability to pay back the money, as well as some confidence in the reliability of the collateral. Also our ability to access interbank lending depends on the confidence other banks have in our collateral.

The acceptance of risk by commercial banks, of multiple times the value of initial cash deposited, is one reason why governments and regulators fear banks failing on a wide scale. In such a failure, the banking system loses the initial million (or trillion) deposited but takes six (or ten) times that value out of circulation. This is money that is financing the working capital cycles of farms, factories, shops and service businesses. The political consequences are severe for governments permitting this to occur.

However, demand deposit banking allows banks to smoothly add financing via lines of credit to replace shortages of cash as is required through the fluctuations of business cycles. Its ability to create money means financing is available to a large number of businesses. This is provided sound standards are applied in risk assessment of cash flows and collateral.

For longer term capital investment cycles, covering many working capital cycles, we have a different requirement from the working capital cycle requirement. We need funds available that will not be curtailed or withdrawn by a commercial bank if trading conditions are difficult for a period. A longer term commitment by the financing party is required.

Investment banks issue debt securities such as bonds or securities with other well defined cash flows contractually set to specific times. However, securities of any type can be replaced with other types with quite different time parameters, providing they have equivalent value at the time of exchange. That value can be determined by appropriate financial engineering, taking into account a range of factors. These include interest rates, maturity dates and probabilities of events such as changes in interest rate and defaults in interest payments or principal. The current value of a fixed interest rate generated cash flow can be equated to the current value of a floating interest rate cash flow.

The net effect of this is that lines of credits can be used to transfer money, from cash flow positive phases of cycles in one set of businesses, into cash flow negative phases of working capital cycles in others. The cycles may have quite different frequencies. We may require a large and complex chain of risk transfer involving multiple financial intermediaries, including investment banks, commercial banks and others. This large chain of risk transfer may require a range of financial engineering techniques that translate financial commitments from one type of instrument to another at equivalent value.

A problem that occurs with financial engineering is that when mathematics is applied incompetently, risk assessments can be catastrophically wrong. A classic and recent example is the assessment of mortgage risk in some Collateralized Debt Obligations (CDOs) prior to the GFC. These were based on the percentage of defaults experienced during a period of rising real estate prices prior to 2007. These did not factor in what the percentage of defaults might be in a cyclical downturn. The securities based on the analysis turned out to grossly undervalue risk.

As markets (for whatever product or asset we deal in) rise, risks to financing parties tend to drop. This is because profitability usually increases on a rising market as economies of scale increase. This risk reduction tails off when economies of scale are negated by diminishing returns. Then financing risks rise increasingly as those markets fall.

Marginal interest rates increase when risks increase. Even if the central bank reduces its interbank rate when the general economy slows down, the marginal rate to borrowers is likely to increase, perhaps by significantly more than the central bank reduction. Financing parties, like sellers of non-financial products, charge more as supplier risk increases.

Financing parties, whether commercial banks, investment banks or other types of financial institution, do not need to provide the bulk of the funds on their own. That is apart from relatively small portions to cover losses. The bulk of the money is transferred from one customer, temporarily in a positive cash flow state, to another customer, temporarily in a negative cash flow state. Temporary may be a day or a decade depending on the length of cycles involved for each party.

The financing party provides a mechanism that accepts risk, using its skills and experience to manage that risk, and transfers the money from a party with one set of needs and risks to a party with different set.

Price/Volume Curves

With only one buyer and one seller for a product, it is difficult to set a price. The seller might sell it for a price far less than the buyer is willing to pay, or can insist on a price that is far beyond the value of the product to the buyer. Discussion about value and negotiation can help but often fails, particularly when trust is low. Often the price is determined by who feels the greatest risk of loss in the event that the other walks away.

With multiple buyers for a product we can set a price and see how many potential buyers reject it completely, how many buy without further investigation, how many seek to more exactly clarify its function and thus value for them, and how many haggle to get the price lower to match the value they see in the product. Not all of these parties are seeking exactly what our product offers. Some want less capabilities and don't want to pay for ones they won't use. Some want more capabilities and would pay more if our product could provide it. By noting these various responses we can better determine a consistent market price than is possible with a single buyer.

On the buy side, having only one product to choose from, even if other parties are buying it, makes setting value difficult if our needs are different from theirs. Is there some other way of getting the benefit we are seeking at a lower price? If there are other similar products to the one we buy, we can use these as a reference to set value. Easiest of all is a commodity where one ton, yard, cubic foot or gallon of a product from one supplier is effectively the same as another ton. This equivalence may be determined by some simple measure or certification process using more technical tests.

Remembering Figs 9 and 9A in Appendix 1, we think of different values seen in a product by different types of buyer. Buyer's risk is a key factor here. A subgroup of customers may be willing to pay a high premium to minimize risk of the product not performing. Another subgroup wants the product but is willing to risk it not performing under certain conditions. The members may be able to adjust to its limitations. There may be a range of levels of adjustment that buyers are willing to make. The other factor is that the product simply does not do what some customers want.

Changing the price up or down will reduce or increase numbers in the various groups as buyers move from one to the next by varying degrees, creating some kind of price/volume curve. Conversely increasing or decreasing the populations of the various groups when supply is limited will drive the price up or down. These behaviors can be seen in the various price/volume curves of Appendix 1.

On the supply side, there is almost always some time spent between investment of funds and delivery - purchasing or hiring resources, awaiting delivery, converting the inputs, assembling the product, holding and transporting (or vice versa) for delivery. This involves a period of exposure to risk and is thus a deterrent to supply.

Some degree of confidence in some level of expected price is required to invest for this period. Confidence in price expectation can be increased with a customer contract or a market price for similar products supplied by other suppliers for other customers. Price leads supply.

There are exceptions to this. Sometimes customers will ask suppliers to build something and agree to pay whatever it costs. Winning markets when time is critical can be such an incentive if the first mover shuts out latecomers who do not comply with its standards. Wars and natural disasters are examples where the cost in life or property of not dealing with a problem are so high compared with the cost of the task, that normal economies for such a task are set aside. However, even then we usually agree to a charging rate or set of rates in advance - per hour, per day, per mile, per ton, etc. Or we provide an estimate, which may not be binding but is an indication. Much higher risk then falls on the buyer. This risk can be reduced with detailed design and specifications but sometimes time to prepare these is limited under these circumstances.

Remembering seller's and buyer's risk:
- The seller wants the cash ideally before creating the product. Next best is cash at delivery time. Next best is cash soon after delivery. This relieves the risk of not getting paid at all, which often increases once the product has been consumed or used.
- The buyer would ideally have the product delivering its benefits before paying for it to confirm its performance (the longer it does this the better). The next best is to pay for it when it is delivered. Next best is to pay in advance but on milestones that relate to visible activities that reduce the probability of the product not performing when it arrives or never arriving at all.

Either buyer or seller can perceive the greater risk from the deal. There is a spectrum of payment timing arrangements from full payment in advance, partial payment in advance, cash on delivery or collection to payment on invoice, and variations of each of these. The payment time relative to delivery will tend to be negotiated according to which party feels the highest risk.

The cyclical nature of pricing and delivery payment leads to two potential failure modes that are intrinsic to the investment and return nature of business. These failure modes can apply regardless of other positive or negative factors applying to a business, its market or the general economy.

Wave Stability and Business Cycles

With an appreciation of the wave behavior of cash flow and price, and the role of risk, it is useful to apply some mathematics describing wave mechanisms to further understand price collapse. This will not allow us to predict exactly when a wave is going to collapse. There are too many waves interacting with each other for that to occur. But it allows us to anticipate how a business of interest, with its particular cost structures, trade and investment cycles will be affected by the market in which it operates. And how it will be affected by the general economy that, in turn, impacts on that market. In addition to our observations above, the mathematics tell us:

- Financing changes the market. Some customers who would normally only buy if the price was cut, will pay a higher price if they are financed into it.
- Financing achieves this because it gives the buyers longer to get value out of the product before they have to pay it, reducing their risk of the product's non-performance.
- There is no indication from the model when a collapse will occur in terms of the number of cycles in the decay process, only the conditions preceding it. If we do get close to collapse

we may be able to reverse the slide. Or we may rush on towards it, convinced it will never happen.
- There is no indication from the model as to how long a collapse will last. It might be a one day fire sale for a shop or a multi decade deflation for a large industrial nation.

We have taken the opportunity to develop an illustrative mathematical model, which models price, volume and risk in waveforms, including the development of bubbles and their role in price collapse. It first deals with products which behave on a market-wide basis such as commodity products and moderately differentiated products. We then look at how it applies to highly differentiated products, which are less susceptible to market-wide price movements. We use complex numbers in the model.

Complex numbers have been used for hundreds of years. They have been used in engineering environments for wave analysis such as ocean engineering[1], telecommunications[2] and electric power systems[3]. They greatly simplify analysis of cyclical systems where key events occur at different points in the cycle.

Why do we do this? Merchants and bankers have been handling financial risk since Medieval times, if not since Babylonian times or earlier, without using complex numbers. The reason is that its use provides a very effective way of modelling time delays between events in a cycle, and seeing what happens when those delays increase or decrease. Those delays (between price setting and delivery and between delivery and payment) are key factors of risk, especially when they start to change for any reason.

The model highlights that there is an underlying mathematical logic to cyclical behavior in business. This relates price and risk for seller and for buyer as they vary with volume. Given the importance in business of economies of scale, this price, risk and volume relationship is critical. We describe it here because understanding the changing balance in price and risk helps provide an analytical framework for understanding scenarios as they evolve.

The model is quite versatile, dealing with waves of any length of time and businesses of any scale. It covers the beach vendor selling $2 drinks on an hourly cycle or the global oil company building $10 billion p.a. supply chains lasting decades. Most of the time we are dealing with working capital cycles which have stability problems. However, longer cycles can have the same issues.

The model does use some trigonometry of complex numbers, so readers who are uncomfortable with this can skip the mathematics and move to Implications of Wave Model below, which covers the implications of the model and its underlying assumptions.

Wave Movement of Cash Flow and Price

Price and volume of product (units, tons, gallons, etc) each fluctuate about some kind of average for each cycle with its particular wavelength. The average for a short wavelength is itself dynamic (see Fig. 1 below) and will be vary as cycles with longer wavelength fluctuate. Wave mathematics allows us to break composite waves with shapes quite unlike sine waves into simple sine wave components and analyze them individually.

For example we can individually analyze the major components in Short, Medium and Long cycle waves in the general economy for the purposes of studying stability in those cycles. In doing so we need to keep in mind that, at any given time, other components will add to, or subtract from, the one we are analyzing. They can then trigger, delay and sometimes nullify critical change points in that wave shape. However, the underlying wave, while possibly hidden by other waves for a while, continues on its path and can emerge, usually unaffected.

The individual wave under analysis is the one whose potential collapse concerns us. However, the composite wave from all the other waves in the system often makes it very difficult to see that wave separately from all the others. This does not mean it is not present, ready to suddenly appear in full force at an unexpected moment. A particular wave may be the one that takes a business out of action, takes its sector into a deep hole or takes the general economy into a recession. At the same time waves representing other parts of the economy may be smoothly and gently fluctuating.

Wave Shapes

Given that our price and volume waves fluctuate around averages, the ups and downs even out. We will not know the average level of a particular wave until after the event and for this analysis it is not of particular importance. The average is likely to be moving itself to some degree or other. The wave we are focusing on may be superimposed on another wave of longer wavelength (the dotted line). And in turn shorter wavelengths may impact on the shape of the one which has caught our interest (not illustrated).

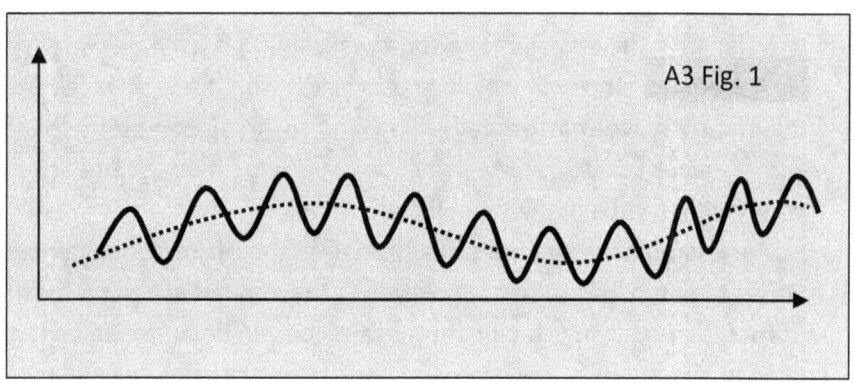

A3 Fig. 1

From a stability perspective we are primarily interested in the movement of the particular wave being analyzed relative to the average, not the average itself. The positives and negatives relative to the average determine the particular wave's behavior and ultimately its potential to collapse. The wave it fluctuates about has its own stability dynamics.

As mentioned in Appendix 1, waves of different wavelengths can pass through each other and leave each other undisturbed, unless one pushes another over some stability limit. Then one wave can trigger a collapse in the other that might not otherwise have occurred. In this case instead of returning to its previous state after the wave passes through it, the collapsed wave stays collapsed.

By analyzing the wave in depth we can understand the fundamental forces occurring that can have a real impact. What we can do about them is another story. Understanding is not the same is predicting but is very valuable for knowing what to watch out for. We do not need to know exactly when a given market will turn to benefit from knowing the risks and opportunities that will come with that turn. Our object with situational intelligence is to understand the state of our business in terms of its sensitivity to changes that we make and changes made by external forces. Fig. 2 shows Price and Volume waves as they move in parallel.

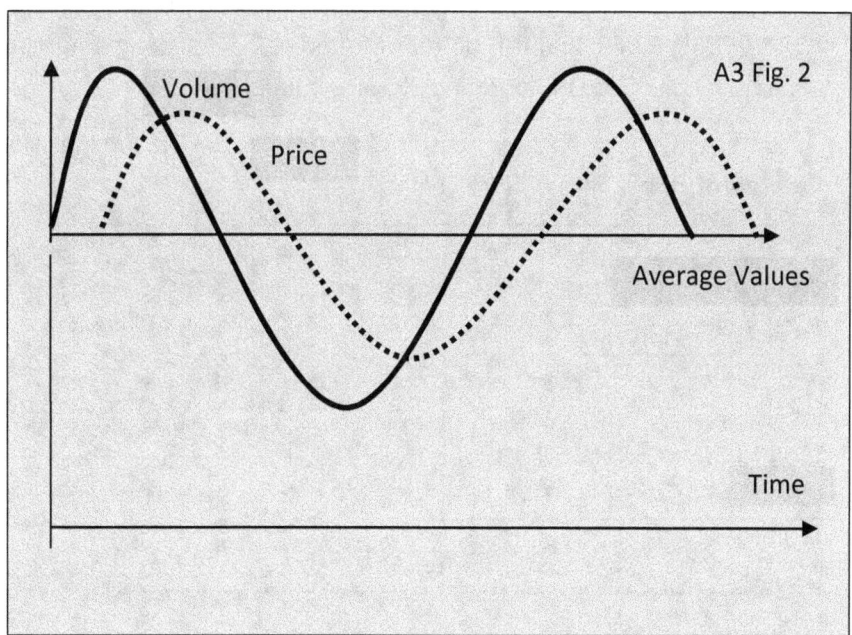

Cash flow equals price multiplied by volume.

If we focus purely on the wave components of volume and price, using their averages as a zero, when both volume and price are positive, cash flow is positive. When either is negative with the other positive, cash flow is negative. When price and volume are negative we have the rather odd result that their cash flow multiple is positive. Volume decreases, price decreases and yet cash flow increases! However, we are only looking at the wave components, not the average components of volume and price, and when these are added to the wave components the total will reflect real values.

Complex Numbers - Imaginary Money

Wave behavior is usefully modelled with complex number mathematics. For those unfamiliar with this field of mathematics, a complex number can be presented as $z = x + iy$, where $i = \sqrt{(-1)}$ and x and y are both real numbers. Real numbers include numbers such as 1, -11, 1.55, ¾, $\sqrt{3}$, and can be represented as points along a number line traversing from minus infinity to plus infinity.

Alternatively $z = \sqrt{(x^2 + y^2)} \cos\theta + \sqrt{(x^2 + y^2)} i \sin\theta$. The $\sqrt{}$ expression represents the length of the z vector.

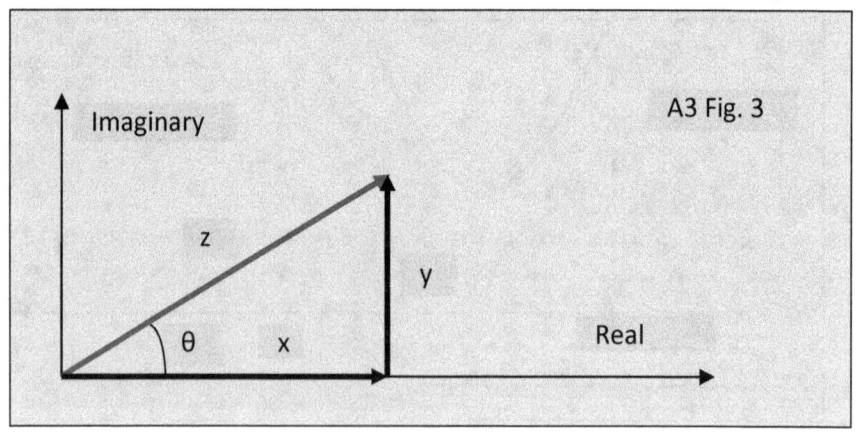

A3 Fig. 3

It can also be presented in polar form, $z = \sqrt{(x^2 + y^2)}e^{i\theta}$ where θ is the angle between the real axis and the z vector. The ability to analyze a wave in polar form that is offered by complex mathematics enhances our ability to relate risk, volume and price as they vary through time.

Imaginary is a slightly unfortunate word in some contexts, particularly in the financial arena. It can imply something fictitious or fantasized, whereas it actually means here that we simply do not (yet) know if something is a fact. We may have a high level of confidence that it is a fact, based on experience and application of a range of risk management processes, but not certainty. We imagine that we will be able to pay back a bank loan but, until we actually do, neither we nor the bank is certain. The money is at risk.

How much it is at risk varies. Rational business decisions allow for a wide range of risk levels. If we lend money to the US Treasury we might feel 99.9% or higher confidence that we will be repaid. Ultimately the US Government can print more money if it runs out. The money may not be worth as much as when we loaned it, due to inflation or reduction in the value of the dollar against other currencies, but at least we get something back.

By contrast if we were venture capitalists we might have less than 50% confidence of repayment on individual investments in a group of ten investments. We know that if one of the ten pays off big it will more than compensate for all the losses with the others. Venture capitalists of course choose investments with the potential for very large gains if they do succeed. The gains are often large when the product does succeed because competition has been deterred by the high risks.

In between these extremes, the financial industry has many financial instruments with varying degrees of confidence in repayment. Generally, bankers have knowledge of the borrower's past performance and the nature of the purchase or investment. That knowledge helps them assess the risk. Generally, they also require the borrower to provide some kind of collateral so that the banker has something to liquidate if the borrower cannot repay. This further reduces the risk of total loss. If the collateral can be sold on to other parties in the market for cash, the risk reduces further again.

However, from a mathematical point of view we consider borrowed or loaned money as imaginary, because for the purposes of analysis we will model it in a separate dimension from money in the bank. This aligns with the mathematical view of imaginary number, where in our example above, the letter i represents a different dimension to the line along which real numbers can be placed.

In the interests of clarity we are not discussing complexity theory here. Complex variable analysis is applied to the price of a single product or asset and the impact of its changes through cycles. While there may be common ground with complexity theory we are not dealing with that.

Price, Cash Flow and Risk

Price, volume and cash flow each include a known component and unknown (imaginary) component. Known and unknown here are, of course, relative. Known is what we expect with a high confidence to maintain a predictable level, at least in the short term, as supply and demand in our market change. Unknown is what we expect to significantly vary up or down as supply and demand change.

In our financial context, the imaginary money is quite independent of the real money, needing no real cash flow from operating business activities to provide it, only a financing party. In the background there will be a financial instrument, defining a commitment to future repayment under specific conditions. We give this to the financing party in exchange for cash now.

For our price and volume waves, we can model these using complex numbers as follows:

- For a sine wave, each wavelength in the graph showing wave height versus time is represented by one 360 degree rotation in the polar view.
- Seller price, P_S, is a complex number with a real component and an imaginary component, which varies as the wave fluctuates.
- Volume, V, is also a complex number with a lag angle, respective to Seller price, of θ.

Taking a polar view of the cycle, we show Seller Price, Ps and Volume, V as two vectors. For simplicity of analysis we shall pick a point in the cycle where the imaginary component is zero.

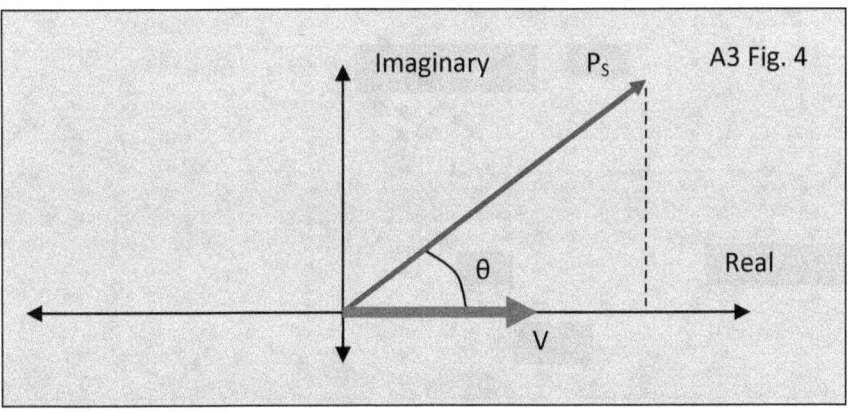

A3 Fig. 4

The angle, θ, which shows the lag between price and volume, is an indication of the risk to seller. From the time the price is accepted and the supply process activates, the seller is spending money, which is at risk of not being paid by the seller until product delivery and acceptance.

Cash flow = Volume x Price

Real cash flow = $P_S \cos\theta V$

Imaginary cash flow = $P_S \sin\theta V$

The Role of Financing

Consider now the impact of an external financing party transferring some funds into the seller's bank account. This allows the seller to get paid earlier with the lender accepting the risk for part or all of the supply costs.

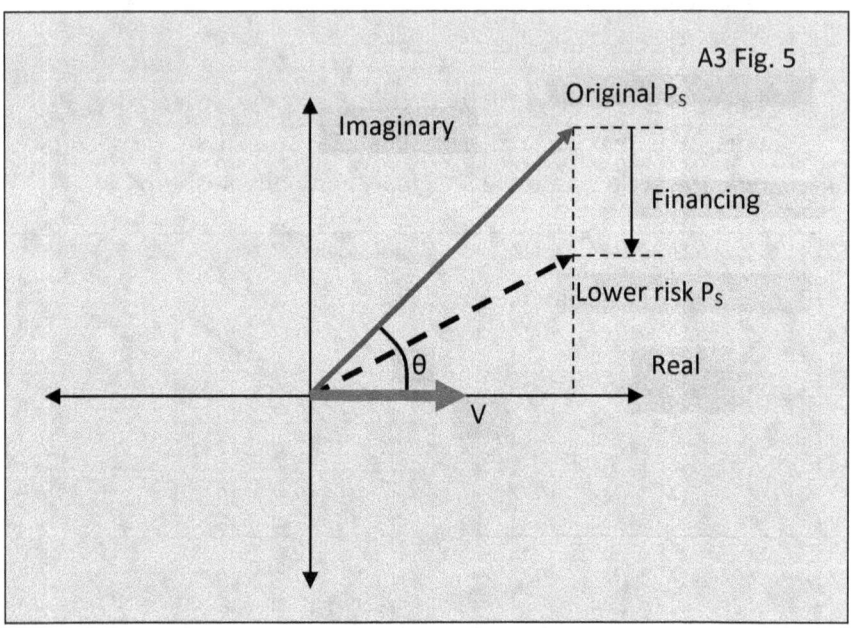

A3 Fig. 5

The dotted line shows the new P_S, with risk reduced for seller due to an injection of finance by an external party accepting that risk. The angle of lag between P_S and V is now smaller than θ, indicating the reduced risk.

Financing here is in the imaginary dimension. Anticipated or imaginary cash flow is the cash flow we need to bridge the gap while we are waiting to be paid. We need real money of course to do this and in practice we exchange a commitment to pay in the future with our financing party for that cash now, using a financial instrument as mentioned before. The financing party accepts the risk that we may not be able to repay it.

Seller's and Buyer's Risk

So far this analysis deals with seller's risks only. This would be applicable if our customer was firstly next door, incurring minimal delivery costs and secondly understood our product as well as we do, or perhaps even better. Then the customer would have no doubt what benefits they will receive from it. For example it might be our product's first customer and we have custom-developed the product to their requirements. They are involved in design, sourcing of components, quality control, logistics and support systems that they would understand and have confidence in. Alternatively we might have developed a product for our own use and proven its effectiveness. Then we decided that we could sell it to other companies with precisely similar requirements if they exist.

Other customers may also be next door, but not understand our product and how it may help them more than at the most limited level. They may have no idea what the total cost of using it in their environment will be even if we can give them a firm price, delivered to their door.

Other customers again may be on the other side of a continent, delivered via roads through mountain passes or deserts, or across an ocean, delivered through sea lanes subject to piracy and typhoons.

Others, in addition to being far away, may speak in a different language and may know very little about our product, how it used, how they could benefit from such use and how we might help them with problems. The risks for them of non-performance of our product may be much higher than for the first group of customers next door, even if we cover all the risks in getting the product to them.

When we consider the demand side, we introduce buyer's risk. This risk plus any additional known costs such as installation and training, creates an impedance to purchase. This impedance is also a complex number, being composed of unknown and known components. The complex impedance will include a real component made up of items such as delivery costs and taxes, and an imaginary component being the value the market adds to price due to risk. As we covered earlier, if risks to the buyer associated with our product are higher, the buyer will want to pay less. If our product eliminates potentially costly risks elsewhere, the buyer will pay more.

In general we will have a spectrum of levels of buyer's risk. As we increase volume we will need to attract buyers with less understanding of the product. These will have increasingly higher exposure to risk of the product not meeting their needs. These later customers will ordinarily need a price reduction to attract them.

Price will also be affected by known supplier costs, which the supplier will tend to pass on in part or full. These known costs will go into the average price. We can remove these from the analysis because we are only focusing on unknown factors in our wave analysis.

The diagram in Fig. 4 applies to a situation with only P_S and no separately valued P_B. Here volume is probably relatively low, limited to just those customers who have no risk that the product will not meet their requirements.

For the buyer side, we add another buyer's risk price vector, P_{BR}, which adds to Ps to produce a buyer price, P_B. P_B and P_{BR} are both complex prices with imaginary (risk finance) and real components. P_B and P_{BR} both start at zero for the very small number of customers who have no risk buying the product as delivered. They increase as the larger numbers of customers with a higher risk of the product not meeting their requirements are attracted by reducing price. P_{BR} is a product of Volume, V of product and an impedance factor, I_{BR}, which is another complex variable that relates price increase to volume increase.

$$P_{BR} = VI_R$$

So for the simple supply chain below, the core product capability incurs costs and risks to reach the price P_S. To meet customer risk reduction requirements, additional known costs and commitments by the supplier to deal with potential problems are required. These add further costs, some known and some unknown, which increases price to P_B. The obligation to pay is confirmed when the product is accepted by the customer.

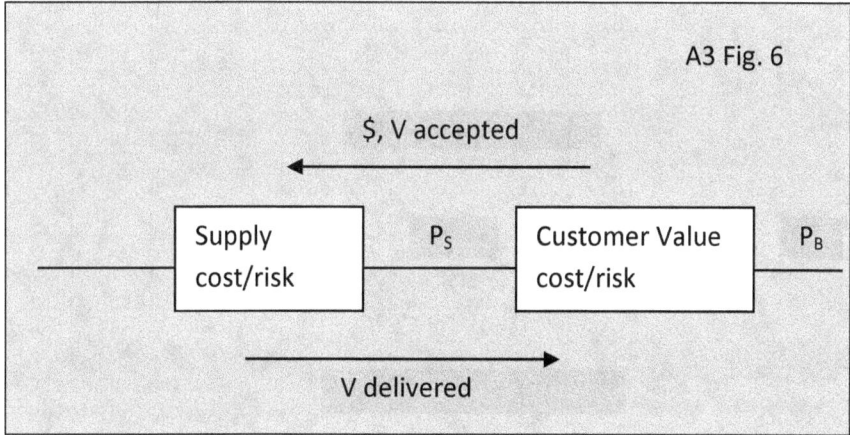

A3 Fig. 6

The polar diagram below shows these new components. Note that this is a snapshot at one point in the cycle. Through the cycle the various vectors will rotate together about the origin (see Figs. 8 and 9 below). The snapshot below shows the condition when volume, V, is oriented along the x axis with real value at maximum and imaginary value at zero.

The polar diagram displays the other price component, P_{BR} in a vertical orientation. P_{BR}, the additional price we need to add if we as the seller are to commit to covering the buyer's risk. At this moment in the cycle it this price has a purely risk component. It pays for things like uncertainties in configuration, customization, warranties and money back guarantees. At other points in the cycle it will include real and imaginary components, i.e. known costs and risks yet to materialize into known costs. In the diagram above we are only showing the imaginary component at the point in the cycle where the known value is zero and the unknown value is at a maximum.

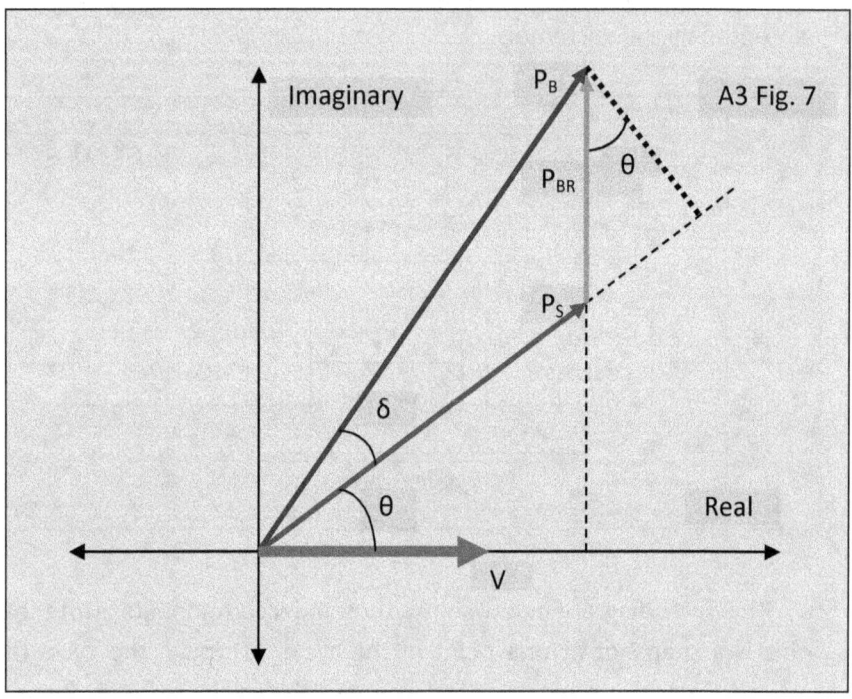

A3 Fig. 7

In a given cycle, the arrangement of these vectors relative to each other will usually not change much. Over multiple cycles as conditions change, the arrangement will change more significantly.

This diagram may seem rather abstract relative to the real world of business. But what this geometry is focused on is actually something very material in business. That is the timing between cash flow and price determination as separately perceived by seller and buyer. And the variations in these do have a very real impact on continuity of business. Just changing these timings, introducing advances or delays in payments, can hit the accelerator in business or hit the brakes, sometimes with dramatic consequences.

The diagram shows two phase angles of particular interest, θ and δ. Each angle represents a key aspect of the business cycle and its changes through the cycle or between cycles is an important indicator of what is happening. Applying some trigonometry we discover some new relationships.

The construction line made of dots (rather than dashes) at an angle of θ to P_{BR} is useful here as it is related to both P_{BR} and P_B. Dotted line length = $P_B \sin\delta$ and line length = $P_{BR} \cos\theta$

or $\cos\theta = (P_B/P_{BR})\sin\delta$

Remembering real cash flow = $P_S V \cos\theta$

And using the relationship above, $P_{BR} = V\, I_{BR}$ or $V = P_{BR}/I_{BR}$

Real cash flow $= P_S (P_{BR}/I_{BR})\cos\theta$

$= P_S (P_{BR}/I_{BR}) (P_B/P_{BR})\sin\delta$

$= (P_S P_B/I_{BR})\sin\delta$

We will come back to these relationships in the analysis of Buyer/Seller Price Lead and Price Collapse below but we need to also understand how these vectors behave as we go through the cycle.

Cyclical Patterns of Price and Volume

Fig. 7 tells us a lot more about the behavior of the cyclical relationships of seller price, buyer price and volume.

Firstly the angle between volume, V, and the real number line indicates where we are in the particular business cycle. This angle is zero in the diagram above but it will rotate from that zero value through 360 degrees as the cycle progresses as will P_S and P_B.

In Fig. 8 below, we focus on seller price, P_S. At various values through the cycle, e.g. 0 degrees, 90 degrees and 180 degrees, P_S, reaches significant values. In the first Panel, at 0 degrees, P_S is at its maximum real value. In the second panel, at 90 degrees the real component is zero, representing an average value through the cycle and the imaginary component is at a maximum, representing peak financing that needs to be provided on supply side. At 180 degrees, the real component is at a most negative or minimum value and imaginary component is zero representing a momentary lack of need for financing.

A3 Fig. 8

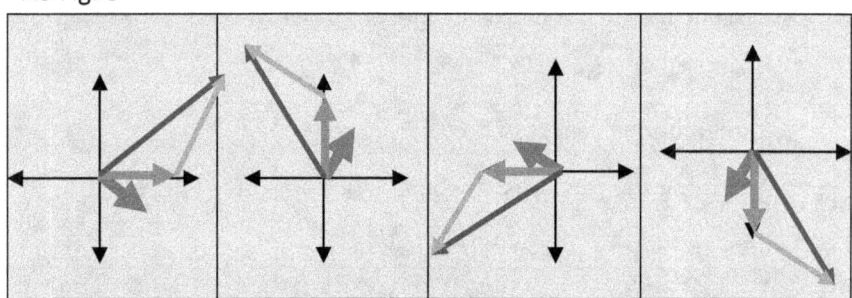

What is the significance of imaginary price here? If we look at the second panel in Fig. 8, when P_S is at 90 degrees, the imaginary (risk) component of P_S is at a maximum, which means the price risk is at its highest point. The risks that threaten a seller with getting a lower price than desired for some of its stock are at their peak here. These risks maximize after V has passed its maximum real quantity and the cycle is on the downside. The *rate* of supplier price reduction is at its peak. Also buyer price is already below average and is heading to its lowest level in the cycle. The really needy customers, who would pay a premium to ensure immediate satisfaction have already purchased, leaving only the marginally needy ones, who may haggle over price or not buy at all.

When P_S is most negative, as in the fourth panel, price risks are at their lowest. Thirsty customers are accumulating faster than they are being supplied and the risks of price reduction are low.

The buyer price, P_B, will go through similar points in its cycle but lead the supplier price. In panels 1 and 2 in Fig. 9, we see buyer price at maximum imaginary (highest price risk) and minimum real.

A3 Fig. 9

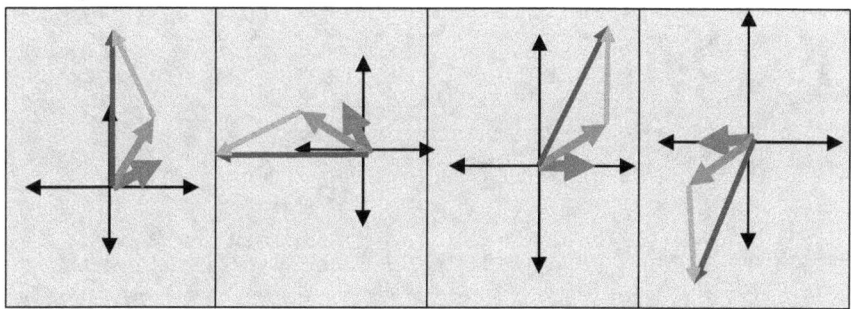

Volume, V will do similar but, in this configuration, lagging behind both the buyer and the supplier prices. Again V goes through maximum and minimum real values and average real values at various points in cycle. In panels 3 and 4 in Fig. 9, we see V at maximum real and minimum real.

Buyer/Seller Price Lead and Price Collapse

The second angle of significance in Fig. 7, δ, represents the lead of buyer price over seller price. When it is 0, we have the situation in Fig. 4 where $P_B = P_S$. Buyer's risk is zero, a theoretical situation, with few if any customers. To add customers whose valuation of the product is less based on known characteristics, or who perceive higher risks of the product not meeting their specific needs, we need to reduce price. As we add customers with a tolerance for some risk, the imaginary component of P_B increases in value and δ increases. P_B (the length) then progressively gets larger than P_S so that the ratio of

P_S/P_B moves down from 1.0. Incidentally, V increases as well along its line θ degrees behind P_S.

As δ increases we move along the curve with increasing volumes, ultimately approaching collapse point. But providing we do not get too close to that point, we will hopefully enjoy prices that are reasonably stable. If we do get too close we slide over the nose and follow the curve in Fig. 10.

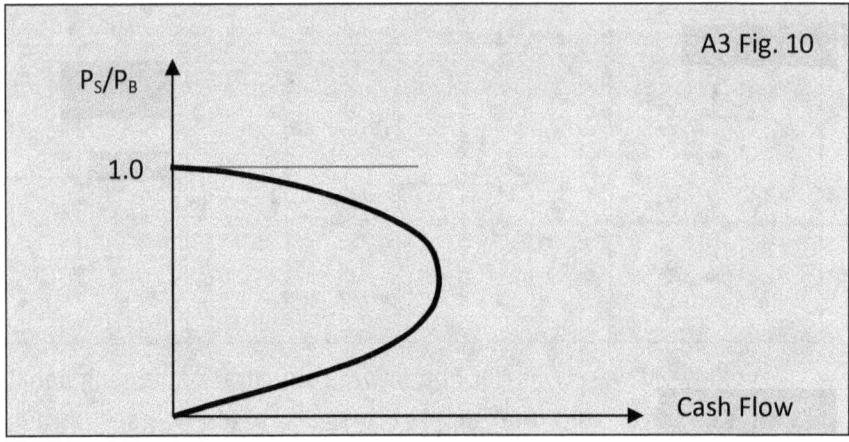

A3 Fig. 10

Why do we collapse following this logic with the curve turning back towards the origin? Why does P_S/P_B not simply steadily decline as price increases, perhaps following a curve like Appendix 1 Fig. 9?

Remember real cash flow = $(P_S P_B/I_{BR})\sin δ$

This equation means real cash flow starts at zero when δ = 0 and increases to $(P_S P_B/I_{BR})$ when δ = 90 degrees and drops back to zero when δ = 180 degrees.

Impact of Financing on Price and Volume

Our first angle of interest, θ, represents the lead of Seller Price over volume, V. So far we have looked only at the situation when Seller Price, P_S, leads V. But this can change.

If we look at Fig. 7 we see P_S leading V by θ. If we progressively reduce θ to zero and then take it into the negative value so that V now leads P_S, Fig. 7 is replaced by Fig. 11.

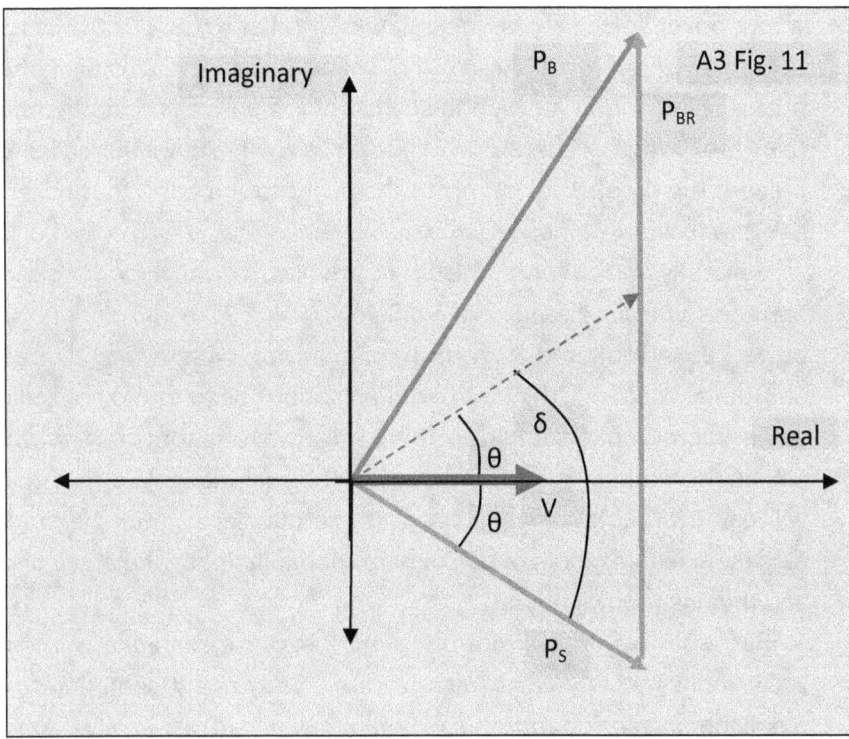

A3 Fig. 11

When product volume, V, leads supplier price, P_S, the shape of the vector configuration changes. With P_S still pointing along the X axis, the V vector is now leading it and the shape of the configuration is quite different.

This kind of change is caused by an external party financing some, or all, of the sale and accepting seller's risk following the principle shown in Fig. 5, where adding finance reduces the angle θ. Financing sales to fill the gap between sale and delivery is a key strategy for increasing sales volume. We can reduce seller's risk dramatically by paying the seller in advance to supply and deliver the product.

We are not talking here of the buyer paying in advance, because this would drive buyer's risks up as seller's risks are reduced. Buyer financing of seller's risk does have a valuable role in some situations where buyer's risk may be low relative to seller's risk, but this is not our focus here. In this case, the financing party is a bank, other financing institution, or even the owner of the business in a role other than the business operator. Whoever it is, it allows the seller to prepare the product for supply to the buyer to the point that buyer's risk is reduced.

Generally it is more difficult to reduce the buyer's risk price premium, which is based on the unknown value of the product to the buyer. Buyers fall into a spectrum of behavior, with varying degrees of rational economic thinking based on various degrees of knowledge and economic understanding. There will always be some buyers who will buy something that they want with no real thought to how they will pay it back, if someone finances the purchase. Multiple credit cards and loan sharks are useful here, particularly for the asset-poor and the financially ignorant.

But wiser buyers will not buy simply because someone will lend them money to buy whatever they like. They might sometimes be overly optimistic about their ability to repay a loan, especially if times are good, but they do know they have to pay it back plus interest. They will balance the value they hope to get from the product with the expected difficulty of repaying the loan. If that value is in doubt, repayment plus interest is much less attractive.

If the supply side is financed risk can now significantly reduced. Having the product in front of us ready to be studied, touched, tasted, listened to, opened up, driven, increased in volume, sat in, tested or checked out in some other way substantially closes the gap. Having other customers using it and commenting positively further reduces risk. Having it ready now, not in three days, three weeks, or three months also reduces some of those uncertainties as our needs may change in that time.

If we do not have to pay for the product until a significant period after delivery, the risk is reduced again. We know that if for any reason we get to payment time and we find it did not meet our requirements we will be in a stronger negotiating position than if we had already paid. This is important should we want to send it back, have it repaired, adjusted, modified or replaced.

The external financing party has accepted the risk of buyer dissatisfaction. The risk for the seller has passed to the financing party and risk for the buyer is now much less.

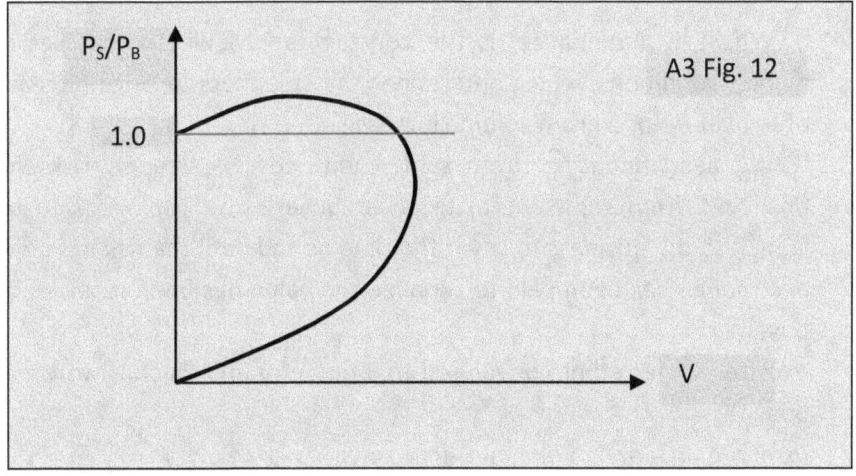

A3 Fig. 12

With this configuration there is an important change in relationship between the relative sizes of P_B and P_S. Previously when P_S led V, P_S was always less than P_B so that the ratio P_S/P_B was always less than 1.0. In this configuration, as P_B increases in angle relative to the X axis and while P_B is between P_S and the dashed line in Fig. 11, or while V leads it by an angle δ with a value less than 2θ, P_B will be shorter than P_S. This means that the ratio P_S/P_B starts at 1.0 and then rises above 1.0 until P_B reaches the dashed line where $P_S = P_B$ in length and then drops below it as the angle δ between P_B and the X axis (not shown on this diagram) continues to increase.

We now look at the general case.

Real cash flow, $C_R = P_S \cos\theta$ Vol, where P_S is the length of the vector P_S

Imaginary cash flow $C_I = P_S \sin\theta$ Vol

We are assuming that, at least at the margin, which is where our wave fluctuates, price increases linearly with demand for a constant supply capability.

Buyer's risk price, $P_{BR} = $ Vol I_R

Where I_R, impedance, is the constant applicable to that set of market conditions, which determines the steepness of price increase of P_B over P_S for a given volume increase.

We need financing (from somewhere) to cover supply risk and financing (from somewhere) to cover buyer's risk. It needs to be loaned to the business to cover the time period until the risk has gone and money has been paid to supplier and value has been received by buyer.

After some rather convoluted trigonometry and algebra we come up with:

$$(P_S/P_B)^2 \sin\theta \cos\theta - P_S/P_B \cos\theta \sqrt{1 - (P_S/P_B)^2 \cos^2\theta} + C_R/(P_T^2/I_R) = 0$$

Those who are mathematically inclined may recognize that the presence of $(P_S/P_B)^2$ in the same equation with $C_R/(P_T^2/I_R)$ means that for each single value of $C_R/(P_T^2/I_R)$ on the horizontal axis there will be two values of (P_S/P_B) on the vertical axis.

This rather complicated equation produces a set of curves shown in Fig. 13. When we plot the curves we need to plot the upper and lower portions of the curves separately. Although they join at the nose of the curve, they have quite distinct behavior.

The four curves each have different values of θ (the lead of supplier price over volume through the cycle), with the second curve from left having θ = 0.

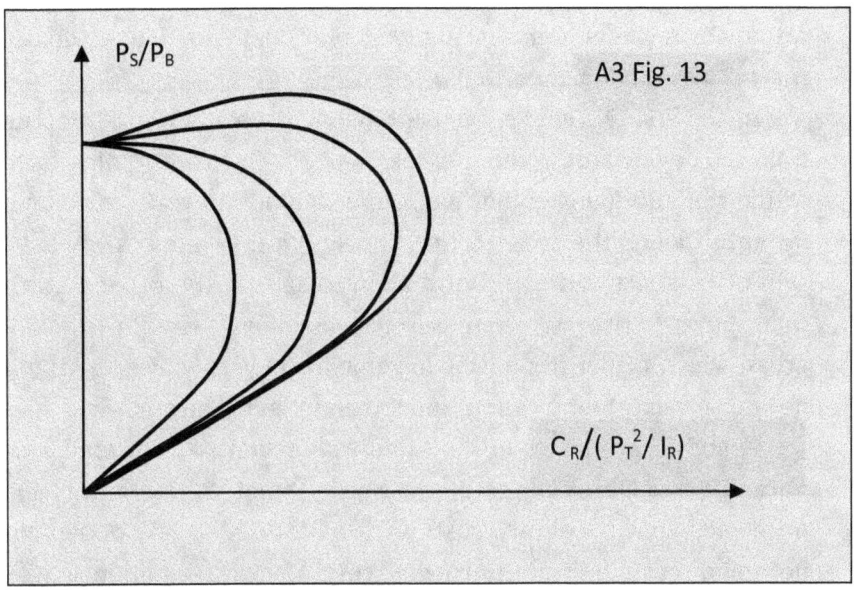

A3 Fig. 13

By using the ratios $C_R/(P_T^2/I_R)$ and P_S/P_B, the curves are scale-independent. They might represent hundred dollar or hundred billion dollar markets.

This set of curves is similar to our price collapse curves in Appendix 2 Fig. 3. The key difference is that, with this curve, price drops to zero whereas the one in Appendix 2 Fig. 3 falls to some nonzero value. This is because this analysis only includes the variable wave component, with the average being excluded from analysis.

Implications of Wave Model

What does our wave-based price collapse model mean in the real world? What is happening when P_S varies in relation to P_B? Does this rather abstract mathematical outcome really have anything to do with real business and finance?

For the first two curves from left in Fig. 13, the ratio P_S/P_B declines from 1.0 downwards without exceeding 1.0. One contributing factor to the ratio declining is that we gain economies of scale as volumes increase though the cycle so that Supply Price, P_S reduces. P_S is the sum of real cost and risk contribution to seller. The other factor is that Buyer Price P_B increases as volumes increase, due to progressively higher risk for the incremental buyers whose needs may be less perfectly met by our product than for initial buyers.

P_S and P_B are prices in the same transactions. P_S represents the price the supplier receives at the supply point. P_B represents that price plus known delivery costs such as transport, tax, duties plus unknown costs. These unknown costs include additional work required to meet specific requirements, fix difficulty of use or improve unreliability and other unknowns associated with a different environment from the one the product was initially designed for.

In the case of the third curve, for financed supply, P_S/P_B initially exceeds 1.0 because P_B initially decreases as financing reduces the risk for buyers (other people's money at relatively low interest) and drives up demand. After that the buyer price P_B increases as newer customers have greater risk of non-satisfaction and it increases faster than reductions in supplier price P_S due to economies of scale.

The fourth curve is a more extreme case of the third curve, where financing is very liberal and buyer's risk is considered low in a rising market. It is expected that asset values will increase to pay financing costs. The common pattern for the four curves is that, as volume increases and we get close to the nose of the curve, we go into a situation where a small additional increase in volume will push us to a point of no return. This could take place over many cycles or just a few. The curve provides no indication of time in terms of number of cycles.

The curves may, but do not necessarily, show a time sequence. The maximum volume of sales in a given cycle will tend to increase steadily as business expands. That maximum will then move steadily from left to right towards the point of no return over a series of cycles, sales volume growing as we go, and then reach the point of price collapse on the final unlucky cycle. However, before we get to the nose, we could also reduce sales for a number of cycles and back up the curve to a more stable point.

This might be because we have some sense of caution. Or some external event or change in market behavior could cause this reversal. It might be some short or medium term change in customer behavior or cost structures. Or it might be caused by some other market wave passing through, in which case we would return to the previous point after that wave has passed. We could then continue along the curve over additional cycles towards collapse. Our natural inclination to feel more confidence as sales expansion leads us to this final point.

Equally we can be pushed by some other external event or change in market behavior closer to the point of collapse. This might be a relatively short term market wave, which pushes us to the right. If it pushes us too far we may go over our nose before it completes its cycle and has the chance to push us back to the left. Of course if we do go over the nose we will not be coming back in the near future.

The pattern is not determined by frequency, so could apply to any cycle from a one hour working capital cycle to a multi-decade technology cycle. It does not deal with the impact of one cycle on another, other than to highlight that as we get close to the nose a small normally reversible movement, which could be caused by another wave passing through, might push us over the tip.

Cash on Delivery

Considering our first option, cash on delivery, Curve 2 from left:
- At very low sales (first buyers off the block) we are selling to those few customers who know exactly what they are getting. For these customers there is no buyer's risk. Customers pay full price on delivery. $P_S = P_B$.
- As volume increases we start to attract customers with less confidence in the product. Buyer's risk starts to increase. They need a price reduction to close the deal.
- As volume increases further, new buyers with less confidence in the product's ability to provide value are emerging but buyer's risk is steadily increasing and further price reductions are required to keep increasing sales volume.

Payment in Advance by Buyer

Considering the next option where the buyer is required to provide an advance payment to reduce supplier risk, Curve 1 from left:
- At very low sales (first buyers off the block) we are selling to those few customers who know exactly what they are getting. For these customers there is no buyer's risk. Customers pay in advance of delivery. $P_S = P_B$. There are less of these customers than those who would be willing to pay cash on delivery but not in advance so the curve drops more steeply.
- The pattern continues as for cash sales but at every value of P_S/P_B the sales volume is less than for the cash sales curve, because a smaller proportion of buyers have cash up front.

Financing of Buyer

Considering next the supplier, or some external financing party, provides advance payment to reduce buyer's risk, Curve 3 from left:
- At very low sales (first buyers off the block) we are selling to those customers who do not need any financing.

- As volume increases we start to attract customers with less confidence in product and/or ability to pay at this time. Buyer's risk is reduced by the financing (someone else risks up front money not being repaid if the product is not satisfactory or if they buyers cannot pay). These buyers need less of a price reduction (or none) to close deal than in the cash sale case. If financing is sufficiently attractive (low interest and extended time to repay) we attract buyers who are willing to pay more than the low volume cash price.
- As volume increases, further price reductions are required.

High Levels of Financing

Considering next when financing is very easy to get and appears to be of low real cost in interest (rising prices may suggest that buying now rather than later will be cheaper than waiting, even if we have to pay at significant interest rates). The classic case for this is a real estate or stock market bubble. Here people take on loans they cannot afford because they believe they will be able to sell the asset for a higher price than they paid and pay the loan back before they have to start paying higher interest costs. This time we are looking at Curve 4 from left.

- At very low sales (first buyers off the block) we are selling to those customers who do not need financing to cover risk.
- As sales increase P_S/P_B becomes significantly greater than 1. A larger number of buyers are buying. This is not for the intrinsic value identified by a customer who can pay cash but because they think someone will buy it from them at a higher price than they pay or that it will cost them more if they wait.
- If for any reason the price stops increasing, even if it only pauses, many of these buyers have the need to sell to meet their commitments before those commitments get bigger. This can activate the collapse.

- This curve does not permit significant price reductions in the event of a need to get additional sales. With the other curves we might be able to drop price by 20% in an emergency without going too close the nose. But on this curve that kind of drop will trigger the collapse because the nose is high. These buyers do not want to even think prices might drop significantly. If they do think that they then realize they have borrowed for an item that has already lost value and panic sets in.

General Observations

This analysis does not predict whether a price collapse will occur in a particular cycle, only the sensitivity of market price to collapse. If we are getting close to the nose of the curve a small disruption may push us into collapse. In theory, many, many cycles can occur without a collapse, even with the system close to stability limits. In practice during the upside of a cycle, people are increasingly tempted by individual profits to collectively push market aggregates too close to the point of collapse. It is hard to believe prices will drop when they have been rising steadily and we stand to profit by continued increase. Or if we do think they might drop, we hope it will only be small and temporary and less of a risk than the risk incurred by missing further increases.

As an example of the Short cycle in the financial markets (3-5 years), it might take two of these cycles (6 – 10 years) before we have a really big collapse or it might take 20 Short cycles (60 – 100 years). But it almost certainly will not take 200 Short cycles (600 – 1000 years) because in that time people will likely come to think collapses are a thing of the past. They will believe collapses are prevented by good regulation and central financial market management, or are prevented by a good lack of regulation and a good lack of central financial management, depending on their ideological persuasion.

There is no probability allocated to extreme events such as price collapse based on recent volatility. Recent volatility is not the determining factor here. If volatility is high it will overlay the cycles above, increasing values at some times and reducing them at others but not change their fundamental behavior. High volatility, like a price spike, could push volumes along the curve past the point of collapse. However, the volatility in itself does not cause the collapse but may help determine when it occurs.

The model also does not define a time period for the collapse in terms of the number of cycles that it lasts before prices get back onto the upper curve, or something near it, if they ever do. It could be a one day clearance sale or a deflation lasting decades. It also does not define the depth of the collapse. It could be total with production and sales stopping dead. But usually there will be some base level sales to keep business moving. Cycles will then continue, albeit at a lower level, one which may be very painful for owners and staff in the business. In this case we drop to some point on another curve. If we do eventually return to an upper curve it may be on a Curve 1 where there is no financing available other than what buyers can provide. Consequently sales volumes may be initially small.

Typically the depth of the collapse and the economic damage done depends on the difference between maximum sales at collapse and the new sales level. When we revert from large sales volumes to small sales volumes, a lot of economies of scale are lost, driving up real costs until at some time in the future when sales volumes pick up. If we have also invested financially to make those economies of scale possible we may also have heavy capital commitments on top of higher per-unit operational costs.

This can take a long time to recover from. Hence recovery from large collapses is usually much longer than from small collapses. Instead of a short term downturn that flushes out incompetents, we have substantial medium or long term cost increases and damage to productivity on a wide scale. Eventually we may need a lot of discarded or downgraded facilities such as derelict factories, junked ships, weed-covered rail tracks and broken roads to remove capacity to the point where it falls below the new lower level of demand so that price can start reviving.

Note the role of economy of scale. Its increases and decreases initially contribute to the wave's creation. Then the larger the economies of scale gets, the greater is the severity of the collapse of the wave when it occurs.

In an imaginary world, some wise and effective regulatory body might regulate financing to support a sustained high level of business activity in financial markets but not so high that we go into the instability zone. In the real world, however, there are wide views held on the wisdom or effectiveness of regulation. Politicians are advised and funded by the financial industry, which naturally seeks to minimize regulations that constrain financing. The industry is of course not always wrong in their justifications. Rules in any sphere are often ineffective or produce unforeseen consequences.

Assumptions of Wave Model

The reader may be suspicious of precise mathematics being applied as above in our little model to the hugely diverse and often chaotic world of global business, and rightly so. A model can be very useful for explaining a certain situation but if, based on that usefulness, we decide the model is always valid then we have replaced business thinking with ideology.

The assumptions in any model are critical. Economists and business analysts develop models based on observed behavior but are sometimes tempted to apply their models outside of the zone where the behavior was originally observed. They often apply it far more generally than is merited.

That temptation increases when ideologists get involved, with political objectives and special interests to be served. Sometimes commercial reality is ignored as they extrapolate their model into zones where it is not accurate or even where it is completely invalid. This is fine for ideologists and politicians, as they can always deflect the blame to their opponents if things go wrong. Losses are paid by the taxpayer.

Several assumptions have been made in our model:
1. Price increase with volume is linear over the range of the cyclical price fluctuation.
2. We are treating each cycle for which the stability analysis can be applied to with its particular wavelength as independent of other cycles. This includes Short, Medium and Long general economic cycles, and our business's own working capital and investment cycles. Waves pass though one and other.
3. There is a smooth transition in response of volume to price.
4. There is a smooth transition between cash in the bank and cash from financing as money is spent and revenue comes in.
5. We are only looking at one price in a single market (perhaps other prices are doing similar things but they are not considered here).
6. We are analyzing cycles where prices fluctuate in response to market forces through the cycle, not where they are fixed across the cycle by contract.

We need to understand these assumptions so that we can use judgement in applying the model to real world situations. We especially need to know three things: when the model is valid, when it is not valid and when it can be made valid, through suitable and clearly understood allowances and adjustments.

Does the model completely cease to be relevant when we cross the boundary of the zone where the original data that was used to develop it came from? Or does it transition into a modified model, (possibly less mathematically precise but in a reasonably predictable way)?

The first four assumptions relate to the mathematical integrity of the model. These assumptions jointly add up to a lot of ifs and buts, which limit the model's use as a forecasting tool. Again, however, our purpose is not to precisely forecast when something happens in a market or to the wider economy. It is to provide ourselves with early warning of conditions that could destroy our own business or offer a great opportunity.

The fifth assumption is fine for many businesses, or parts of businesses, where the product has low differentiation from other products in the market. However, there are many products which do not comply. We want to assess how these products relate to the model, if at all.

The sixth assumption has particular relevance when we are looking at price collapses that occur at the working capital cycle level. Some working capital cycles last years, e.g. those associated with the construction of very large supply facilities such as petrochemical plants and nuclear power stations. However, most are much shorter, being weeks or months. Wider markets move in slower cycles, such as Short, Medium and Long cycles, and market-wide price collapses follow the dynamics of these longer cycles. But even with shorter working capital cycles, individual firms can get into a price collapse situation within a few cycles, even one cycle, so we need to understand how long contracts affect the cycle.

Mathematical Integrity, Assumption 1: Linear Price Variation with Volume

This assumption of linear behavior is not always valid. Prices can increase or decrease with demand in non-linear ways. If our wave component levels of price and volume are large relative to our average levels we may go well out of the linear behavior zone and our math may cease to be valid. The classic case here is the price spike. If a supply or demand constraint occurs price may spike up or down in a highly non-linear fashion. At this point we move into another framework entirely until the constraint is removed.

However, most markets have average volumes much larger than the wave component so, at least for these markets, the assumption is reasonable for our purpose. Again we are not trying to forecast when a collapse will occur within 1% error or even 10% error, only to recognize the conditions that support a collapse so that we can prepare to deal with this to our advantage.

Mathematical Integrity, Assumption 2: Interaction of Wavelengths

Waves of different frequencies in many systems pass through each other, usually leaving each other largely unchanged. People working in the electronic and telecommunications industries involving wave behavior such as fiber optics and wireless communications may be familiar with this. Observers of the ocean will see similar wave behavior. Two large waves fed from different storm systems can pass through each other, briefly creating a giant wave. If you are on a fishing boat at that location this is not good. However, after the waves have passed, previous conditions return for the sea itself. We are assuming that the waves are following a mechanism where wave amplitudes can be simply added in a linear way (see Assumption 1).

This means that a shorter cycle can support relatively healthy prices during a longer cycle that is depressed, even in a state of price collapse. Inventory (Short) cycle prices might be strong for a period of some quarters during a multi-year phase when Fixed Investment (Medium) cycle capital investment prices have collapsed. And vice versa, the longer cycle can be buoyant while the shorter cycle is undergoing price collapse. Of course a Short cycle high during a longer cycle high will be higher than one during a longer cycle low.

The above applies to individual markets and the general economy. Some industries may thrive when the general economy is depressed. Some will be impacted more by the general economy than others.

Housing values are generally not tightly bound to the fortunes of just one industry unless that industry dominates a local economy. People in manufacturing businesses may live next door to people in construction, retail, law, banking, software, shipping, etc. Manufacturing may be slow but the other sectors may be strong. Real estate values reflect the health of the total economy in an area rather than just one industry.

Similarly for financing charges, diverse industries such manufacturers, farmers, construction, distribution, energy and communications need funding from the same pool. Interest rates typically reflect the health of the total economy rather than just one industry.

Mathematical Integrity, Assumption 3: Smooth Response of Volume to Price

This is valid where a company has many buyers and at any given time a portion of the buyers will be ready to buy when price reaches some threshold point. The size of that portion is variable and will be influenced by many external factors. If the market is small and there is just one buyer in a given tier, that variable portion will be either 100% or 0%, resulting in a very lumpy curve.

Mathematical Integrity, Assumption 4: Smooth Transition between Cash and Financing

The model assumes that, as expenditures are incurred and revenue comes in, we only borrow just the amount we need at a given time, and that we get the funding as soon as our cash runs out. In fact of course financing may be delayed, disrupting operations, and may come in lumps. However, modern financial engineering techniques provide a wide range of instruments to transfer financing from one structure to another and blend in any lumps in a relatively smooth way.

Significant Deviations from Assumptions, Assumption 5: One Market Price

For the fifth assumption we assume that a company's product *competes against businesses with sufficiently similar products that they share the same price.* This is fine for commodity products but commodities are an important but limited portion of the economy. A large number of competitive situations between similar products deal with multiple prices in tiers. Others deal with situations where, even within a tier, some business's products have an ability to resist price reduction by their competitors. At first glance these are exceptions to our assumption and would seem to undermine application of the model to these situations.

Multiple price tiers are actually the lesser problem. We can simply treat each tier as a separate entity for analysis, with its own cycle. Volume may bleed from one tier to another but essentially the associated loss (or gain) is not unique. It is not different from loss (or gain) of demand due to any number of other market factors such as product substitution, deferred expenditure or the behavior of other competitors. The price responds to cyclical pressures normally.

However, within a particular market or tier we can have products that are differentiated from the rest by some essential capability for a particular purpose. So sales for a particular company may drop with reduction in demand as the market contracts but, if it holds its price, other suppliers cannot simply step in and undercut it, taking what sales are available. The wider market price is still important as an indication of demand and an inspiration for customers to apply pressure to have price reduced, but that market price does not dictate price for this product. Examples include:

- Key functions. The product can perform the functions of other products in its market but has some specific function they do not. Customers will have to achieve the result some other way.

- Local monopoly. If we have the minimart store in a big city neighborhood where people do not drive on a day to day basis, and the next store is a five or ten minute walk away, there is real time saving to people nearby using our store. There is nothing to stop them using the next shop but it costs them time, which they might consider increases the total product cost to them.
- Other total cost factors. The product works in some way that reduces overall cost to the customer of using the product (saves a lot of staff or equipment time, materials, energy, pollution, space) compared to competitor products.
- Complex dependencies. The product works with other parts of the customers' systems in a way our competitors' products do not. Decisions made on such systems previously, perhaps years ago, may determine our customers' cost structures. These may include long term support and maintenance, repair and replacement, integration with external systems. If the systems supported, maintained repaired and replaced need our product, whereas our competitors' products are incompatible with these systems, we then have a protection from competitor price drops.
- Aggregation. Our particular aggregation of product components may hit a sweet spot, or several sweet spots, Here customers get more value from our product than another aggregation of similar cost components.

A company's sales staff need to understand these issues and to communicate factors impacting the total benefit customers receive from the product. At the higher end of this spectrum, with large complex solutions, sales interactions may involve many people and many meetings per person. Some of these people will have much longer timeframes in mind than others, and be less concerned about short term price factors than long term ones.

Products with these qualities can resist market cycles to a large degree and avoid price collapse when their competitors are undercutting each other in a downwards spiral towards insolvency.

We should note that all the above means only that the product cannot be replaced at the point of collapse in *this cycle.* By a similar point in the next cycle a competitor may have developed equivalent functionality in their product, perhaps by reverse engineering the other product. Then this protection against replacement will be gone. One day we have a premium product, essential to all top-of-the-line customers. The next day we just have a commodity product under constant price pressure from multiple competitors.

But as long as it lasts, how is this differentiation likely to impact on sales volume? If they cannot get a lower price by going to our competitor, they can still reduce purchases. Deferral of purchase is one obvious option for large deals. Conversely suppose the customer has committed to a product line, perhaps years before, and needs components or services to keep a major investment operational. They are then less likely to defer purchasing these components and put at risk a far greater investment. With differentiation we would usually expect we can hold prices and margins even if we incur some reduction of sales.

Say the wider market volume drops with a price collapse of 40% and a sales volume drop of 30%, we have options:

1. We can lower price and hope to minimize loss of volume. Given a strong product differentiation we might lose 10% price for a 10% sales drop. Depending on where we are in our own investment cycle, 10% price reduction may be easily manageable or disastrous (if we are close to survival limits). With a lesser product differentiation we might lose 20% of price and 20% volume.

2. We can hold price and let volume drop. Again given a strong product differentiation we might lose 20% volume, and with a lesser differentiation we might lose 30% of volume.

All of the above numbers are hypothetical and serve only to indicate that, with strong product differentiation, the impact of a market-wide price collapse is likely to be less than without that differentiation, to some degree or other. The other thing to consider is that although our competitors may be suffering far more, as they are forced to compete on price with each other, we are usually still under some cyclical cash flow pressure. If we are highly exposed to financial pressures we can be tempted to create our own price collapse situation.

Assumption 6: Price Fluctuation through Cycle - Contracted Price and Contingent Price

We know that cash flow follows some kind of wave form for our internal trade cycle and for each capital cycle we go through. We invest and earn, each Working capital cycle and each capacity, market or technology investment cycle. And if we start to fall behind in our payments, our cycle starts to stall and sooner or later our suppliers stop supplying and we are out of business. While a market downturn or general economic downturn kills off many businesses, we don't need either downturn to go broke, if we do not manage our business properly. We can do it by ourselves.

We can have cash flow problems in times when our competitors, suppliers and customers have no such problems. In fact a large number of small businesses die of this in their first few years, even months. The internal investment cycles of the product need to be considered as well as the wider market and general economic cycles. These cycles are diverse and each has its own risks.

But it would appear that price does not necessarily follow a wave pattern over the Working capital cycle. Typically, we set a price in advance, sign a contract for that price and get paid when we deliver. The price for a standard product is fixed and does not vary through the order to delivery cycle. Even if a discount is negotiated, this is set at time of sale and from then the price is fixed.

And some deals follow fixed price contacts over many working capital cycles. For example, large construction projects and large technology projects may take place over many working capital cycles. Each month or quarter, work may be carried out and payments may be made but these are subject to a long term contract which ties these into completion milestones and retention payments. The price, putting aside variations, is fixed over the contractual period.

However, there is a price that does follow a wave through the individual company's working capital cycle, as well as the longer market cycles. This is a price underlying the contracted price that is uncovered by asking a question: What would happen if for some reason the production and delivery process was stopped at a point during the cycle before completion? This might happen in several ways:

- Buyers pull out of the purchase deal due to their own cash flow difficulties or a due to a perception the deal is no longer a good one. This is a classic construction industry real estate development problem when an economic downturn occurs before construction is complete.
- We find out that the buyer is bankrupt and we decide not to sink any more money to complete delivery.
- We run out of cash and cannot find money to complete delivery.
- A supplier cannot supply and the contract is cancelled.
- A force majeure event occurs that will prevent the buyer from taking delivery.

Each of these events leaves a collection of resources that cannot now be delivered in its completed form for payment. What would be the market value of the resources put into the product then?
- Standard sizes of material have been cut, shaped to purpose and may be of only scrap value on market if product is not completed.
- Discrete components may be in resalable condition but may need to be sold by an agent for a margin and transported to the new customer.
- Man hours have been paid for to produce an unfinished product, which may not be easily finished by another party without the equipment, processes and systems normally used to create it.
- Code has been written for a program but not finished, tested and documented.

Each of these contributes to a reduction of market value down to some composite price below contract value. This price will vary according to the point in the cycle where the supply and delivery process stopped. The price will drop as potential loss of value of inputs increases through the process and then increase as completion becomes more certain. It converges with the contact price if and when we complete the product, deliver it and get paid.

All this is hypothetical until the supply or payment process is disrupted at some point in the cycle and cannot be re-established. Then it becomes real.

We are very familiar with this in the financial sector where financial assets are used for collateral at a certain value for a loan period. If the market value of the asset reduces for some reason or other, e.g. rumors of increased credit risk, the lender may make a margin call. It demands a top up from the borrower to match the reduction in collateral value. But the principle applies to other sectors as well, as an underlying value in the event of planned event falling through. The financial sector simply structures this as routine business practice. Private equity firms often specifically contract out of the normal application of contingent price during the loan. This would apply when cash flow or profitability levels breach the bank's usual covenants. Of course if things do go bad the contingent price will activate at the end of the loan.

If a contingent variation does occur and our product is a commodity item, we may quickly find another buyer, but our profit margin may be eaten into with transaction costs. Suppose we cannot quickly find a new buyer, or we cannot deliver to the original buyer. Then that underlying price, the contingent price, goes from being hypothetical and ignorable to being an unavoidable reality. Depending on where in the cycle this occurs, the contingent price may be much less than the contract price.

We may have had some understandings between ourselves and the original buyer, covering specific buyer requirements and discussions about how the product meets those requirements. Whatever was the price, determined through those discussions and negotiation, it is replaced by what is available on the market, less whatever new costs are incurred in getting it to that market. As our product gets more comparable to other products in terms of function it is more easily compared in terms of price and value with these other products. After making appropriate allowances and assumptions it can be sold in a liquid market for the price that market delivers.

The contingent price is cyclical, following a wave shape. It may be a very lumpy wave (as in Appendix 2 Fig. 9, showing a cycle whose shape is far from a simple sine wave). But it can still be deconstructed into sinusoidal waves as components, although this may require many components. We would not bother with such a deconstruction but in principle it is possible. It is thus logically subject to the same wave mathematics, including collapse, as applies to our market wave. So while we have less pressure from competitors to collapse our price than for the less differentiated product, the risk of collapse is still real. Lose a significant deal, or have a project go wrong, and things can rapidly unravel.

Similarly we are never really sure how long our strong differentiation mentioned in Assumption 5, will last. Even if it is only partially eroded by new developments of our competitors that part may be critical. It may be the part that our customers were unwilling to sacrifice in a market-wide collapse but now will do so. Uncertainty about this eats away at our confidence to hold price on our highly differentiated product.

This is in some respects the converse of the situation in Assumption 6. We can sometimes resist price collapse with strongly differentiated products when the wider market price collapses. Conversely we can have a price collapse for a highly differentiated product when the wider market price does not collapse. A moderate downturn in the wider market may be all we need to push us into the collapse zone if our internal business cycle is already approaching instability. In fact we can easily put ourselves into that zone even when the wider market is buoyant if we are short of cash.

In essence highly differentiated products are exposed to the same mechanisms as less differentiated products and commodity products. Their actual waves are separate from those of the wider market but interact to varying degrees. They need just as much care to avoid disaster as do less differentiated products.

By understanding how changes in buyers risk translate to changes in financing risk, upside and downside, we can identify potential for financial instability. Both upside and downside financial risks offer opportunities for financial killings. Typically one will dominate the other during one part of the relevant cycle. Then the dominance will reverse as we move into another part of the cycle. That cycle may be a single investment cycle or a composite cycle. If we can see the cycle change before the rest of the market, we can make the killing.

1. "Wave Prediction Models For Coastal Engineering Applications" Vijay G. Panchang, Bingyi Xu, Zeki Demirbilek, Offshore Engineering
2. "An Introduction to Fourier And Complex Analysis With Applications to the spectral Analysis of Signals" Russell L. Herman
3. "Power System Dynamics Stability and Control" Jan Machowski, Janusz W. Bialek, James R. Bumby

APPENDIX 4: MACRO-ECONOMIC STABILITY

Our focus has been on the effects on individual firms, a microeconomic view. There are a number of reasons to consider macroeconomic behavior as well:

Some of our greatest opportunities for financial killings come from large scale price collapses and there are further excellent opportunities during recessions. But without growth at some time there is nothing to collapse and no wealth to capture. So we need periods of growth in the general economic system, particularly in sectors where we have businesses that can benefit from that growth. And even if we make our best killings in the collapse we want to further build that money gained by capitalizing on growth.

In addition, the seeds of collapse are always present in the growth. So the more we understand about growth the better we can see the cracks appearing and hear the groans of the buckling structure. We need to understand the factors leading to business growth with its increasing investor and consumer confidence, its improving economies of scale and its appetite for financing. And we need to understand the mechanisms that are involved in revival of growth after collapses.

Organic Growth Mechanisms

In Appendix 3 we looked at growth and collapse in terms of organic growth within a business in a cyclical environment. Here, looking from the perspective of the operators of a company that is a target for a financial killing, we grow within our existing territory (whatever and wherever that is). We carry out business as usual, accumulate a surplus and invest some of it in new tools and facilities. These allow us to enjoy economies of scale greater than we had previously and thus allow us to make products less costly and thus to make a bigger profit contribution on each unit of product. Hopefully this justifies the capital investment in the new tools and facilities.

But this is just the beginning. The economies of scale gained by expanded production offer additional opportunities:
- They also allow us to make more products than before with a larger economy of scale again. We can sell these at a lower price than previously to attract new customers and still make the same profit margin.
- Or we can sell at even lower prices and make a smaller margin on individual units but a bigger total contribution towards capital expenses.
- We can finance additional customers who cannot pay cash. Perhaps we were financing some before but we increase the proportion. The additional sales give us increased economies of scale. In addition, customers enjoying financing are often less aggressive about asking for low prices so our margins may improve.

In this organic growth model, we grow indefinitely until we and our competitors saturate the market. At that time we cannot entice any more buyers into the market, we collectively build too much supply capacity and the price collapses. At some future time with less capacity or more buyers we can start growing again.

There are other growth mechanisms:

We can expand into a new territory – a plain or a river valley, an island or continent. We replicate what we are doing in our existing territory and simply by doing more of it we generate more wealth. Empires have done this for thousands of years.

Often this territorial expansion is given a jump start with new technology.

New transport technology to get there, take the resources we need to exploit it and bring back product.

New agricultural technology makes the new territory useable, whereas previously we may not have had the tools to exploit it. For example, the land may be hilly and hard, and only be productive if we use the plough we have just invented. Prior to that we could only plant in alluvial valleys with soft easily planted ground.

New military technology to subjugate the existing inhabitants.

This mode of growth does not happen as often as it did once on a large scale in the Western world. There are not a lot of foreign territories left that we can freely invade without getting resistance from some existing inhabitants.

A variation occurs where we do not simply take over a new territory but find a new market in a new territory for a product made by us. We do not simply take over the territory but sell our products to it and/or set up production capacity within it with the inhabitants' agreement. We have to offer them products made by us that they want. Or we have to offer them production capacity that they want, which we set up to operate for mutual benefit.

In the post-colonialization era of globalization this is a more common situation than simply taking over another territory. Of course political pressures and short military involvements can help win business in other countries. The simple expansion still has a role.

The above growth mechanisms are not mutually exclusive. Geographically expanded territories and markets can also enjoy the benefits of economies of scale. These economies are a fundamental mechanism of technological advancement. Increases of productivity and globalization feed technological advancement and are fed by it. Such growth can and does continue indefinitely but there are limits.

Our primary focus has been on the working capital cycle and expansion of capacity the fixed investment cycle, which provides additional supply capacity. We also have the other cyclical investments contributing to growth:

- We develop a new product because we believe buyers will get more value from its functions than what it substitutes. This will hopefully attract more business.
- We develop new technology for the delivered product because we believe it will make our products deliver those functions better. This could be by being stronger, faster, longer lasting or more resource-efficient and thus attract more business.
- We develop new technology for the supply process because we believe it will increase throughput from a given size of plant and thus have more capacity, last longer, be less prone to out of operations.
- We reengineer our supply processes because we can reduce inventory, reduce labor, make new technology work more effectively.
- We discover a new oil field, mine, fishing area or other extraction resource and consume its production as long as it is economic to keep extracting. The infrastructure we build may aid the economics of other industries during and after the life of the extraction resource.

These investments are variously made to increase demand and/or increase supply capacity. They work in conjunction with expansions in geographic markets. We can do them without necessarily depending on assistance from outside forces.

Macroeconomic Effects

So far we have not thought too much about the influence of government-controlled or influenced mechanisms such as taxation, regulations, interest rates and currency rates. Again looking from the perspective of the operators of a company that is a target for a financial killing, we have seen our success in achieving growth as being determined by various factors. These include how attractive our products are to customers, how many additional customers we can attract by reducing price, adding functions, making the product more reliable and longer lasting.

We have considered the specific market sector for a product, whether a commodity or a designed product. We have considered how that market grows, how prices can spike upwards or downwards due to limitations in supply or demand and how, in the event of saturation, prices can collapse.

We have not thought much about the wider economy. Our company may be growing, as may be others. We may be feeding off their growth and vice versa. In addition other companies again may be declining, perhaps due to our competitive strength, and some of these will be going out of business. The total business of the economy as a whole may be increasing or declining as we grow.

We experience government-controlled or influenced mechanisms at the microeconomic level. As we embark on these various growth modes we will discover that macroeconomic factors can aid or obstruct us. Taxes, central bank interest rates, currency rates, government spending and regulations can all have big impacts on our business.

Governments and central banks make changes to these factors so as to impact on the wider economy based on how their macro-based models predict the total economy will behave. These models are complex, include many variables and equations, but are still major simplifications of the economy. Models exclude variables on the expectation that they are less important than the variables that are included. They are also at times scarce in the input data they require to operate and users must make assumptions as best as their knowledge and judgement makes possible.

Policy setters base their policies on macroeconomic analysis and we need to understand when they are likely to be effective and thus useful for our own analysis.

If there are limitations in the capabilities of macroeconomic analysis carried out by these bodies, we should understand these. Then we can focus on developing strategies and techniques which pick up where they stop.

We need to consider the success of forecasts using these models because the macro variable such as tax rates and interest rates imposed by government and central banks will be influenced by them and thus influence our business. We also need to understand the forecasts to see if they can be tools that directly help us or provide results that we bet against, confident that they will be wrong.

One thing that we should understand is that what is good for one sector is not necessarily good for another. The supporters of a particular sector may of course tell us that it is good for all, or if not good for all, good for the economy at large. A big rise in oil prices is not good for manufacturers of certain autos, possibly the most profitable ones to build. Nor is it good for developers of suburban real estate significant distances from the city where the suburbanites work.

Governments develop policies based on their forecasts. If the forecasts are wrong, due to limitations of their models, this may have results different from what they claim:

What is good for large corporations may be bad for small business.

What is good for some industry or market sectors may be bad for other sectors.

Governments can inadvertently cripple industries with misguided legislation or regulation. It is often much easier for them to do this to legitimate businesses than to criminal ones such as illegal drugs trafficking.

In a global economy, governments can disrupt business with trade policies in ways they sometimes fail to anticipate. Parties who seek to gain from a particular trade policy will seek to downplay potential damage to other parties and support models that help their case.

As long as we understand that models can produce outputs that are divergent from reality, we can gain from the opportunities presented by government policies based on erroneous macroeconomic models. Government policies, claimed as boosting the economy, may do the opposite while they enrich the government's supporters. Some of the best opportunities come from collapsing markets and prices.

Macroeconomic Analysis and Forecasting Models

What we need to know about the macroeconomy for the purposes of identifying opportunities for financial killings is:

- The current state of macro conditions that can have an impact on a business that we are targeting in some way or other for the killing.
- Forecasts of major indicators that indicate changes in these conditions.
- The confidence we can have in those forecasts and the potential variation from those forecasts.
- What changes that we could use in our analysis in preparation for a killing are out of scope of the particular forecasting system.

We have mentioned the Fed's model-based forecasts.

The US Federal Reserve US Economy model, FRB/US[1] is a large scale model of the economy with hundreds of equations and identities. These equations are built up from experience of macro movements. FRB/US is used to identify the impacts of various shocks on the economy in terms of how they affect the Federal Funds Rate, GDP Growth, the unemployment rate and inflation.

The Fed also uses a range of Dynamic Stochastic General Equilibrium (DSGE) models. These are models which are smaller than FRB/US and are easier to use for policy analysis by modifying components of the model to focus on particular areas of interest.

They are also more rigorously tied to economic theory than the FRB/US, which is more pragmatic in mixing equations based on observations with those based on microeconomic theory. The DSGE model also imposes cross-equation restrictions that FRB/US does not.

DSGE models split the macroeconomy into a number of economic units made up of groups of similar entities. The Fed EDO large scale DSGE model[2] includes:

- Slow growing (mostly consumption goods) final good sector, CBI
- Fast growing (capital goods) final good sector, KB
- Intermediate Goods Producers, CBI
- Intermediate Goods Producers, KB
- Residential Capital Owners
- Non-residential Capital Owners
- Consumer Durable Capital Owners
- Households
- Central bank

With DSGE models, each of these economic units follows equations based on microfoundations. The logic of these microfoundations is to base the behavior of macroeconomic units on microeconomic behavior. The microfoundation rules and equations are sufficiently general to be applicable to multiple industry and market sectors. Rather than deducing equations to simply align with observed data, we require them to follow business logic at the individual company level. This will avoid a change in government policy distorting the mathematical equations.

The microfoundations involve a concept called the Representative Agent. Because we may have millions of different entities in some of our groups that make up economic units, we pick on one to represent the rest.

This at first sounds absurd. Just considering intermediate goods producers, how does an agent representing a small business represent a large business? How does a business in one sector represent a business in a completely different sector? The back street foundry does not represent the steel rolling mill even though they both melt and shape metal. It certainly does not represent the flour mill even though they and the steel rolling mill are all intermediate good producers. Both raw materials and final outputs are totally different.

However, if we put aside all those issues, and we focus purely on market price for a given product type, then the concept is not quite so crazy. What the agent is then representing is the entity buying, selling or financing at the market price. That market price may be quite fluid so the representative agency will move from one company to another, deal by deal, second by second.

There are two aspects of market price here. The first relates to the products that our different units in the group do not share. The second relates to the products that our different units do share.

We do not have a few product types we have millions. But at any one time, prices of all these millions of products will form some kind of array. The shape of that array will change with time but much of it relatively slowly when the economy is in steady state. Products require other products as inputs and products sell in competition with other products. There are all kinds of relativities between prices, each relativity being definable by a set of rules and parameters. From Appendices 3 and 6 we know that supply costs, buyer risk premium, financing and variations on each of these across geoeconomic links will all contribute to price relativities.

There will be some kind of price relativity between the foundry equipment, the steel mill equipment and the flour mill equipment. There will be some kind of price relativity between the steel mill rolled steel joists and the metal castings. There will be some kind of price relativity between the joists or the castings and the flour bags.

The relativity linkages may not be direct. They may go through multiple steps and convoluted routes. A product may be made of physical assemblies and software. The assemblies may be made of components. The component may be made of refined materials. The refined materials may be made from processed minerals or processed vegetable fibers. The software may be made from modules. The modules may be made from code objects. The code objects will be made from code. Each step may be carried out by a different company subcontracting to the next company in the supply chain. The companies may be in different counties and the supply chain may move back and forth across the globe. No matter how complex the linkages are that feed price relativities, and no matter how visible or not they are, they do exist in the real world so can be treated as legitimate context for our model.

Following these relativities, each price will pull related prices when it moves one way or another. So when our representative agent makes a transaction and sets a price the related prices adjust accordingly to a greater or lesser degree. Of course the DSGE model does not include the rules and parameters of these relativities. We just need to know that out in the real microeconomic world this activity is going on.

Some might call this array of prices a general equilibrium. However, general equilibrium is a huge simplification of what is really happening in economics and finance at the micro or macro level. Nobel Memorial Prize winner, Friedrich Hayek described the pricing mechanism in a market economy as a System of Telecommunications. Here buyers and sellers communicated by setting prices and thus determined what was produced and by how much. Input in the way of a selected price from the person most knowledgeable about the value of a product or asset, whether buyer or seller, was fed into the supply system by this mechanism. Hayek explained this as why the market economy far out-performed central planning at delivering what people actually required. The committee that set prices and volumes worked in a room with little knowledge of what happened in the field

But such a pricing system is dynamic. Every communication adjusts prices in some way, large or small, even if it just holds a price for the moment while another unit of inventory or supply capacity is consumed.

We can now regard market price for a single product knowing that it connects to all the other products. The market price for a given product or asset will typically follow a price volume curve. Buyers who are not willing to pay the price will not buy. Buyers who are willing to pay more will buy. Buyers who are willing to pay just the market price, but no more, will set the price. Combined with those willing to pay more, these who are willing to pay just the market price will set the volume of sales.

These buyers are the representative agents for that group for that moment. Similarly suppliers will have a representative agent who will sell at the market price but not less. Financers of working capital, e.g. commercial banks, will provide finance for those cash flows that meet their standards for credit risk and decline those that do not.

Based on this our representative agent model makes some sense. However, it reinforces the situation that while the model may be conceptually sound in its reflection of micro level transactions amongst many agents, it does not explicitly model these. So it cannot itself analyze at the micro level. It cannot tell us anything about the individual company or firm other than the state of general variables such as interest rates and gross economic growth, which influence those companies and firms. While the model reflects the behavior of millions of buyers it does not forecast their behavior at the individual level.

We should also be aware that the timings of price changes may be totally different between different poducts even if they are related.

Within a sector, price may be moving in a relatively linear way during steady state conditions. But between sectors the price signal may be delayed. Our flour mill above may use metal components shaped in the foundry or in the steel rolling mill. However, significant price changes in their inputs may not come through to the flour mill for months or years. Conversely, an increase in the price of flower may flow into the price of food and on into the wages of workers making steel components but again these flows may be slow.

This time delay can lead to instability. Instead of a price signal being immediately responded by some adjustment to it may grow much larger before another sector responding gets the message. Hayek's system of telecommunications has recorded messages with delayed listenings as well as real time conversations.

Model Scope

It is important that DSGE models have the right types of economic units for a given purpose. These models are famous for failing to forecast the Global Financial Crisis and Great Recession. One reason is that many model designers did not see the need to include banks in their set of economic units. The logic here was that underlying economic forces were not dependent on finance. So finance as a sector responded to economic forces but did not have much power to change these forces. The key function of commercial banks to carry risk during lending activities was omitted.

We would suggest that financing is utterly critical to economics because of its effect on economies of scale, price and economic stability but we will put that aside for the moment.

A cynic might have said if the designers treated the finance sector as more than a background service, the government might need to regulate it more severely to avoid economic instability. Early users of DSGE were Real Business Cycle theorists. They were strong believers that governments should not interfere in the economy and used the models to support their theories. Explaining business cycles as being due to shocks (see below) and having the financial sector providing only a transaction processing role in the wider economy supported their beliefs.

For those of us with an interest in financial killings, this lack of focus on the financial sector is a big limitation of a forecasting model. The good thing is that its absence means the model does not identify in advance crises that create excellent financial killing opportunities.

However, the financial sector can be included as an active economic unit in a DSGE model. The Fed EDO model above includes a central bank, although its primary focus is to apply interest rate responses to inflation rather than to focus on lending risk.

The New York Fed has developed another DSGE model[3]. It has fewer economic units than the full EDO. These include households, final good producers, intermediate good produces, capital producers, banks, entrepreneurs and the government sector. This responds to leverage ratio constraints by increasing interest rate spread and thus the cost of lending after a shock, which reduces output.

The Bank of England has developed another DSGE model that focuses on provision of working capital by banks to the non-financial sector[4]. Here the requirement of banks to maintain leverage ratios at regulated levels creates shocks for producers due to reductions in working capital. This reduction in working capital causes persistent reductions in economic activity.

These models respond to high levels of loan failures, which reduce bank reserves, with availability reduction in loans.

Shocks

Another aspect of DSGE models is the role of shocks. Shocks occur all the time in business and come from many sources. Examples include natural disasters, epidemics, political crises, terrorist strikes, wars, system failures, the impacts of new products, discoveries of previously unknown material resources, unexpected declines of such resources, government policy shocks and technology change shocks.

In an equilibrium model, shocks rapidly dissipate and the system soon returns to normal conditions. We see this when we drop a stone into a still pond. There are ripples for a short time and then smooth water returns.

DSGE models use shocks to stimulate change in states of general equilibrium. Early versions of DSGE focused on demonstrating Real Business Cycle theory, which suggested that business cycles are caused by shocks, particularly technology shocks, leading to changes in productivity. The logic was that if productivity reduced due to a negative technology shock, people would lose the desire to work, at that particular time and wait for productivity to increase when presumably their efforts would be more worthwhile. This would lead to an increase in unemployment and a reduction in output!

Our own perspective is that while shocks do activate cycles we do not need them to do so. Investment cycles such as working capital, product development and technology development cycles, are self-regenerating, with no shocks required. As long as we keep getting our money back at the end of the relevant cycle with a satisfactory profit, we keep reinvesting and the cycle continues. With the right financial conditions, cycles will grow until they collapse (see Appendix 3). These collapses can create a shock of great severity without the need for technology or other external shocks. So shocks can create cycles but cycles can also create shocks.

DSGE Models and Financial Stability

We have mentioned the microfoundation and shock aspects of DSGE models because they have a particular significance for financial killings based on financial instability. There are two considerations:
- What they will probably be right about.
- What they might be wrong about because the model has not yet had the relevant component added.

- What are they not even looking at because it is outside the scope of the model.

What government agencies and central banks believe will happen is important even if it is wrong. In fact it is important especially if it is wrong. If we understand how their policies will lead to certain events happening, which they have not seen coming, then we can benefit. The economic and financial environment before the GFC is a classic case. Governments and central banks believed severe financial crises were a thing of the past in suitably managed economies. Their failure to see the GFC coming created a series of excellent opportunities for financial killings for those suitably prepared.

Government agencies and central banks also believed that economies would recover from crises much faster than they have done during the Great Recession. They believed that they just needed to flood the markets with cash at low interest rates and the global economic system would pick up speed again. This expectation has created continuing opportunities for financial killings of the types helped by depressed markets and excess capital.

Newer models, which explicitly include the behavior of banks and the impact they have on the wide economy should do better in these areas. Models get better and better as people learn from unforeseen events and extend the models to allow for the newly discovered dynamics. The number of different approaches to modelling the impact of bank leverage is an indication of the awareness that central banks have developed for this issue.

However, successful these models are though, they are essentially policy tools. The central bank wants to influence macroeconomic variables such as interest rates, inflation rates, unemployment levels and growth. It does an analysis, makes adjustments to its control variables and monitors responses over the following weeks and months.

These are not supposed to be a real time control systems where changes are identified and rapidly responded to as might apply to maintain the stability of a nuclear power plant, oil refinery or power system. DSGE models are based on an assumption of general equilibrium. This is at best an extreme simplification of economic reality. However, it provides a mathematical framework that is solvable so is useful providing we bear in mind its limitations. General equilibrium assumes a steady state condition, which is disrupted by shocks. This is at best a partial view of economic reality and one which specifically ignores the driving force for working capital and other investment cycles, that is the recurring opportunity for profit.

In a real economy, volumes and prices are changing all the time according to changes in supply and demand (remember Hayek's System of Telecommunications above). Steady state in markets requires liquidity and a smooth relationship between price and volume. This means prices and volumes can move back and forth along a curve without destabilizing jolts when buyers leave in a panic or enter in a frenzy. Buyers and sellers can have their respective deal or no deal prices and the representative agent role moves between them.

In the diagram below, similar to those seen in Appendices 2 and 3, only small changes in price, $\Delta P1$, occur in response to moderate changes in demand volume for most of the curve. This means no radical change in buyer type is required to restore equilibrium. A general equilibrium model should produce reasonable results where the slope is moderate as the system can respond to moderate changes in demand in a stable manner.

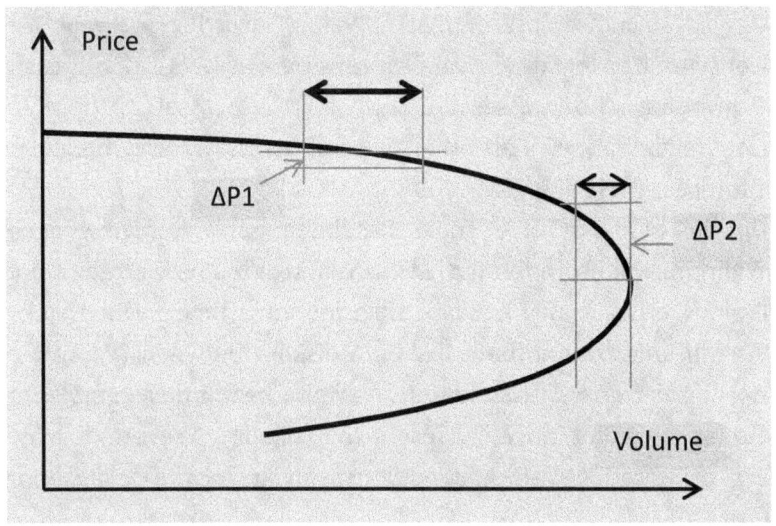

This applies until we get near the nose and then small changes in volume result in large changes in price, ΔP2. Near the nose, general equilibrium is no longer valid. The nose is the zone of price collapse. Up to this point the market offers steady state conditions, where growth (or decline) can occur incrementally each working capital cycle. We do not need for this purpose to know the details within working capital cycles, just whether at the end of the cycle we have grown or contracted and made a profit.

When we get near the nose, everything changes. We are approaching price collapse where the rules of steady state cease to apply. A normal movement along the curve due to some short term change, e.g. a shock, can, instead of returning to its previous position or nearby, can go past the point of no return. We go from linear responses to change to highly non-linear response to change.

The pricing array relativities apply when a sector or subsector goes into a price collapse situation and incurs a major price change for a product or asset. This price change can pull other sectors or subsectors that were previously quite stable into the instability. The classic case occurs when a financial firm holds a lot of a particular asset that incurs a loss of market value, incurring a threat to its solvency and/or liquidity. The firm sells other assets to raise cash to and in doing so depresses the price for these assets. These then create demands to sell off other types of assets. Macro models may not forecast these situations.

In the model after a shock has been applied, a new general equilibrium will be generated. In the real world a new array of prices will emerge but it may not be stable for some time. When stability returns in due course there will be a disjoint between the new one and its predecessor. Its conditions may also bear little resemblance to the ones preceding price collapse if the collapse is severe. It may be years or decades before conditions similar to pre-collapse ones return.

For parties with an interest in monitoring instability situations that DSGE models miss, other tools are needed. This is not a criticism of DSGE models. In most technical fields we use different tools for different purposes. Ocean engineers will have one wave model for analyzing the continuing wave-driven movement of sand and shingle along a coast over a period of years to block shipping channels. They will have another model for analyzing freak waves in the open sea that could capsize a containership, demolish an off-shore oil platform or wind farm. Power system engineers will have one wave model for analyzing steady state conditions on a large network. They will have another for analyzing sudden system collapses triggered by a local plant outage in a hurricane or by an equipment failure.

DSGE models analyze at the macro scale and typically use time intervals of one or three months between estimations. This is reasonable as they are designed to test policies by implementing them in the model then using it to forecast changes over several years. If we want to track changes, which occur at the specific market sector or subsector level, and can occur much more rapidly, we need other tools.

The tools need to focus on sectors and subsectors which affect a company or firm of interest. These include those changes that appear when some small volume variation occurs but one which reaches a capacity or demand limit. The financial elite build their own tools and methodologies for this purpose.

1   "The FRB/US Model: A Tool for Macroeconomic Policy Analysis" Flint Brayton, Thomas Laubach, and David Reifschneider

2   "Documentation of the Estimated, Dynamic, Optimization-based (EDO) Model of the US Economy: 2010 Version" Hess T, Chung, Michael T. Kiley and Jean-Philippe Laforte

3   "The FRBNY DSGE Model" Marco Del Negro, Stefano Eusepi, Marc Giannoni, Argia Sbordone, Andrea Tambalotti, Matthew Cocci, Raiden Hasegawa, M. Henry Linder, Federal Reserve Bank of New York Staff Reports

4   "Understanding the macroeconomics of working capital in the United Kingdom" Emilio Fernandez-Corugedo, Michael McMahon, Stephen Millard and Lukasz Rachel

APPENDIX 5: MORE ON SPECIFIC CYCLES

We have briefly mentioned the different business cycles that can contribute to financial killing opportunities. Some of these are useful to understand in greater detail. Individual types of cycles can be complex, affected by many factors and have combined effects. The more we understand about what is likely to affect their timing or size, the better we can use them to our advantage.

These factors can vary the timing and the size of a cycle peak or trough but they do not stop the cycle. People who do not follow these factors can easily think the cycle is not relevant or non-existent. They may think it is a thing of the past, made irrelevant due to advances in technology or markets. They are then taken by surprise when the cycle moves into a critical phase.

Different types of cycle have different impacts on different sectors. If we are looking at instability in a given sector, or subsector, we need to understand how important a particular type of cycle is likely to be for that sector. We also need to understand how such cycles combine with other cycles. A particular combination may create the rogue wave that creates chaos in that sector or subsector and thus create opportunity for financial killings.

Working Capital Cycle

There are many variations of working capital cycles in terms of the sequence of order, delivery and payment. Payment may be made after use for a period, on proof of performance, on proof of delivery, and on order. From the perspective of stability of this cycle, we are very interested in the period of time between payment by the supplier for materials, labor, services, etc, and the time when benefits flow to the customer. There are various points in between, e.g., shipment of parts, delivery to customer, completion of testing, usage for a certain period. There are various part payment or full payment possibilities at such points.

This period of time requires financing to cover the supplier's costs of delivering the product. That financing may be provided in part or full by the buyer, by the supplier or by a third party financing firm. If the supplier or a third party provides it, buyers will tend to buy greater volume of product. This role of financing in expanding sales affects price and economies of scale. Ultimately it can have a major role on stability of the working capital cycle. The stability of the working capital cycle and the involvement of its financing are described in Appendix 3.

Instability of the working capital cycle provides great opportunities for financial killings. The working capital cycle is the single most critical cycle for parties seeking opportunities from price collapse. It can also be influenced should any of the other cycles, or combinations of them, go into a downturn. These downturns lead to pressures on key components of the working capital cycle including price, cash flow, liquidity and profitability, which can trigger its collapse.

These components of the working capital cycle are described in more detail in Appendix 2.

Typical cycle periods are from days to months from order to payment after delivery. Extended payment periods of months or years can be added to this with hire purchase or leasing arrangements if financing is provided for use of the product before final payment.

The working capital cycle is typically financed by commercial banks or shadow banks carrying out commercial banking activities. Disruption of other investment cycles can cause turmoil and extensive change of ownerships in production assets. But disruption of commercial banking activities will stop those production assets from working and large numbers of workers from getting paid

Typically the working capital cycle is the only business cycle that is predictably regular in its frequency. The others are themselves combinations of many smaller cycles so cycle lengths can vary.

Inventory Cycle

The inventory cycle occurs because suppliers risk losing sales and market share to competitors if they cannot deliver quickly. Quickly for one sector and set of customers may mean in minutes but not hours. For another sector and set of customers it may mean weeks but not months. To ensure they have stock ready for delivery in minutes, or weeks as the case may be, the suppliers build up their inventory, which may be quite costly.

When supply exceeds demand as a result of too many suppliers building up their inventory, and/or demand dropping off, prices have to drop. If there is a lot of excess inventory it will take time to be cleared and supplies with cash flow problems and who have to sell will drive prices down and if enough start competing for sales, prices will collapse. This applies for autos, oil, financial securities and others.

If there is only excess inventory, not excess capacity, prices are likely to collapse to a smaller degree than for the case when there is excess supply capacity (see fixed investment cycle below). Suppliers can reduce output without reducing throughput below economic levels for the fixed investment, inventory can be run down. But it can still be very painful and, if liquidity is low, fatal for businesses.

Fixed Investment Cycle

This is often referred to as the Juglar cycle, the Trade cycle or The Business cycle.

Supply capacity is our capacity to deliver our company's product, whatever that product may be, whether goods or service. It is the capacity of the factory production line, the excavator in a mine, the service van, the truck, the ship, the phone network fiber optic circuit or mobile phone tower. We define it by the maximum quantity of product we can supply to customers in a given period or via a given delivery: 1000 autos per week, two tons per scoop, ten technicians and equipment available at a site for service calls, 10 tons per load,

18,000 containers per ship, 50,000 calls per hour, 40GB per second etc.

This is usually a physical capacity but where such a physical limit does not apply, it might be one set by some safety limit. In a banking environment, one supply capacity which determines the amount of lending that we can do is capital. For example, if we have capital of $10 billion we might be able to take deposits from depositors and lend up to $120 billion. Beyond that we exceed the permitted leverage ratio. If some of our borrowers do not pay us back and they exceed the normal % allowed for bad debts, our capital will be reduced. We need to raise more capital or can cut back on loans made to customers to restore the leverage ratio.

Infrastructural Investment Cycle

With infrastructural facilities we typically have limited choice where to build it them. By contrast, industrial plant can usually be built in a variety of sites. The ground may need to be flat and stable. It may need to be on or near a major transport route. But such requirements usually have options. We pick a site and then design the plant much as we would for another similar site.

Infrastructure location tends to be dictated to by geography including terrain and the accumulated structures of centuries of human development. A road may need to go over a particular mountain pass or across a river at the most economic location for a bridge. A rail link may need to go through a tunnel under the mountain. A port will usually need to go on a deep water harbor and/or at a river mouth. Often a lot of consulting, planning and seeking of approvals is required. There may be issues with connecting to existing infrastructure. We cannot usually build a standard unit elsewhere and move it on site. Perhaps we can install components but generally we are dealing with purpose-built facilities with long assessment and design times. Payback periods can be in decades.

Politics also often has a big role. Infrastructure may be publicly or privately owned according to type and to prevailing political beliefs. If public health is the dominant driver, as with sewerage systems, it is more likely to be publically owned. If there are revenue-earning opportunities, as with water supply or toll roads, private ownership may enter the picture. This creates opportunities for the politically well-connected. It may help reduction in public investment if politicians see it more logical to have new developments done by private operators than taxation-based investment.

Like real estate, infrastructure requires a lot of resources in the way of skilled manpower. This may drift away when construction levels are low, as with lot of heavy equipment. If there is a large expansion of infrastructure, this may take time to build up over multiple companies, particularly if the equipment has extended lead times. While the buildup occurs, the construction companies who can deliver projects may have low levels of competition and prices may be high. As more companies build resources, prices should ease. Then as the bulk of a project or projects are completed, there will be an excess of equipment and manpower seeking work. This will drive prices down to the point that companies cut their resources back to the level required for maintenance work.

Infrastructural developments may incur long delays once their need has been identified because of the long lead time that often occurs. Their need for completion may become much more severe because of these delays. When they are delivered they can have a significant impact on capacities. This can in turn have significant financial impact on activities dependent on infrastructure. Land values may increase rapidly when transport or environmental services are upgraded (see Appendix 6). Certain types of businesses may become much more economically sound. Other businesses may then incur competition that can put them out of business.

Real Estate Cycle

There is an underlying property cycle associated with growth of population and an expanding need for housing. Steady growth of population is not necessarily followed by steady growth of house construction. The price of existing housing needs to be high enough to justify extensive construction of new houses. So we tend to have intensive periods of construction when prices reach that level. This continues until too many new houses have been built for available customers. Then prices drop, which panics some owners who may have high levels of debt and prices collapse. They stay down until excess houses have been populated and the cycle starts again. The prices of older houses fall with the prices of the new ones.

This gets more complex when we add other cycles to the mix than simple population growth:

Other local industry and market sectors will have their own growth/decline cycles. This will cause populations to expand and contract, increasing and reducing demand for housing. This adds to the natural cycle caused by population growth.

The supply of skilled builders also moves in a cycle. When there is a lot of construction going on, construction companies hire workers who may have been underemployed, and wages increase. Young people see building as a well-paid career and undertake training to join the work force. The delay in expanding workforce capacity means construction is slow to start, restricting house supply and driving up real estate prices further. When prices collapse, and the rate of construction drops off, some workers will leave the construction industry. This will delay the industry's ability to respond to future surges in demand.

The above cycles impact on the real estate cycle for a specific locality. This is the Area Price Relativity Change Cycle, which tracks how that locality has a particular level of price relative to other localities is determined by geoeconomic factors. See Appendix 6. These compound the local factors.

New Product Version or Process Cycle

We are talking here about using an existing, proven technology platform in new applications. It may be a new product - a mouse trap using electronic detection and control to switch on and target a laser beam to kill the mouse. Or it may be some variation of a product already developed using the same technology platform. We build a bigger metal spring-driven mouse trap large enough to catch rats.

Or it might be a new supply process, again a variation of a process already built using the technology platform: A change in sequence of operations, additional storage near bottlenecks, enhanced automation; a wider bridge to let more traffic through or a smaller tank to mix smaller batches of chemicals are examples.

Design of new products and processes is typically much shorter in time than development of new technology platforms (see below). It is similar to development of minor upgrades to the platform. We are already dealing with something which we know works effectively in a different product and which we know how to put into practice. Typically we also enhance the platform when we apply it to new products or processes. Each time we do so we test and refine the platform in some way so that it occurs in close coordination with minor upgrades.

Construction may of course take years longer than design for facilities like large factories, chemical plants or nuclear power plants. And then it may take years of operations before new designs are fully proven against events whose effect may take a long period to eventuate like big storms, floods, earthquakes. Development of such facilities requires first getting them working effectively in normal conditions and only then seeing whether they withstand the forces of nature over time.

In the case of products, quite small enhancements can often make dramatic differences to market acceptance. A 5% increase in product functionality might be the functionality that is needed for 60% of the market to buy the product. Conversely previous increases, which might have been ten times as extensive, but left out that particular enhancement, may have made almost no difference to sales. At the edge, small changes can be very important. But the rise and fall of cycles can hide changes so that we may not know what new function actually gives the product its sales boost.

The market response to a new product of course may be very different. Two restaurants may use the same kitchen equipment but one restaurant may be full every night and the other nearly empty. Two mobile phone manufacturers may use identical or near identical equipment and software platform but one may sell ten times the number of units as the other. There are always different factors in how products are applied in different situations.

New Technology Platform Cycle, Major and Minor

Technology has always been an integral part of business. People use tools to produce things more efficiently than they can produce things without them. In addition, people specialize in the use of certain tools and gain expertise that makes them more efficient than others with less training and practice in using those tools. The butcher has his unique tools and expertise as do the baker and candlestick maker. People's productivity with a particular set of tools usually follows an experience curve, which is a type of economy of scale curve.

As we use tools over the years and increasingly understand the things we can do with them, we think about how we might make them better. We experiment with changes to materials, components, to arrangements of tools and to the methods, processes and systems with which we use them. Thus we develop the underlying technology platform our tools use.

Periodically we make major changes to the technology platform. We replace the stone-tipped spear with the bronze spear then the bronze spear with the iron spear. We replace the cog ship with the more maneuverable caravel ship. We replace the lateen caravel ship with a faster square sale caravel ship. The function remains the same but there is a key gain in some aspect of the technology.

We can make small incremental changes to the platform, refining the lateen sale perhaps. This is usually less costly and less risky. But periodically we need to make a more fundamental change to the platform if we are to make big productivity gains.

Changes to develop a new technology platform starting from initial ideas on what the underlying science of a technology now makes possible to full operational condition take time (typically years) and money. We thus have an initial investment, initial revenue as the product using the new technology is released, then we have increasing revenues as the technology is proved to be dependable and to offer new benefits.

The new platform is technically better in some way than the old one – faster, lighter, stronger, more corrosion resistant, uses cheaper raw materials, easier to work with, or just uses a better method – more accurate, more reliable, quicker, more easily learnt. However, we must rebuild the goods or service with the new technology platform, which takes time and resources.

Typically there are early applications that get the biggest payoff from the new advantage, big enough to charge them a price that can support development costs spread over a low volume. As additional applications follow they can be delivered at a lower price. This is due to accumulating economies of scale and building of experience so they do not need such a big economic benefit for a limited number of buyers as applies to the early applications.

The Major technology cycle involves stages such as:

- Assessing the potential of the new platform to achieve commercial advantages through the new platform's technical superiority.
- Picking initial application(s) which will achieve maximum commercial advantage early in the development cycle.
- Designing and building the application(s) in prototype form.
- Testing the prototype in the market.
- Refining the application(s) based on that feedback.
- Putting it into production.

This cycle can suffer many failures and be very expensive. It brings many companies down, even if they have succeeded in it multiple times before. Common reasons for failure include:

- Overestimating the benefits offered to potential customers by the new platform.
- Taking too long to bring it to a reliable, usable form.
- Undermining the perceived quality of the existing platform before the new one is ready so that customers move to alternatives.
- Making it too difficult for users of the existing platform to transfer their processes to the new platform.

The Minor technology cycle involves stages such as:

- Developing the next group of applications based on commercial potential and experience gained with the first application(s). The platform is now proven in terms of capability in other area(s).
- Developing better application support based on experience, better documentation and training, simplification.

Even developments which ultimately turn out to be very successful can have difficult periods in early stages. New technology is developed to do some task of the old technology much better, typically ten times as well – faster, stronger or for longer. But often, at least in its first version(s), it does not do all the tasks of the old technology well. It may need a lot of skilled handling by the user to do them. Often it does not do them at all. Early users tend to be technically advanced people who can create tools to fill in gaps.

As consumers we may be familiar with this. New personal computer operating systems such as Microsoft Windows Vista and Windows 8 made major changes but removed the previous interface, making some users very unhappy. Following versions returned previous capabilities after much user pain. Very often minor technology platform upgrades are driven by user feedback pointing out key capabilities in the old system. These have not been brought over to the first version of the major upgrade. Their absence could be because the developers did not see the necessity or did not have time to include them.

Experienced users of the previous generation find the new system is difficult to learn. It is also unreliable and inefficient at carrying out the work processes they have developed for the old system. Newer (typically younger) users do not care because they have never been that familiar with the old processes. They care less about reliability and efficiency of work processes because they find new technology much more interesting than established work processes. They know where their career development lies.

The initial difficulties of early versions can lead to catastrophic results for certain customers who rely on it. The difficulty that users experienced in earlier technology have understanding the new on can hide its limitations. The familiar patterns have gone and they do not see odd behavior. To them it is all odd.

For the business implementing a new technology platform, expecting great performance from the new platform or from a significant upgrade missing capabilities can have dire results. Key things necessary for a particular business environment may not have made to into the delivered version.

A variation of this occurs where the functions are developed but are not reliable. Or they work effectively on their own but do not get effectively integrated with other parts of the business process. The architecture of integration may have been started but the critical components may not be in place.

This can have a huge impact on process reengineering during private equity buyouts. If the efficiencies gained required to make the business profitable do not arrive, the profitability of the project may not be delivered. This killing will not be made by the initial PE firm but by the one that buys them out, and implements the technology when it is ready. Any business depending on new technology to maintain its competiveness and profitability may suffer seriously when a new version fails to deliver the required advantages. Arriving a year or two later may be too late.

We have discussed the role of technology for creating economic shocks in Appendix 4. Technology can have large impacts on economics but it does not necessarily do so quickly. Technology developments take time and their uptake can take longer. What can take extremely short periods of time, however, are combinations of technology. Combinations have historically had big impacts, with advances in one of agriculture, transport, commerce or industry triggering advances in one or more of the others.

Combinations of Technology

Technology has advanced in cycles over millennia in a number of areas, each feeding the others.

A given technology advance does not typically occur in isolation. We mentioned in Appendix 4 how combinations of technology can lead to large shocks.

- Agrarian technology started with animal husbandry, plantable grains, grain storage and aqueducts.

- Commercial technology started with contracts, bills of exchange, money changing, sea loans, letters of credit, deposit banking, insurance.
- Industrial technology started with hand tools, craft specialization, mechanization (wagon wheels, pulleys, windmills, waterwheels, etc.).
- With the introduction of carbon fuels for machinery, industrial technology continued with steam engines, internal combustion engines, electrification, mass production, automation, process integration.
- Information systems have developed through clay, fabrics, paper, printing, photography and electronic information.
- Transport technology has developed the use of pack animals, timber span bridges, roads, wagons, stone arc bridges, canals, rail, steel bridges. On the water transport side, galleys, sailing ships and motor ships. These tended to take long periods of time to be developed and to proliferate. For example, the medieval cog type of sailing ship lasted for centuries prior to being replaced by the caravel. The caravel opened up the Indian Ocean and East Indies to Portuguese explorers, prior to the caravel itself being replaced by the carrack.

Each major development such as these in a given technology changes the economics of the technology. Wealth increases significantly for those who benefit. Each of these key developments may be separated by generations, even centuries. Each is proliferated around the world via trade routes such as the Silk Road and the Indian Ocean, again sometimes taking decades, sometimes centuries.

Developments in one technology group often stimulate them in others. An advance in commercial technology might dramatically increase trade, financing developments in transport technology. This then leads to further increases in wealth, which will reinforce the developments in commercial technology. If a new technology in one group is already under away, just needing a big customer base to expand it, the stimulation may be a trigger for an explosion as the two technologies combine and feed each other.

With these developments, the entire structure of society typically changes. The wealth generated needs to be protected so security and military forces are funded on a growing scale. For example, the development of grain storage reinforces the need for military forces to protect the store from raiders. Military and political leaders grow more powerful and society gets more hierarchical.

Transport gets progressively lower in cost with economies of scale. Engines get more efficient. Container and tankers get larger with associated economies of scale. These change the balance between shopping and shipping. See Appendix 6.

Each advance typically opens up a set of new business streams with their own financial cycles.

We mention these fragments of historical development because they highlight a consistent pattern in terms of investment cycle life. Technologies develop in waves, which ripple out across the world and waves in different groups combine. What has changed is that once these major developments appeared centuries apart and were then refined over generations. Then they appeared decades apart and then years apart but with the internet they evolve far faster.

Extractive Cycle

Often extractive cycles lead to a combination of a one-off pulse generated by the extractive industry itself, or series of such pulses, and self-generating cycles from other businesses. Many self-generating businesses cannot get established if it takes several years before they pay for the infrastructure they need to function. Or if it needs multiple businesses to share that infrastructure and they are unlikely to start at the same time. Having an extractive business pay for the initial infrastructure provides a nursery environment for the establishment of businesses which themselves could not fund costly facilities.

We develop a mine to extract mineral ore and the ore price and ease of extraction justifies the cost of building a deep water wharf to transport the minerals via sea to their markets. Smaller businesses who could not justify building such a wharf - fishing, tourism, agriculture and horticulture perhaps – use the wharf and pay a portion of the wharf operating and maintenance costs.

This goes both ways. The ore price drops and/or the easily extracted ore runs out. Now the wharf construction could not now be justified and even operations and maintenance are too expensive for the mine on its own. However, the wharf's capital cost has been paid for by the mine in its better times and the other businesses now contribute to operations and maintenance costs.

With multiple parties sharing infrastructure, second phases of the extractive business may not need to be so profitable. That lower margin may be due to lower prices, to lower levels of productivity associated with lower extraction rates, to higher variable costs associated with digging deeper, sailing further, hauling further or pumping harder. An example is the mining of a mineral in lower concentration than the concentration available when first mined. The profit per ton may be less but if there ae other parties contributing to infrastructure costs, the mines can survive at that gross lower profit margin.

The mine in good times has created a nursery environment for the other businesses to grow to the point where they are self-sustaining. Once they are self-sustaining they permit the mine to operate in less favorable conditions.

Continued extraction in a new cycle may be possible on an economic basis if the price increases (perhaps as part of the material's commodity price cycle) or new technology makes it possible to extract the product at a lower cost. Until we decide to invest in that new cycle we have a one-off pulse of investment and return on investment.

Extractive cycles can also be good for technology development. For example, the commercial imperative for early steam engines, the killer app, was to pump mines, a relatively simple, static application. As the technology was developed, it was used in manufacturing and then trains and ships.

Leverage Cycle

The leverage cycle[1] is an important cycle for financial killings. Other cycles combine to create a financial killing opportunity but the leverage cycle is often critical to the timing of that opportunity. The leverage ratio for assets or companies is that of the amount borrowed to buy an asset, e.g. a house, to the amount of equity provided by the borrower. The leverage ratio varies through the leverage cycle. When lenders and borrowers are confident about rising asset values, they become comfortable with low deposits and high leverage ratios. When confidence drops for some reason, such as high levels of credit failures, investors start selling assets and the asset price drops.

In the case below, the leverage cycle precedes price for an asset. When lenders become concerned about credit failures they cut back on lending, forcing buyers to pull out of the market and this then affects the price. With an absence of buyers who need financing to borrow, the price plummets. Eventually when credit failures have receded after a difficult period, lenders increase lending again and asset prices start to rise.

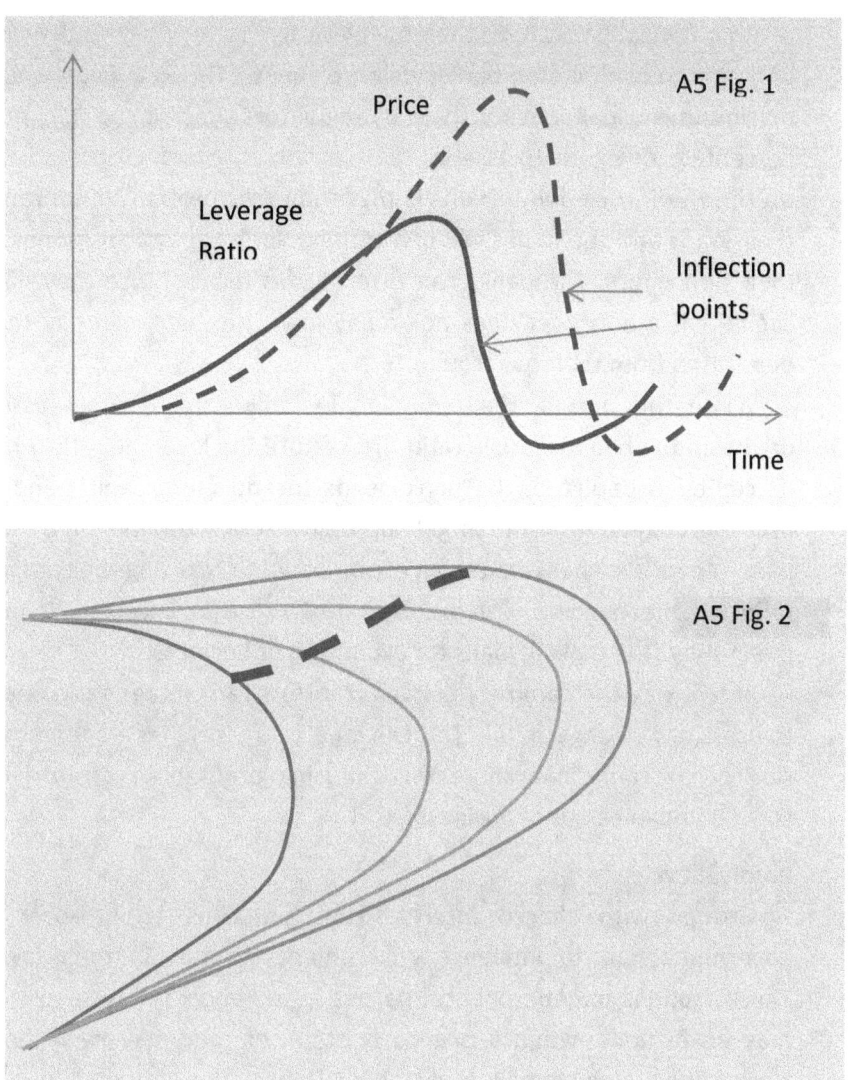

The price/time curve here is connected to the price/volume curves in Fig. 4 in Appendix 2. But instead of doubling back after reaching a peak volume, it moves in one direction with time. The dotted line curve in Fig. 2 above indicates a progression from low leverage (lower curve) to high leverage (upper curve).

Commercial banks have their own leverage ratio, which is the ratio of assets to capital on a bank's balance sheet. This is a value whose maximum is usually set for them by regulators specifying a minimum percentage of capital to assets.

The risk incurred in banking is that some borrowers will not repay their loans and the banks will be not be able to repay that money to their depositors. The banks can take on this risk because they have capital. If a borrower does not repay loan, the bank can pay their depositors from their own capital.

When this occurs, the reduction in bank capital versus assets drives up the bank leverage ratio. To restore the leverage ratio when its capital is depleted, the bank needs to add more capital and/or reduce outstanding loans to get the ratio back below the limit. This may mean the bank cuts back on loans to existing businesses, reducing the ongoing working capital of those businesses. It may mean they stop making loans for expansion of businesses.

In this way the commercial bank transfers its leverage ratio issues to users of working capital. This can create stresses in the operational side of the non-financial sector, reducing profitability and driving some companies out of business.

Political Cycle

Groups with shared interests form factions to be part of governments or to influence governments to rule in their favor. These factions may be political parties in a democratic system, they may be factions within a one party state, or they may be factions supporting a king or military dictator. The relative strengths of such factions shift as situations change and their supporters are happy or unhappy with their shares of the economic pie.

Political parties are funded by those who think that those parties will protect and advance their interests. That includes their personal interests, the interests of the economic group or class they identify with, and the interests of those who may be outside of that group but who may be allies for some reason or other. It also includes a third group. That includes those whom they perceive as deserving of a better deal for cultural or religious reasons than would be dealt out by another political party. And politicians attempt to convince a wider group again that they are in that third group.

The key driver of the cycle is that factions in power use their power for the benefit of their supporters while pretending to use it for a wide benefit. Eventually reality shows through and they are replaced by another faction. The new faction takes power, reversing some or all of the previous adjustments and gain approval of the wider group for doing so,. Naturally as they do this they favor their own supporters most. They keep improving things for their own supporters claiming to offer benefits for a wide group while actually delivering them to its own supporters. This continues until the reality of the favorable treatment to some and less favorable to others again shows through and a new faction, usually the first one regains power. The cycle starts again

What varies the length of the cycle is the expertise of the politicians. There may be a regular election cycle applying in some kind of democratic system and here the aim is to maintain the political cycle length for multiple election cycles. In other systems groups may be much more fluid. They may be factions surrounding a king, dictator or military junta which awards civilian power to its faction of choice at a given time. They may be groups within the wider military and security forces who have economic interests, direct or through providing protection to civilian businesses. The faction needs to keep the populace from rebelling and threatening the realm.

Whatever the system, talented politicians can convince groups of people that they are helping them when they are actually disadvantaging them. This is a complex game that is fed by diverse business cycles and feeds back to diverse business cycles. The interactions create numerous opportunities for financial killings.

From the business person's perspective, when our faction gets into power it protects and advances our interests to a greater or lesser degree. Some groups always benefit more than others. Those who benefit less may eventually come to believe another party will do better for them and transfer their votes to them. The other party comes into power and starts to protect and advance the interests of those it represents. How long this takes will depend on the skill of the politicians. If things go wrong and the benefit-less camp suffers more than they think is fair, politicians may still be able to blame the other party.

Alternatively they may convince the voters that, yes through no fault of the government, times are hard but they would be far worse if the other party got into power. Smart politicians can benefit from catastrophes, even if their policies created or permitted them. They declare war on the problem, call for large amounts of money to pay for the solution, and feed that money through their own supporters to deliver the solution.

The left/right divide is always good material for politicians to exploit. The excesses of the rich can periodically be highlighted to disgust the voters in the middle classes as can the excesses of the poor.

The rich spend on large houses, exotic autos and boats, high fashion clothing and accessories, expensive restaurants, large and ostentatious parties in exotic and public locations. This is generally accepted as natural behavior displaying success and influence. If we are seen to be successful we are more likely to be entrusted with powerful positions, big projects or investment funds. And the more success we display the better. Driving a four cylinder Mercedes is more convincing than driving a four cylinder Toyota. Driving a six cylinder Mercedes is more convincing again, and driving an eight cylinder Mercedes is even more convincing than that. Occupation of these tiers in the pecking order implies access to resources that can help or damage those we can encounter.

However, conspicuous expenditure can earn the anger of the voters if they see the rich enjoying these pleasures after causing a financial disaster, which wipes out pension funds or middle class jobs.

The poor in turn earn the anger of voters by having multiple children to earn welfare, spending their money on alcohol, drugs and gambling instead of good food for those children, and letting them go to school with little food and poor clothing.

Adept politicians can point to extreme examples of behavior of either class as a reason to implement programs curtailing the economic advantages of their chosen villains. Increase income taxes or slash welfare as is applicable. They can also point to the criminal activities of their selected targets. The rich use fraud to boost their wealth when legal methods fail. The poor use street theft. Both are good for interesting the voters in tougher laws and police resources.

But politics is not always as simple as left and right. Political divisions come in many shapes. It may simply be the pro-business party vs the other party, which may be pro-worker, pro-poor peasant, pro-environment, etc. But it is not always this simple. Some business sectors are more supportive of egalitarian parties than others. For example, the Construction sector may benefit from a government that supports low income housing or building of public roads. Some businesses in sectors such as tourism and renewable energy are environmentalists.

Different sectors also have very different perspectives on what is good for business. A software developer in California may have a very different perspective from a mining company in Nevada. A plane builder in Washington State may have a very different perspective from a corn grower in Iowa. Major risks will be different for each and what they can do to manage those risks will be different. Their requirements from politicians will thus be different.

Another political differentiator is that between suppliers for commodity markets and suppliers of purpose designed products. When producing for a commodity market, our competitiveness depends on cost because the price is the same for all. Our focus in investment goes into reducing variable costs.

When producing a purpose designed product there is typically more tolerance by customers for price variation and associated cost variation, sometimes a lot. What is critical is functionality. There can be a big downside risk for offering a less functional product than our competitors as we could slide into a lower level of product attractiveness – losing price and volume. There can be a big upside risk for offering a more functional product than our competitors as we could slide into a higher lower level of product attractiveness – increasing price and volume. It is worth paying more for many types of products if this can move product attractiveness in the right direction.

The difference is on the type of risk where we focus our efforts. If variable costs are critical, we may be very interested in minimizing wages. This might mean fighting unionization and the legislation of minimum wages. If usability and incremental functionality is critical, we will probably pay staff a premium for skills in product development and support. We will be keen to develop relationships with people in other countries to attract talented staff, expand markets and increase economies of scale.

Both political parties in the US are supported by the financial sector and take their interests into account. Even if politicians did not actively promote the interests of the financial sector, it would dangerous to their political survival to act in ways that risk the survival of that sector. In Appendix 4 we mentioned how commercial banks, for example, are closely involved in the decision making of producers of goods at the working capital cycle level. Other types of financial firms are closely involved in capacity expansion, product and process development and technology advancement. All of this slows down if the financial sector is not making its share (as much as 40%) of overall profits.

And failure of even one significantly sized financial firm can lead to ripple effects that might damage many more. If the ripple continues, Main Street firms that employ tens of millions of people may have financing problems. Then they may have cash flow problems, then problems with suppliers, then problems delivering to customers, then problems paying their staff. Those staff vote for politicians so need to be treated carefully. Whatever interests politicians work for they must always be seen to be in favor of jobs and growth.

Stimulation of the economy is a good thing to do before an election. Promote the message that things are improving due to good management through a difficult period (caused by wastage and mismanagement by an earlier government). The middle classes will not want to threaten the stability of the recovery by voting for those who might disrupt the economy and lose the gains that follow the pain.

Tax reduction is also always a good thing to promote. We reduce the taxes (on our supporters) in the interests of stimulating the economy for the benefit of all. This is very credible because tax reductions do genuinely stimulate the economy. Of course different tax reductions stimulate different parts of the economy and their impact is greater or lesser under different circumstances. See Appendix 4, Macroeconomic Effects on Stability.

The political cycle is complex because political policies do not instantly and neatly produce the benefits for the greater good that are claimed by politicians. There are delays in implementation, delays in taking effect, inefficiencies, siphoning off of funds and resources by allies and opportunists, and unforeseen (or foreseen but not discussed) consequences which counteract the policy. All of these have their respective time frames so the end result of policies may occur years after their introduction.

Lobbyists and lawyers write the actual legislation. This frees up politicians to keep close to their funders and to sell the benefits of package. Research shows that we only need to cater to the top 30% of income earners. The rest are too powerless to worry about. Many of these people are conscious of their powerlessness and do not want to risk drawing the attention of those with the power to hurt them in some way. In depressed times they are conscious of how easy it would be to lose their job or business if they threatened the wrong party. They are also conscious of how hard it would be to replace that job or business, especially if labelled as a troublemaker and/or liar if they do rebel.

Bureaucrats implement policies though rules that are supposed to derive from the policies. Bureaucrats live by rules. The rules may achieve their original purpose or may be counterproductive to achieving that purpose. Which occurs is much less important to bureaucrats than whether their authority is respected and whether the extent of their authority expands rather than contracts. Bureaucrats naturally have their own ambitions for career growth. For example, if it is good to make some rules to put some limits on greedy capitalists (or power mad trade unionists) then making more rules is better. If individual bureaucrats are doing good work implementing those rules, then managing ten people implementing rules with their guidance must be better. Better yet would be managing 100 other people to implement the rules.

The fact that the rules are sometimes are counterproductive is first something to be denied. Then, if accepted in the face of overwhelming evidence and popular outrage, the bureaucrats will need a budget and a team to improve the rules. Ideally this improvement will occur by extending the rules, not by reducing them.

In all this, there is much opportunity for people who understand political processes and administrative systems to achieve their objectives without it being clear to others what is going on.

Interest Rate Cycle

Interest rates respond to supply and demand for money. Generally this has meant that when the economy expands investment is required in additional working capital, inventory and fixed investment. The need for money to fund this investment causes an increase in borrowing. Interest rates rise to attract more lending funds. When demand drops, these investments reduce, reducing the need for borrowed money, and interest rates drop.

Central banks stimulate and control the behavior of privately owned banks. They stimulate by printing a core quantity of paper money and control by regulating how much the banks may lend in relation to deposits, and in relation to bank capital.

However, the dominant supply and demand factors have changed in the last few decades. Interest rates regulated by central banks have steadily declined. Historically this would have caused inflation of consumable product prices but there have been economic forces at work that have driven down interest rates.

From the 1980s there have been a number of significant changes in markets:

- Automation has reduced employment opportunities in many industries, particularly for lower income earners. This has forced them to compete harder for what jobs are left, driving down their rates.
- Many markets have been deregulated, allowing businesses to reduce labor inputs.
- Globalization has meant labor can be supplied by workers in foreign countries at lower wages, driving down wages for lower income earners in western countries.

- Taxation has been moved from income tax to sales taxes, increasing the portion of tax that lower income earners pay.
- Income tax rates have been flattened, reducing taxes paid by higher income earners.
- Labor unions that previously fought for pay rises when companies made more money, have been restricted and removed from many business places.

The net effect of all of these has contributed to a reduction in income levels for lower income earners relative to higher income earners. This has meant that high income earners, who have the ability and inclination to save and invest, have more money to do so. From an investment growth perspective this is very good because there is more money available for the purpose.

Conversely those who struggle to save and invest at the best of times, and can only buy capital assets such as electrical goods, cars and real estate by borrowing, have now less ability to borrow for those items.

It does not matter whether we think these lower income people deserve to be poorer because they are lazy/stupid/immoral wastrels or we think they deserve to maintain the living standard they once had. Either way they cannot borrow as much as they once could at interest rates at the time. But meanwhile the upper income earners are saving more. They can no longer lend as much as they once could at the interest rates at the time On the consumption side of the economy, savings increase and borrowings decrease.

On the production side of the economy, if the upper income earners have good investment opportunities they will invest more of it. They can invest in makers of luxury products because they and their peers can afford to buy more of these so there is likely to be market growth and need for additional supply capacity. But there is a limit to how much of these products can be sold. They can invest in companies which make products governments buy like weapons and security services. The markets for these have periodic growth phases. But for other sectors, depending on lower income earners buying, growth may be limited.

When there is excess supply capacity, it is smarter to buy existing production assets than to build new ones That is unless there is a significant improvement in economics offered by new technology in those new assets. In a recessionary environment there are likely to be fire sale opportunities as weaker companies get squeezed. Money then moves from bank account to bank account with transfers of ownership without being converted into assets. The net effect of this is that money stays in the bank seeking interest earnings.

Market logic tells us that, in the absence of other demands for money such as expanded business investment, interest rates must drop. This allows reduction in the cost of borrowing far enough for the lower income people to borrow that money saved by upper income people. Otherwise they cannot borrow. If they do not borrow and if business also does not borrow to invest, there is a shortage of borrowers. Central banks can keep rates up but if they do the economy slows down. If it is already slow, central banks are under pressure to keep rates down or recessions will deepen.

No doubt one of these days some other market force will create a demand for money that will dramatically drive up interest rates. This will counteract changes influence on interest rates caused by income redistribution . But in 2017 that force has yet to appear.

A big plus of low interest rates is that it makes it less costly to make investments that take a long time to make an economic return. New technology platforms, complex products and processes can benefit from this. This supports the development of life saving drugs, greater energy efficiency and less environmentally destructive human activities. So the sacrifices of the less affluent will eventually be rewarded with benefits in health and the environment when economies of scale bring costs down for them to enjoy these.

Currency Cycle

Currency values rise and fall under a number of influences including:

- Excess of sales of products to other countries over purchase of products from other countries. If more people buy a currency than sell it for normal trading activities, its price will be influenced upwards until there is a better balance.
- Excess of investment from other countries over investment to other countries. If more people buy a currency than sell it for investment activities, its price will be influenced upwards until there is a better balance.
- If prevailing interest rates paid on borrowings in one currency increase compared with rates paid in another the currency with the higher interest rates will tend to move up.
- If currency traders see patterns developing in one direction or another they may speculate on further change, which accelerates the movement in value.

As the general level of economic activity moves with other cycles, e.g., inventory, capacity or technology cycles, there will also be an impact on currency values. If people are feeling affluent at a given time they may buy more foreign luxury goods. If they are feeling less affluent they may buy more low cost foreign goods. Either of these can increase imports.

Currency value movement is driven by net sales across borders and net investment across borders for all sectors. But if one particular exporting sector is relatively large and undergoes an expansion, it can affect that total and thus affect the currency value. This change in value can affect net export sales in the other sectors. Sometimes this is favorable when the particular companies import more than they export and thus reduce costs. Sometimes this is unfavorable when the companies export more than they import and sales drop more than cost drops.

If an industry sector has been particularly successful with exports it will drive up currency values. Its success earns money for the sector which allows it to invest and gain further economies of scale. This allows it to hold prices to foreign buyers in spite of currency value increases and to increase exports further. If it is of significant size relative to the rest of export trade, this drives up the value of the local currency disadvantage.

Meanwhile other net exporting sectors in the currency zone suffer from the higher value of the currency as their prices in local currency drop while their costs in local currency increase. Their sales volume falls and, as it falls, they lose economies of scale aggravating their problems.

If this continues, they go into sustained decline. Usually sunk capital in production capacity keeps industries going to some degree (albeit with new owners if the old ones have borrowed funds they cannot repay). This continues until the time when reinvestment is required and then they simply stop producing.

The losses of these sectors now start negating the gains of the successful sector for the total economy and exports in total fall back. If imports do not reduce in quantity at the same time, this leads to foreign exchange deficits or larger deficits if there were already deficits. These deficits accumulate and sooner or later traders lose confidence in the currency. A rapid decline in currency value can then occur.

After a period, the lower currency values makes export of other products (new or resuscitated old ones) more economic, leading to export of these after initial investigation, development and marketing effort. Continued investment in their capacity and sales, based on success in new or revived markets, leads to continued growth in exports and an improved surplus/deficit situation.

Eventually this impacts on currency value and the cycle starts again. The previous strong sector may lead the way, having come out of its down cycle, or it may be another sector in growth mode for whatever reason.

The timing of the currency cycle is usually years or decades as some industries develop markets and build capacity while other industries lose markets and abandon capacity.

Changes in direction in currency cycles, like other cycles, can be initiated through a shock event or through recurring business drivers. They can also be initiated through combinations of shocks and recurring business cycles. A shock surge of revenue in one sector, such as opening up an oil, mining or forestry resource, initially pays for facilities, e.g. in transportation. Their presence supports recurring businesses in other sectors. A currency value cycle occurs, typically a long one lasting years.

The currency cycle is more or less important to various countries depending on their size and industry mix. If we have a small/medium country with just a few major exporting sectors, and exporting is a large part of our economy, our currency is likely to fluctuate a lot relative to more stable currencies like the US dollar. If one of our export industries starts to do well – increased capacity or higher world market prices – money starts pouring into that industry.

For example Australia has close cultural, language, political, military and economic links with the US. But its dollar moves substantially in value against the US dollar. The value of the Australian dollar has varied between 1990 and 2017 from a low of US$0.4829 to a high of US$1.1054. Australia's top five exports in one year were Oil (25.6% of total exports), Ores, slag, ash (25.2%), Gems, precious metals billion (6.6%), Meat (5.2%), Cereals (3.4%). Any of these can quickly rise significantly in value, increasing the value of the A$. Conversely rapid declines in these sectors foreign earnings can occur, with falls in value of the A$.

The extreme case of the sudden rise of one industry is known as the Revenue Curse. Here one sector is so dominant its rise causes increase in currency value that crushes the rest of the economy. It becomes cheaper to import products than buy locally. The other sectors do not necessarily bounce back when the dominant sector goes into a quiet phase and the currency value drops. Their staff may be gone, their equipment may be derelict and their real estate may be sold. The classic example is a third world economy with a large extraction industry such as minerals, oil and gas or forestry. But it can occur for a first world company as well.

Typically currency cycles follow a long term cycle due to competitive advantage in one or more sectors. But on the way we are likely to see the usual patterns of multiple cycles interacting with this long cycle. We may have big cash flows from working capital cycles in seasonal sectors – agriculture, tourism, etc. - or from capacity investment cycles. At the time the cash flows the currency is likely to move up and then fall back later in the season.

The currency value cycle may be relatively smooth or involve sudden collapses in value. These occur when misplaced optimism is suddenly replaced with a realization that things have deteriorated and may not improve in the foreseeable future. This often occurs after trade deficits accumulate or a collapse occurs in the price of a big export earning product. A rapid decline in currency value can then occur. A shock or an accumulated cyclical effect can be equally effective.

The effects of changing interest rates can also have a large impact leading to a collapse. The interest rate differential between two counties that trade a lot may rise quickly, perhaps due to one's central bank policy change. That country's currency value may then rise rapidly. If the other country's currency value moves up with it, it may incur a decline in exports to other counties followed by a sudden fall in currency value.

Currency cycles of course have a particular impact on geoeconomic forces, just as they are influenced by them.

Financial Risk Perception Cycle

An important cycle relates to the market perception of financial risk. Marvin Minsky described how people get more and more comfortable with risk as time goes by from the last financial crash[2]. The more time elapses, the less intense are the memories of the last crash and the less influential are the people are who do remember them. There are always plausible reasons why this time is different: There is better technology, the market is more fluid, the risk mathematics are better now, the last crash was caused by government intervention or by lack of government intervention.

The cycle goes something like this:

After a financial collapse when lenders do not get their money paid back, lenders become very cautious. Only borrowers who have good collateral and reliable earnings will get loans.

As time goes by, with only these borrowers who are good risks getting loans, loan default rates drop, historic bad debts gradually get paid or get written off, and confidence builds in the system. There may be still bad debts incurred here and there but they are less likely to trigger cascades of failures.

Financing expands further over the years, with continued low levels of bad debt and confidence grows. Loans are made to expand capacity gaining increased economies of scale and higher profitability. Bad debt levels are still moderate. Prices gained by suppliers of products and assets are good as the number of buyers who would not buy without financing increases as a portion of total buyers.

Loans are made to buyers who expect prices to increase and see it advantageous to buy now. The level of bad debts increases but products and assets can be sold to other buyers with only moderate losses.

Capacity of new products and assets exceeds demand and suppliers who need to pay back financing costs reduce prices to get more market share. A price collapse of financial assets occurs.

After a large financial collapse, when perceived financial risk is high, politicians will often regulate the financial sector to prevent recurrence. Some will have more enthusiasm than others but the majority may see the need to be seen by voters to be doing something. The less keen can publically accept the need for changes but work behind the scenes take the teeth out of the regulations (see Political Cycles above).

As perceived risk reduces, politicians will promote the benefits of deregulation for various reasons, each of which can be legitimate to some extent or other:

- Regulation is ineffective.
- Regulation is stopping economic growth.
- Regulation is not necessary any more with a liberated market or with more advanced technology.
- Other methods of reducing risky behavior are better than regulation.
- The original cause of the applicable past financial disaster was not risky behavior by the financial sector but errors by government agencies.

High levels of real financial risk can create opportunities for financial killings gained by going short if the market perceives risk to be less. Conversely high levels of perceived financial risk can create opportunities for financial killings gained through going long if we can identify factors that actually minimize real risk.

General

All of the above cycles need to be understand in depth if they have an impact on a particular financial killing opportunity. Their interactions must also be understood. This extends to interactions between regions. We may have a particular cycle at a certain point in one region but at another point with very different characteristics in another region. This can change the viability of a product in one region competing with a similar product from another. It also can change the viability of a product in one region supplied with components from another region. Those components might be materials, energy, parts, subassemblies, code or design factors.

1. "The Leverage Cycle" John Geanakoplos
2. "Stabilizing An Unstable Economy" Hyman P. Minsky

APPENDIX 6: GEOECONOMIC FACTORS – STABILITY OF LINKS

We have discussed the various cycles that can contribute to a specific financial killing opportunity. These can apply in any location. Buyer's risk and known supply costs are also significantly influenced by geographic factors. These in turn have an impact (sometimes dominating) on price in addition to local cost factors. This applies to the trade of goods and services between locations around the world and to investment of supply facilities that contribute to that trade. It also applies to real estate prices, which are influenced by trade flows and which support trade via collateral for financing.

We discuss buyer's risk between regions in depth here and elsewhere because it is the source of a type of transaction risk shared by buyer, seller and financing party. The transfer of part or all of buyer's risk to the seller and financing party is a key component of the growth of business and ultimately of its collapse.

The seller steps up to take on buyer's risk because this will make the buyer buy more and make other potential buyers buy when they previously would never have bought. Economies of scale are gained. The financing party steps up to help the seller transfer more risk from the buyer than the seller can provide alone and buyers buys more. And again new types of potential buyer start buying. Ultimately it ends in tragedy for some because some buyers can never repay the financing but until it does this is the market system working.

Geoeconomics and Trade

In Appendix 3 we described at an overview level how price was affected by both known transport costs and a buyer's risk premium for differences between regions. This is in addition to production cost and buyer's risk in the production region. Buyer's risk combines with economies of scale and financing to generate business cycles and to generate opportunities for financial killings when the cycles become unstable. Transport links can also play a big role in events that destabilize the financial system. We look to the study of geoeconomics to help us understand these processes.

Geoeconomics has multiple definitions and one is "The combination of economic and geographic factors relating to international trade." For our purposes we would vary this slightly and use the term inter-regional rather than international trade. This is because the trade between regions within multi-region nations such the US, Russia, India or China may be just as significant from our perspective as that between nations in the same region such as Belgium and France.

We are also particularly interested in sudden changes in geographic factors which influence price.

In a global economy, many cyclical factors are affected by the forces of geoeconomics, which determine the relationships of trade and finance between regions.

Geoeconomics might be seen as a subset of spatial economics. The book The Spatial Economy[1], describes a diverse field of knowledge including such areas as:
- The development of cities
- The development of local markets for a supply center alongside its export markets
- The balance between economies of scale for a supply center and transport costs to and from the center
- Size distribution of cities
- The development of ports and transport hubs and their relationship with city location
- International trade and specialization by country
- Industrial clustering

The mathematical foundations of analysis and modelling for these subjects are described in the book. Its focus is on economic development over time, not on how sudden changes in demand and how this might affect prices. However, it establishes underlying cost structures relating to transport networks connecting supply and market hubs.

The other insight we get on transport routes is from the study of geopolitics. And this is not just where trade and financial centers will be likely to form along a given transport route but which transport routes will be most effective in the first place as a result of natural features. From this follows which centers will be big in global trade and finance.

The geopolitical forecasting company, STRATFOR, observes that countries with geographies supporting low cost bulk transport systems are historically much more effective at formation of capital. Historically navigable rivers have offered the lowest cost transport. River transport typically is an order of magnitude lower in cost for bulk than road transport[2]. So regions with such navigable rivers have been strong in forming capital, leading to accumulated wealth and strong banking centers. This geopolitical view does not go into the elaborate mathematics of spatial theory but identifies a clear pattern.

Capital centers in Europe to this day are largely found in the river valleys that defined medieval capital flows. Milan, Frankfurt, Amsterdam, Rotterdam, London, Paris, Stockholm and Vienna all represent different capital systems on different waterways. This is not just a Medieval Europe pattern. Great trading cities around the world are usually based on river systems connected to the oceans. Shanghai, Tokyo, London, Frankfurt, New York City and Chicago are examples. This gives a perspective on what regions of the world are rich and what are poor, with associated implications on where big pools of money circulate with opportunities for capture.

However, both the spatial economic and geopolitical schools of thought are focusing on developments that take place over years, decades and centuries, accumulation effects. Our focus is on sudden changes that occur over transport links once the links are created.

The Influence of Bulk Transport on Price

We have talked about changes in transport technology in Appendix 5. Associated with these technology cycles are gains in economies of scale. Usually a new technology supports some kind of increased scale of operation. The first implementation may take some advantage of the increase, within existing demand. Then as demand expands, ongoing increases in economy of scale take further advantage of the advance in technology. The capacities of transport links have increased by many orders of magnitude over the centuries.

When we put product on a pack animal, transport by road is lower in cost than when we had to carry them on our own backs because we can carry several times the load per trip. Transport costs of humans walking and carrying goods would have high variable consumption costs per pound of goods carried by the merchant – eating and lodging.

When we put them on a horse-drawn wagon, we scale up again, further reducing variable cost. When we put it on a horse-towed river barge, we scale up again, further reducing variable cost. Capital costs ae increasing but if the volumes increase sufficiently we can pay for that out of the saving invariable cost.

But geography starts to have an impact as we start introducing these higher capital cost components. If we have to traverse a mountain pass up a narrow track we are probably limited to the pack horse, or, if it is really narrow, a load on our back. Wagons need relatively level surfaces such as plains and river valleys. Barges need rivers or canals. The perfect land route is a wide river valley where we can have wide flat roads or railroads and easily accessible deep, wide water channels. The Rhine, the Yangtze, the Mississippi are examples with much of their route like this. Economically developed areas along them provide supply and demand for bulk products being transported along them.

We may increase economies of scale on a single link many times. Our merchant increases his load of merchandise for a trip by a factor of ten by switching from a packhorse to a horse-drawn five ton river barge. His descendants transition from the five ton barge to a 30 ton barge. Their great grandchildren may transition from a 30 ton barge to 100 ton barge and theirs may transition to a 1,000 ton barge. When we move to ocean transport, capacity has evolved through even more orders of magnitude. The cog of the middle ages carried up to 200 tons while modern mega container ships carry nearly 200,000 tons, nearly 1,000 times the cog's load.

Static facilities such as canals supporting the boats and ships follow the same pattern. And introduction of a new, larger canal can reroute the largest of these ships which may have outgrown the existing canal. For example, the Panama canal became too small for very large ships. The fuel savings of very large ships make it economic for ships coming from Asia to go around South America to reach the east coast of the US rather than using the Canal. When the canal gets upgraded to handle bigger ships, the economic relationships will change again.

The variable cost of transport per ton-mile moves down steadily. To make this all happen, in addition to advances in the transportation equipment itself, great advances in logistics and finance must occur to coordinate millions of transactions.

Transport in bulk is inherently attractive due to its potential economies of scale. Instead of the cost of multiple transactions we have the cost of one. Instead of the cost of multiple transport vehicles, with a driver or team for each, we have the cost of one. It will be bigger of course and more costly to operate than one little one, but not more costly than multiple ones.

If we do not inherit favorable terrain to provide favorable physical conditions for transport links, we have to improve the resources we have, often at a high cost. Railroads and multilane highways are both difficult to build over steep terrain. They tend to get built overpasses over or through tunnels if they are to cross mountain ranges. There needs to be such a pass or suitable geology for a potential tunnel for this to happen. Not every mountain range makes this possible.

Distribution scale transport can always occur in parallel to bulk transport. An intrepid merchant can walk over a mountain, through a swamp or dense forest with a small package for someone. Or the merchant carry it on board an aircraft or boat. But its weight and volume will usually be a fraction of that which is carried by bulk transport. Its movement will generally have a small impact on price compared to bulk shipments.

As bulk transport is introduced, reducing the variable cost of consumption, there is a surplus to pay for transport facilities such as river boats and wharves, and in taxes to the local prince. Lower unit cost is incurred by a big reduction in variable cost and an increase in fixed cost. The fixed cost goes to pay for transport facilities, which are capital items located along the transport route. They may be fixed facilities such as wharves, locks, roads, bridges and rail tracks. Or they may be mobile facilities such as boats and barges, trucks and trains, operating along the transport route. Payments for the transport service go into building the facilities, which remain as fixed assets for years, decades, even centuries. Capital is formed and centers along the transport route become richer. With more wealth they become more powerful.

Some mathematical modelling of this has been done for us. In the New York Fed DSGE model[3] outlined in Appendix 4, one of the components of the model is an intermediate goods producer. From our perspective, a transport link is equivalent to a production facility in its ability to add known cost and buyer's risk premium to equivalent components of price for a product sold right at the production facility.

A port, a railroad, a train, a highway, a bridge, a container ship will probably have very different cost structures and revenue models from a farm, a food factory, a chemical plant or a software development company. However at a high level, there is a similar pattern where as capital investment accumulates, fixed costs replace labor-linked variable costs.

The microfoundations for Intermediate Good Producers are modelled with a Cobb-Douglas production function with capital elasticity a.

$$Y_t(i) = K_t(i)^\alpha Z_t L_t(i))^{1-\alpha}$$

K_t represents capital input, L_t represents labor input and Z_t represents exogenous technological progress.

As capital content, α increases, labor content (1- α) decreases. So as capital accumulates, variable costs reduce.

This variable cost reduction inevitably has an impact on the price of transport. Even a monopoly can increase profits by reducing price to increase economies of scale. There is usually an alternative to the product (in this case a transport service). Merchants can always continue using their pack horses rather than using the river barge if they do not share some of the cost savings. So it is better to get five times the business at half the profit margin than one amount of business at maximum profit margin.

The merchants also pass some of their cost savings to their customers via price cuts to attract more trade from buyers who do not get value at higher prices. The net effect of all this is that bulk transportation systems level prices between supply and consumption points as well as forming capital at key service points along the routes. The greater is the potential market, and the greater is the transport capacity, the greater will be the price levelling.

Either way they accumulate and offer the ability to generate long term income. If they pass on some of the savings to the merchants they can expand volume. If transport cost reduces we can justify moving products that would previously not have enough value to the buyer to pay for the transport. We start with silk and spices, which are light high value items, and eventually move to shipping grain and iron ore. As we add products to the range and as we ship to customers with relatively less spending power, volume increases. In a global economy, there may be many links in the chain from supplier to final customer.

Transport links tend to grow over centuries. If they are built for one purpose, other users tend to come along and use them, adding funds for expansion and maintenance.

The more links there are, the greater the competition between links, driving down the price. The more capacity each link has, the greater the need for that capacity to be utilized at a high level, driving down the price.

This price levelling leveling can apply to the value of the product being delivered or to the value of a site that accesses resources via transport links. The other aspect of this is real estate pricing. Here the product is made up of many components that accumulate over generations. The principles of real estate prices levelling with improved transport connections applies as with other products.

Buyer's Risk

In the Appendix 3, we discuss the premium a buyer is willing to pay over the lowest price available in order to reduce the risk of poor product performance. There are many factors that would stop a buyer from getting the benefits from a product that it is designed to provide. For example, difficulty of use, poor quality or unreliability can all prevent buyers from getting the utility they expect. Buyers will usually be willing to pay a premium in price for a product that they believe is more certain of providing the utility they are expecting.

Depending on the consequences of failure to receive the utility, that price premium may be small or large. If failure would be very costly they may pay multiple times the minimum price to ensure they get the performance they need.

This buyer's risk premium has components of risk imposed by the supplier at its point of supply and components of risk imposed by the transport linkage to the customer. If a product is supplied from a region on the other side of the world with different language and culture, these risks tend to be much higher. This is simply because we often do not know as much about the product and its supplier. There are more possibilities for things to go wrong.

This applies to both the point of production and the transport chain. Buyer's risk can be high in one of these and low in the other or vice versa. Either can be negative.

The price premium incurred by buyer's risk is normally higher as geographic separation increases. Buyers will usually pay a premium for a known and proven solution to their needs over a less known solution from distant places. However, this premium can be reduced, even made negative, with particular financing arrangements. If we offer later payment options to buyers, they will increase the price they pay. Ultimately if we let buyers try the product out for a period and then pay we allow buyers to reduce their risk that the product will not work as they need it to.

In the event of a supply constraint over a link, supply can be constricted. This is a type of buyer's risk. Delivery might be delayed and/or incur transport cost spikes much higher than normal transport costs. Ongoing support might be obstructed.

Money is transferred electronically around the globe by the billion. It no longer needs a wagonload (or shipload) of coins. But transport networks still factor large in finance because the price of products is heavily influenced by transport costs and transport times. Changes in price can have big effects on profitability and cash flow. As a consequence they can impact on a range of financial risks.

Buyer's risk, as we discussed in Appendix 3, does not necessarily require a geoeconomic component. It occurs if we are buying from the supplier in the building next door who may speak our language, share our religion and values, belong to the same ethnic groups. They may even be a blood relative. There is always uncertainty about how a product we are not familiar with will work to meet or individual needs. That applies even when made by the most reputable supplier in an industry, one whose other products we may have used with great satisfaction. Our needs may simply be different from other users.

But if suppose add physical separation by mountain range, great river, desert or ocean to create separate regions inhabited by people who may have different language, values, religion and ethnicity. Then in addition to increased known transport costs, buyer's risk can increase dramatically:

- Target purpose of a product – end users in different cultures may use products to achieve quite different end results.
- Method of use of product - end users in different cultures may use products in quite different ways.
- Use with complementary products and resources - costs of these may vary widely between regions.
- Level of wealth. It may be a widely and frequently used product in one economic area and one used only for special occasions in another area.
- If used as part of a business operation, business processes may be different in different regions. Sequences of tasks may be quite different according to consumption tastes and ways of sharing work.
- Economy of scale – suppose we have a product designed for a region with 300 million people and large economies of scale.

It may offer different benefits, either in end use or production, from a region with 3 million people and much smaller economies of scale in many areas.
- Training and support requirements may vary widely between regions if a product is similar in operation to other products used in one region but not in another.

The amount buyers are willing to pay to reduce risk by buying the lowest risk alternative, the buyer's risk premium can vary dramatically. It may be worth paying just 1% more, 10% more, 100% more or 1000% more. The amount depends on the consequences of buying a product that does not meet desired characteristics. Different buyers have different risks in the event of a product's poor performance.

Poor performance may involve a few minutes minor inconvenience for one customer with little measurable cost. But it may involve a major system collapse for a second customer. This could involve millions (or billions) of dollars lost in revenue, angry customers and lawsuits. In the worst cases it may involve loss of life, destruction of reputation and bankruptcy. The second customer will be willing to pay a far larger premium to avoid the poor performance than the first.

Buyer's risk applies to a supplier next door, just as it applies to one on the other side of the world. The questions are the same: Does the product work the way we expect? Does it deliver the throughput we expect? Does it integrate with other systems we use? Is it reliable? Is it safe? Is the supplier trustworthy? Do they respond to our concerns? Such questions are always valid. However, if the supplier is next door we are more likely to be able to talk face to face with its designers in our first or second language. And we can see production processes, see their working environment and rely on our own legal system if there are disputes. Buyer's risk is usually less, sometimes a lot less when we know the supplier well.

We may need to buy a product and use it for some time before we really know these things. If it is a make or break decision for our business, a new technology, a new production facility, a new brand, we may decide to go with the one from the other side of the ocean if we know its suppliers are really proven in this area. They might have funny eyes, a funny language and behaviors which seem bizarre to us. But their equipment is works brilliantly, lasts for years, is fuel efficient and their after-sales service is thorough, friendly and respectful.

In the internet age this gaining of confidence in a product can take a very short time for products that can be electronically distributed and supported.

Regarding point of production, if the product is a commodity such as oil with a particular specification or a type of grain, we may have a lot of confidence about its characteristics. For a designed and manufactured product such as a Japanese auto or a German machine tool we may have a high level of confidence. This is based on world-wide knowledge about the quality and performance of these products. However, suppose the product is made in a county renowned for bad quality, corrupt inspection processes or it is unclear from documentation how exactly it performs. Then we will be less confident. Then we may be willing to pay a high premium to a supplier whose past offerings give us confidence it will deliver a product that meets our needs this time.

In a global world, a product can change from strange to familiar over time as we see people using it and getting good results from it. If we try it ourselves and it does everything we want, then we may gain as much confidence in it as in a locally supplied product. If it has a wider set of capabilities, as global products often do, we may gain more confidence in it than in the local product. In some cases, where our local industry is less advanced, we may have a low opinion the local product.

Regarding the transport chain, many things can occur between sending a product in good condition and its arrival at the customer site. Product damage in transport, theft, piracy, storms at sea, floods on land, bottlenecks, blockades and acts of war can all occur. Most of these may be of low probability much of the time but can still occur from time to time and sometimes with critical impacts.

Generally customers are concerned with total known cost and total buyer's risk premium for a product. They add point production costs to transport costs and they add point buyer's risk premium to geo-economic buyer's risk premium when they make buying decisions. This may be a simple analysis (we don't trust product quality from Country X so we are willing to pay twice the price for a product from Country Y, whose product quality we do trust). Country Y here may be our own country or another one.

Or the analysis may be much more complex: A port in the Gulf of Mexico is more prone to Caribbean weather problems than one on the in the Persian Gulf. However, the Persian Gulf port may be more prone to military conflict. If we have Caribbean weather problems AND Persian gulf conflict this could have a different outcome to if we have one OR the other. And all of this may be irrelevant until there is an increase in demand for our commodity of interest in a large growing market such as India or China, AND/OR a failure in supply due to an earthquake in half a dozen other localities.

If certain events or combinations of events occur, constraints on transport capacity (bottlenecks) can suddenly occur and prices can leap dramatically until the constraints are relieved. Conversely if a long term constraint is suddenly released there may be a surge of lower cost product available. This can be very good if we are the buyer or very bad if we are another supplier competing with the supplier which has just had the transport constraint released. So the transport network becomes very important, not just in terms of known transport costs but risk factors.

Geopolitical Parallels - Products

This aspect of risk due to our knowledge being constrained by geographic proximity is well established in the sphere of geopolitics, which has many overlaps with geoeconomics. We have seen how our geopolitical colleagues at STRATFOR refer to the ability of bulk transport routes to accumulate capital. They also offer insights on the forces behind buyer's risk between regions.[4]

In geopolitics we are concerned with whom we ally with and whom we are likely to ally against. We ally with those we know well due to family ties, living in the same village, city, region or nation and thus interacting with on a regular basis. Nations themselves are formed from these alliances between people who know each other well. We fear those we do not know because lack of knowledge inherently increases risk. We go to war with those who we do not know well and whom we feel threaten us and the things we value.

Geographic barriers create this separation which prevents us knowing certain people well. The barriers may be rivers, mountain ranges or seas. Whatever the barrier, if it prevents us mixing with them on a regular basis, they will be unknown to us and thus a source of risk. We fear they may attack us to steal our wealth, to enslave us, to enforce an alien religion upon us, to impose their language and/or their culture on us, crushing our own language and culture.

Geopolitics analyses the grouping of people due to their geographic location and how that leads to the formation of religious groupings, nations and to the military struggles between nations based on their geographical interests. Our Venetian traders may not have shared religion and culture with the Muslims but they sailed in the Eastern Mediterranean and got to know the products that the Muslims had for sale and the products that the Muslims would buy.

The key commonality between people in a locality is risk of adverse forces coming from other localities. But risk comes in many, many types. For geopolitics it is the risk that people we do not know will do bad things to us. For buyer's risk it is that we waste our money on buying something that does not function as required.

These geopolitical risks may align with buyer's risk but they do not have to. We may not care if we love or hate the suppliers of our product, only whether it meets our needs. We may prefer to buy off people we like rather than people we fear and hate, but it is not essential. Our urgent question is does it meet our product needs in the way we love or do we fear its unknown quantities, which may let us down in a critical situation. Ultimately if the product meets our needs we will buy it, if necessary from our enemy, and if it does not meet our needs we will not buy it, even from our friends.

The timing of acquiring trust in products from other regions may also be very different from the timing of acquiring trust in people from other regions. Typically people learn to trust products from other regions a lot faster than they learn to trust the inhabitants of those regions. We may buy spices from the Orient and trust these to meet our needs for food enhancement and odor enhancement. But after centuries of trading with them we may still see the suppliers as heathens who are not to be trusted in any other areas. Typically buyer's risk changes much faster than geopolitical risk.

Currency Crises

Markets for individual products sold across the world can collapse in months, even weeks. Prices for real estate can surge (or collapse) in weeks or months. But if we are looking for very rapid changes in price from geoeconomic forces, we come back to the currency crisis, such as the one outlined in Example 1. Loss of balance of imports, exports and investments may not initially attract much attention because trade and investment can be lumpy. But then the imbalance becomes increasingly obvious, indicating some cyclical or structural change. Then some event triggers a sense of urgency and the currency value moves rapidly.

Currency crises occur when particular economies have problems such as going into a rapid export decline due to commodity price collapses or having high levels of foreign debt with interest rates rising rapidly. Future examples might include:

- US restrictions on trade with other countries, if they occur due to changes imposed by the Trump administration, may cause exports from these countries to deteriorate and their currencies to weaken, with sudden declines periodically occurring.
- China struggles to reorient its economy from being highly export-driven to being more driven by internal consumption. Since the GFC China has spent large amounts on public investments of dubious return to keep its economy growing and population calm. The debt increase this has incurred puts downwards pressure on the value of its currency. Its currency becomes less stable with sudden changes in value occurring.
- The Euro zone disintegrates when its Mediterranean country economies can no longer survive their industries being squeezed by the value of the Euro. Individual countries such as Greece, Spain and Italy incur large fluctuations in the value of their currencies as they leave the stabilizing force of the Euro.
- Russia's currency collapses when sustained low revenues from oil exports deplete its reserves.
- Latin American countries experience their periodic crises due to commodity prices falling.

These are just some of the more obvious sources of instability in currency values. None of the above may occur but if these ones do not occur there are many other countries that can get into situations where their currency value slides.

Real Estate and Geoeconomics

Real estate has major importance to the economy for a number of reasons including:
- It is a widely used store of wealth, which offers returns from its use (by owner or by other parties who pay to use it) as it simultaneously holds value for future resale.
- When people's real estate significantly increases in value for any reason they often feel confident in spending a lot more than usual on consumer items.
- It is a widely used form of collateral for loans to operate businesses in many different sectors.
- It offers the opportunity for many people to make long term capital gains through physical improvements and changes in value of the areas where the real estate is located.
- It offers the opportunity to make large financial killings through changes in price that are not expected by wider market.

Real estate is a product that behaves in many ways like any other product but has particular characteristics because it is sold and resold over generations. Every instance of the product is unique in location and may be built by a different company from the product next door. Or it may share many standard components, such as materials, design, and services provided to it, to the product next door.

As mentioned above, real estate has multiple roles in the economy and financial arena. Changes in its value can have a large effect on business. People who have enjoyed increases of value feel more confident in spending on consumer goods, borrowing against their real estate if they do not have the cash.

In Appendix 5, we discussed real estate cycles in a given locality, without focusing on the relative differences in price of between localities. Geoeconomic factors add a new dimension to prices.

Residential Real Estate

The great majority of us have experience of residential real estate prices, either as buyers/sellers or renters, and of how those prices vary with location. What makes one location worth more than another typically falls into three areas:

1. Where the site offers in terms of local intrinsic benefits such as stable land to allow easy construction, nice views, a pleasant microclimate, good soil supporting nice gardens. The more of these benefits we have, the higher the price that our real estate will sell for.
2. Who else lives nearby and what resources are close. We may be able to chat with the rich and powerful when we go for an evening stroll. We may have easy access to highly paid jobs, financial centers, specialist advisors, elite schools, shopping complexes, specialist retailers, hospitality, leisure pursuits (beaches, golf courses, spots fields, parks), entertainment and health services. These will improve our real estate price. By contrast, neighborhoods which might have thieves, rapists and murderers seeking opportunities for gratification will not achieve such good prices.
3. What such resources we can easily access via an arterial transport link. If we can drive along an uncongested route for ten minutes in our late model car to access these resources, our real estate will have a certain value. That is likely to be higher than if we have to drive for two hours or stand in overcrowded public transport rubbing up against dirty and hostile people to access these resources.

The premium locations will have all the features of local intrinsic benefits, proximity to people with power and wealth and easy access to other resources. Its real estate values will be highest. If a property is not in premium location, its value will depend on how easy it is to access those resources via transport links. If the links are fast, safe and comfortable, the value will be higher.

The more desired resources may not all be in the same location. Business centers may be in different locations from, preferred schools, shopping complexes, beaches, parks, etc. A location may require multiple transport links to access these resources. Every good transport link adds value and provides upwards pressure on the price of real estate.

These links do not all have to be ones that a given buyer would use. The buyer may only ever expect to use a subset of the links available but if other buyers value links that one buyer does not use they will still drive up the price. We may not have children going to school in the zone of a particular school. We may live in that zone for proximity to work, for the view, the sunshine, the parklike surroundings or the relative safety from criminal attack. But we will usually still have to pay for the easy access to that school when we buy the property. Others who do value it will drive up the price.

These location factors can improve completely independently of each other so it is easy to miss changes on one if we are focusing on one or two of the others.

If we are developing new residential areas, whether in suburbs or in city, the above factors drive price as for when we are buying a single residence.

Location determines how much it is worth spending on a particular site. In one part of town it may be worth building a twelve room house. In another part, a small transportable home may be the maximum sensible level of capital addition.

Again these location factors can improve completely independently of each other so it is easy to miss the potential of a locality for improved value.

To make killings in real estate, we do not need to have marketing skills such as those of Donald Trump applied when in Trump Towers,

Manhattan. A seven story waterfall and a rose marble lobby requires a particular instinct for the market. Nor do we need to have his business operational skills in areas such as hotels, casinos and branding. We can simply buy an asset which produces an income stream from the operators of these businesses. But we need to buy it before other players realize that it will produce that income stream.

Commercial and industrial Real Estate

Commercial and industrial real estate follows similar geoeconomic logic to residential real estate. Parks and schools may be less important and access by heavy vehicles may be more important. However, access to valuable resources via transport links remains fundamental to real estate prices. Large cities are great nests of connections between diverse physical and financial resources, specialist skills and services, customer tastes, needs and volume of demand. These connections drive their real estate prices much higher than those of smaller cities without the scale and diversity of connections.

Equivalent price-driving locational factors to those for residential real estate are:

1. The local core benefits move from being a fine view or a sunny garden to the size of the market for our commercial activities, or to a key supply source. The market might be based on a good location for a bridge across a major river, for a port, or for a road or rail junction. The supply source might be a mine, a refinery, a fishery, a forest, an agricultural or horticultural center.

2. The valuable local neighbors move from being useful and influential people you might meet on a stroll around the block, or at the local café, to the other local businesses that are of value to have in the locality. These are those that help to pay for local resources, those that attract customers to our premises and those that provide us with various specialist services. Typically the

bigger the center, the deeper those specialist services are likely to be.
3. The accessible resources move from schools and parks to other markets and supply sources that we can easily access via a bulk transport link. These are over and above those originally making the location valuable. Or focus here goes from what is available within an hour or two to what allows us to connect to places across the globe. A port which can berth a 20,000 unit container ship will add more value than one which can berth only a 2,000 unit ship. That will add more value than a winding 2 lane road link over a mountain range or desert.

When change occurs to any of these connections, price will be affected. If a transport connection is strengthened, price between either side of the connection will be levelled to some degree or other. This applies to real estate as it does to traded products. It is not always obvious to what degree this will occur, and how quickly it will occur.

The transport facilities that we have discussed earlier such as roads, railroads, bridges, wharves are themselves an example of real estate with a very specific purpose. If these are owned by the private sector normal opportunities for sudden and profitable value changes can apply.

Real estate in general is a product whose price depends on how many and how valuable are the services and resources it can access. If something changes in the cost structure of transportation links, real estate values can change dramatically with huge ripple-on effects throughout the financial sector and wider economy. The role of real estate prices in their contribution to collateral for mortgages, bonds and derivatives is very large.

Area Price Relativity Change Cycle

There is an associated cycle alongside the real estate cycle, the area price relativity change cycle. Typically over time, certain areas achieve higher prices than others. This happens at the regional level. Major cities on the east and west coasts of the US tend to be have higher prices of real estate than in other less globally connected regions.

This applies at the neighborhood level. Within a city, there will typically be a wide range of real estate values. There is the hill with the big houses bathed in winter sunshine with grand views of the river or harbor. Then there is the damp swamp land near the chemical plant packed with slum housing. In between the extremes there will be a spectrum of values.

These localities tend to hold their relative values over time as the real estate cycle fluctuates. The putrid swamp land does not suddenly become more attractive than the hill bathed in sun. The looming walls of the old factory does not suddenly become more attractive than a leafy park.

But values can change when one or more of those location factors changes. The swamp gets better drainage and the old chemical plant is shut down. Suddenly that gully is no longer perceived as damp and foul smelling but attractive for its proximity to the central city. A lot of slums start in unattractive areas close to the business center. They provide somewhere for the laborers and servants to live. Later when the area gets cleaned up with the decline of old industries, the middle classes pour in and drive out the old inhabitants by paying more for the real estate than their predecessors can afford.

Changes in real estate prices can be expected based on changes in the locational factors we have discussed. Improved potential business opportunities in a locality can increase real estate prices substantially. Better transport links from portions of real estate to major supply and demand centers can do the same. If we can pick the changes in advance of the market, the financial killings can be large. But the timing is not necessarily simple. The challenge is dealing with buyer's risk, which is present in real estate as it is in consumable and durable products.

For residential real estate, if we follow changes in the key locational factors we should be able to pick how values will increase for a certain type of customer. If we can anticipate correctly we can buy real estate before it lifts in price. We may need to upgrade the property and/or redefine it for a new type of customer but we are doing this for a specific and known type. The variables are limited in number.

It is much more complex for commercial and industrial real estate. Here we have chunks of real estate servicing many parties. It may be a suburban subdivision with many lots, an apartment building with many tenants, a hotel with many guests, a shopping center with many shops, an entertainment center with many customers, an office block with many companies or many departments within one company.

It may involve entities that involve several of these chunks. Residential apartments, shops and a hotel may be combined in a single entity. They may be combined to provide a lifestyle package for a particular type of owner.

The land involved may need to be assembled from many previously separate items of real estate. They may need to be bought separately and over a period of time to avoid costly purchases. It may start as a type of land and need to be rebuilt for its new set of purposes. Factories, docklands, warehouses, refuse dumps may have all ceased to function in their previous roles but be ready for transformation.

All those different uses, before and after a purchase, create a lot of buyer's risk.

Sometimes the price drops before it rises. The demise of the dirty old factory may mean loss of jobs and oncomes for workers and small businesses. Until something new fills the gap there is less money for rents and purchases by residents, not more. The absence of the factory may attract new businesses. But it may need some other link to be improved to combine with that availability of space to activate the big change.

The complexities of commercial and industrial real estate may take years to work through. They are comparable to a new product development in a goods or services production environment in terms of market appraisal, design and execution. They often have components of fixed investment and/or infrastructure investment. The cyclical behavior of these types of investments needs to be factored into the evaluation, planning and execution.

Changes in real estate prices follow changes in their locational factors, which of course vary by locality. One region may have rising real estate prices while another may have reducing prices. However, the stronger that the transport linkages between properties get, the more likely are their prices to move together to a greater or lesser extent.

Real estate prices have many kinds of linkages. Suppose one property increases dramatically in price because it has gained in its attractiveness to buyers due to one or multiple characteristics, which other properties do not share. Owners of other properties in the vicinity will see financial justification to invest to somehow try and add those characteristics in part or whole. A better drive on access, a new garage, a better heating system, a more modern kitchen or bathroom, a new décor, a better security system, transplanting ready-grown trees or improved landscaping are examples. If the cost of making these enhancements is less than the potential price difference, the price difference will narrow.

Real Estate Buyer's Risk

Buyer's risk has a particular role in real estate when it comes to price movements. We are not just thinking about what value we might get (or not get if our doubts are justified) as applies for a manufactured product. We are also factoring what price other buyers are willing to pay now and what price we might get paid when we sell in the future. If other buyers are willing to pay more than us for a property we will miss out.

This is not the case with a mass produced item. Then some customers might be annoyed if someone else gets a better deal. But one buyer getting the product does not stop another buyer from getting it unless there is a stock shortage. But with real estate we have a risk of missing out if we do not value it highly enough. We also risk losing money on future resale if we pay too much. The consequence if this that we have a high interest in how other people value a piece of real estate when we set the price we are willing to pay.

This can have some dramatic effects. As buyers of real estate in a one-to-one situation we can make our usual assessments and negotiate a price. But in an auction situation, when we see other buyers bidding at prices more than we have assessed it, we may reassess our previous assessments. Perhaps this locality has now changed value and we have missed it.

Equally, a lack of other buyers at an auction may discourage us from bidding, even at a significantly lower level than we would be prepared to pay in a one-on-one negotiation. The valuation others place on real estate is a large part of buyer's risk. With real estate, when we have finished its use, it is typically not consumed or depreciated like most products. It is often worth more than we paid for it. The resale value of real estate is usually an important component of its value when it is purchased. So its value to others in the future, in addition to its value to us while we use it, is an important contributor to its price.

Real Estate Price Stability

For our buyers and renters of real estate, the question comes up: If complex variable logic and its significance for price stability applies in the bulk transport world of geoeconomics do they also apply in real estate within regions? Do price and volume waves occur as a consequence of buyer's risk as they do for products traded across the world? And the simple answer is yes. One scenario goes as follows:

Neighborhood A real estate values have always been well below those of Neighborhood B next door. Neighborhood A used to have a smokestack factory area nearby where its inhabitants worked and a long but dreary shopping street. Neighborhood B is greener and has a smaller shopping area.

Then one day the factories closed down due to globalization and both neighborhoods' property values stagnated relative to those of the port city ten miles down the highway.

Over the years following, the lower cost real estate in Neighborhood A attracted people who liked renovating old houses and values slowly increased until there were fewer and fewer properties left to renovate. Meanwhile the dreary shops started to include cafes and restaurants which this new crowd liked to frequent. Real estate prices moved up slowly but Neighborhood B maintained a price premium over Neighborhood A.

This occurred until there were very few houses to renovate in Neighborhood A and, at an auction, a house, which had been renovated very nicely got a premium of 20% over the expected price due to an unexpected bidding war between several buyers. When we see other bidders bidding at similar levels to ourselves we are reassured that we are not suckers paying a higher price than would normally be achieved. The next week a similar house also at an auction sold at 30% over the previous expectation. Disappointed bidders from the week before had come with more money, confident that they could safely spend more as prices were clearly rising. The following week at an auction there were more bidders and the price went to 40% over the level expected just a few weeks before.

In the following months all prices achieved for sales of nicely renovated house in Neighborhood A were at 30 to 50% above the previous level. The price of the few remaining yet to be renovated houses also leapt by a similar amount, even taking into account that renovation work still needed to be done on them. On average Neighborhood A real estate was now achieving prices 15% over Neighborhood B, whereas previously its prices were well below it.

People started to analyze the new relative price levels and decided that key factors were the café, bar and restaurant culture that had sprung up. This attracted young affluent professionals as did the fact that Neighborhood A was closer to the port city down the highway. Real estate prices in the city were much higher, having risen steadily relative to Neighborhoods A and B for two decades.

There were now stronger linkages to the port city for income purposes and stronger linkages to lifestyle activities in the café/restaurant area. Our location factors 2, being in an area where we gain benefit from other inhabitants also applied here. We not only want to have easy access to cafes and restaurants we want to go there where people we value, for whatever reason, go. This can change quite quickly if an area suddenly becomes popular with a particular group. It might be the very affluent or it might be the artistic.

The trigger might be any of the three locational factors. It might have been removal of a stinking, polluting factory from the environment. It might have been having a colony of artistic people develop a new culture in the neighborhood. It might have been adding new lanes or interchange to the highway or a new link to the metro public transport system. Whatever it was, the neighborhood affected incurred a rise in real estate prices and started the wave.

In general the timing for the actual surge comes down to when an initial excess of demand over supply leads to a belief amongst the particular buyers at the time that if they do not buy now they will miss their chance. Then a perception emerges across the market that the price was at a new permanent level.

Waves ripple out from the first locality of high demand. The new equilibrium is achieved in a moving wave, which finds a path through the city. The new equilibrium might just follow the old one with everything scaled up but is likely to have at least some changes. The suburb that boomed first will probably achieve a permanently higher position than before. Prices in Neighborhood B above will rise as well as the wave ripples out, just not as much as Neighborhood A.

The Killing

We have talked about how residential real estate can undergo sudden price surges. Periodic wide scale surges can be magnified by relative price changes between localities. This is good for home owners who catch the wave. It offers a kind of mini killing for the middle classes, which can help set them up for a more affluent lifestyle. But the upgrading of residential areas does not on its own lead to a killing of the scale we have talked about previously.

For the real financial killing, we would look to the area occupied by the stinking old factory and the other factories, workshops and warehouses that spring up around that initial factory.

The areas that need concreting over to cover up contaminants, and do not specifically need sunshine, are suitable for commercial developments. They will enjoy the new affluent customer base living nearby. They will also expand it with customers attracted to the café, bar and restaurant culture.

The areas which have had less ground contamination, are sunny and can have clusters of trees transplanted can be developed as large scale up-market residential real estate. The prices will reflect the new price levels of the area plus its proximity to the shopping and entertainment complex.

General Geoeconomic Comments

Links between supply and demand hubs have their own investment cycles which interact with the investment cycles at the local hub level. Both cost factors associated with physical transport systems and price premiums for buyer's risk can contribute to sudden and large changes in price of products and assets between hubs. These can add to and magnify opportunities for financial killings at the local level.

Traded goods prices, currency values, accumulated capital values of transport facilities and real estate prices all depend on a complex geographically distributed chain of contributing components. These components include known cost components of production and transport. They also include buyer's risk premiums for product function and different confidence with products in different geographic regions.

When any of these components change there can be sudden destabilizing effects on the value chain that lead to large changes in price. These changes are often unexpected by the market because they seem random, due to unpredictable increases/decreases in demand or increases/decreases in supply capacity. If demand changes are close to a capacity threshold then price may change far out of proportion to the demand change. If supply changes are close to a demand threshold then price may change far out of proportion to the supply change.

For those watching the relevant group of cyclical factors, patterns can be seen that highlight sensitivities of price to changes in components. We may not know when a specific component in the chain is going to behave in a way that increases or decreases price. But we should know if it is in the zone where it could do so. We can then put financial instruments in place to capture the change in price should it occur over a period of sensitivity. A few examples of components which contribute in this way are:

- A port is at risk of major damage by an impending storm.
- A rail line is at risk of damage by equipment failure.

- An inter-regional highway is becoming severely congested at certain times due to traffic growth, or it has suddenly been relieved of congestion due to an upgrade.
- A shipping canal has undergone a capacity expansion.
- Fuel prices have suddenly shot up or collapsed.
- A declining industrial area has been redeveloped as a trade center, causing a boom in local real estate prices.
- A foreign product has suddenly gained acceptance in the local market.
- A locally developed product has suddenly gained acceptance in foreign markets.
- A new version of a product, process or technology platform has a major impact on product demand. If it is a local product it creates a local boom. If it is another region's product that competes with the local product, it creates a local recession.
- A new mobile phone app makes a local business grow rapidly.
- A new mobile phone app allows businesses based in other regions to substitute on-line information for local knowledge offered by staff in local businesses. This greatly reduces demand for local businesses.
- Social media awakens customers in other regions to the attractiveness of the local region's products.
- Social media awakens customers in other regions to the attractiveness of a nearby region's products, drawing demand from the local region.

There are a vast number of these changes going on in the economy and they have a wide range of sizes and periods of impact. Some have a lasting and large effect. Some have a lasting effect, which does not immediately cause instability but pushes conditions close to the point of instability. The system may be then sensitive to a relatively small change which activates a major instability. Some have a short term effect. If it is large it may activate instability even in previously relatively stable conditions   If it is small it may trigger instability if the system is close to a limit.

As we see changes move supply capacity and demand towards upper or lower limits in a sector, we should be looking for possible changes that would push them across those limits.

We should also be looking for cascade effects: A commodity market price collapse, a tourist scare or a technology problem in one of the potentially unstable major regions could lead to a decline in business volume after a boom period. This could lead to a real estate maket price collapse. This could lead to a financial panic in that region, which could lead to a decline in local business, imports and a currency crisis.

The financial panic could lead to fire sale selling of securities and a currency price collapse. Investors in other regions who had holdings for the securites as collateral for trade or investment would need to sell securities and currency from other regions to cover shortfalls. Similarly holders of that currency would need to sell securities and currency from other regions to cover shortfalls.

 If any other regions were in fragile states at the time, they could similarly suffer fire sales of securities, loss of export business to the initally affected region and a weakening of currency. A real estate market price collapse might follow, compounding the previous difficulties.

There are many combinations of initial events triggering price collapses, which start a cascade of collapses in a local region which in turn cascade to other regions which are closely connected with that region.

1. "The Spatial Economy Cities, Regions and International Trade" Masahisa Fujita, Paul Krugman, Anthony J. Venables
2. "Europe's North-South Divide on Infrastructure" Stratfor
3. "The FRBNY DSGE Model" Marco Del Negro, Stefano Eusepi, Marc Giannoni, Argia Sbordone, Andrea Tambalotti, Matthew Cocci, Raiden Hasegawa, M. Henry Linder, Federal Reserve Bank of New York Staff Reports

INDEX

2007/2008 financial crisis, 146
3D printing, 93
Additive Manufacturing, 93, 98
Alan Greenspan, 19, 34
Amazon, 96
area price relativity change cycle, 311
Area Price Relativity Change Cycle, 262, 311
Assumptions of Wave Model, 222
Automation, 123
Bank of England, 249
bulk transport, 296
Bureaucrats, 280
BUSINESS CYCLES ILLUSTRATED – CYCLE GENERATION, 109
Buyer Price and Risk, 182
Buyer/Seller Price Lead and Price Collapse, 209
buyer's risk, 100, 136, 170, 212, 218, 291, 299
Buyer's risk, 184, 219, 301
Buyer's Risk Between Regions, 95
buyer's risk premium, 299
buyer's risk price premium, 212
canals, 295
Capital centers in Europe, 293
cash flow, 135
Cash Flow and Price Stability, 168
Cash on Delivery, 218
CDO, 45
CDS, 45
Charter Banking, 147
Cloud, 89
collateral, 187
Collateralized Debt Obligations (CDOs), 40, 189
Combinations of Cycles, 60
Combinations of Cycles or Waves, 111
Combinations of Technology, 268
Combinatorial Innovation, 61
commercial and industrial real estate, 313
Commercial and industrial Real Estate, 310
Complex numbers, 194
Complex Numbers - Imaginary Money, 198
Complex Variable Analysis, 66
COMPLEX VARIABLES AND PRICE COLLAPSE, 173
composite wave, 164, 165
composite waves, 162
constraints, 156
contingent price, 233
cost/volume curves, 119
Credit Default Swap (CDS), 20, 84
Currency Crises, 305
Currency cycle, 17
Currency Cycle, 58, 284
cycle and *wave*, 110
Cyclical Patterns of Price and Volume, 207
David Tepper, 11, 20

delivery lags or leads payment, 152
demand deposit banking, 188
Donald Rumsfeld, 32
Donald Trump, 26, 47, 309
DSGE Models and Financial Stability, 250
economies of scale, 122, 124, 125
Economies of Scale and Cycles, 176
economy of scale, 122
EDO, 244
Exchange Marketization, 123
experience curve, 122
external bottlenecks, 134
Extractive Cycle, 270
Extractive Cycles, 54
Fed Board of Governors, 74
Federal Deposit Insurance Corporation (FDIC), 42
Federal Reserve, 43
Federal Reserve era, 147
financial engineering, 189
Financial Institutions, 146
Financial Risk Perception cycle, 39, 40, 42, 44
Financial Risk Perception Cycle, 58, 288
Financing, 123
Financing Business, 135
Financing of Buyer, 218
fixed investment cycle, 18
Fixed Investment Cycle, 50, 259
$^{FRB/US}$, 243
Free Banking, 147

Friedrich Hayek, 246
general equilibrium, 246
Generation of Business Cycles, 116
Geoeconomic, 95
Geoeconomic Cycles, 53
GEOECONOMIC FACTORS, 291
Geoeconomics, 98
Geoeconomics and Trade, 291
Geographic barriers, 304
Geopolitical Parallels, 304
geopolitics, 293, 304
George Soros, 87
GFC, 251
Global Financial Crisis, 11, 21, 43, 248
Government policies, 243
Great Recession, 248, 251
Great trading cities, 293
Hayek's System of Telecommunications, 252
High Levels of Financing, 219
Hong Kong, 17
Impact of Financing on Financial Stability, 143
Impact of Financing on Price and Volume, 210
Impact of Market Collapses on the General Economy and Financial Sector, 145
Implications of Wave Model, 216
income distribution influence on interest rates, 283
Infrastructural Investment Cycle, 50, 260

Interaction of Wavelengths, 225
interbank lending, 187, 188
Interest rate cycle, 18
Interest Rate cycle, 39, 41, 44
Interest Rate Cycle, 57, 281
Internet of Things, 94, 99
Inter-temporal Flows, 115
Inventory (Short) cycle, 177
Inventory cycle, 18
Inventory Cycle, 259
John Paulson, 18
Kitchin (Inventory) Cycle, 49
LBO, 23
Leverage cycle, 42
Leverage Cycle, 55, 272
leverage ratio, 149, 187, 249, 260, 272, 274
Linear Price Variation with Volume, 224
liquidity, 148
Lobbyists and lawyers, 280
locational factors, 317
Logistics, 123
Long Call Option, 82
Long Position, 80
Macroeconomic Analysis and Forecasting Models, 243
Macroeconomic Effects, 240
MACRO-ECONOMIC STABILITY, 237
Major technology cycle, 265
Manufacturing Capacity (Medium) or Fixed Investment cycle, 177
market hubs, 293
Marketization, 122
Mechanization, 123
Minor technology cycle, 266
Mississippi, 294
Model Scope, 248
Monetary Policy Report, 74
mortgage, 37
National Banking, 147
navigable rivers, 293
New agricultural technology, 239
New military technology, 239
New Process Cycle, 51
New Product Version Cycle, 51
New Product Version or Process Cycle, 263
New Technology Platform Cycle, 264
New Technology Platform Cycle – Major Upgrade, 52
New Technology Platform Cycle – Minor Upgrade, 53
new territory, 238
New transport technology, 238
One Market Price, 227
Organic Growth Mechanisms, 237
Organization, 123
Paul Krugman, 17
Payment in Advance by Buyer, 218
polar view of the cycle, 201
Political cycle, 39, 44
Political Cycle, 56, 274
Pounds, 15
price acceptance, 135
Price and Volume waves, 197
price collapse, 140

Price collapse, 139
price collapse curves, 215
Price Collapses, 63
Price Fluctuation through Cycle - Contracted Price and Contingent Price, 230
price levelling, 297
price spikes, 132, 157
Price spikes, 131
Price Spikes, 63
Price Spikes, Collapses and Triggers, 62
Price, Cash Flow and Risk, 200
price/volume curves, 119
Price/Volume Curves, 190
Product Development cycle, 42
production capacity cycle, 129
Production Integration, 123
Quantum, 15
Quiet Period, 147
Real Business Cycle, 248, 250
Real Estate and Geoeconomics, 307
Real Estate Buyer's Risk, 314
Real Estate cycle, 39, 40, 44
Real Estate Cycle, 262
Real Estate Price Stability, 315
real estate prices levelling, 298
renewable energy, 89
Renewable Energy, 99
representative agent, 247
Representative Agent, 244
Residential Real Estate, 308
Rhine, 294
Risk For Supplier, Buyer and Financing Party, 181

Risk to Financing Party, 186
river valleys, 293
Robotics, 91
Salih Neftci's Principles of Financial Engineering, 80
seller's and buyer's risk, 192
Seller's and Buyer's Risk, 203
seller's risk, 170, 211, 212
Shadow banks, 42
shock, 118
Shocks, 59, 249
Short Position, 81
Short Put Option, 82
Smooth Response of Volume to Price, 226
Smooth Transition between Cash and Financing, 226
solvency, 148
Soros, 17
Specialization, 123
Spikes, 133
Stanley Druckmiller, 14
Stephen Schwarzman, 22
STRATFOR, 293, 304
Summary of Economic Projections, 74
Supplier Price and Risk, 181
supply capacity, 132
Supply Chain Costs, 95
systemic crises, 147
Technology cycle, 39
Technology cycle (Long), 177
Technology Platform cycle, 42
The Big Short, 18
The Cloud, 88
The Collapse - Diseconomies of Scale, 160

The Destabilization Phase - Limits, 152
The Influence of Bulk Transport on Price, 294
The political cycle, 18
The Role of Financing, 202
Transport links, 292
Type 1 financial asset, 155
Type 2 financial asset, 155
Type 3 buyers, 154
Type 3 financial asset, 155
Type 4 buyers, 154
Type 4 financial asset, 156
UK currency short, 81
UK Pound, 17
UNDERLYING MATHEMATICS OF LIQUIDITY AND SOLVENCY, 162
US Federal Reserve, 19
US Federal Reserve Beige Book, 73
US Treasury, 21, 43
Warren Buffet, 27
wave, 111
Wave Movement of Cash Flow and Price, 195
Wave Patterns in Cash Flow and Price, 174
Wave Shapes, 196
Wave Stability and Business Cycles, 193
Winston S. Churchill, 30
working capital, 249
working capital cycle, 121, 129
Working capital cycle, 110
Working Capital cycle, 176
Working Capital Cycle, 48, 257
Yangtze, 294

www.ingramcontent.com/pod-product-compliance
Lightning Source LLC
Chambersburg PA
CBHW071156240526
45470CB00016BA/123